Praise
Evil D

Captain Dean Olson (retired) and I started our careers with the Douglas County Sheriff's Office in Omaha, Nebraska within days of one another in July of 1978 as two members of a class of 10 new hires. Over the next 25 years, 3 months and 7 days Dean and I worked with, around and for one another in the various bureaus, divisions and units of that department. We have been coworkers and friends over these past 40 plus years and have learned a lot from each other. The cases presented in this book I was familiar with or worked on as an investigator at the time of their occurrence except for two of them. To this day I truly believe that had the Michael Cullen cases been assigned to any other investigator for follow-up they would have gone unsolved. Dean is a tenacious and talented professional on a never ending quest to update himself and expand his knowledge base on all subjects related to law enforcement, not for himself but for the benefit of others, to use to assist him in the successful resolution of crimes so that the victims may find a modicum of peace. Dean is one of the very best investigators I have had the pleasure to work with.

William (Bill) W Black
Office of the Attorney General
Nebraska Department of Justice
Chief of Investigators
Criminal Prosecution Bureau
Criminal Investigation Division
Chief of Violent Crimes Unit

Captain Dean Olson comes from the time of old school cops who lived and breathed the job. Every police officer has their talents and Dean's intelligence, investigative skills, and courage made him one of the finest officers I have ever known. The reader will be exposed to the harsh realities of heinous crime and the dedicated investigator who had an innate need to get justice for each victim. A great opportunity to be brought into the real world of police investigation.

Captain Art Nolan (retired)
Newport News, Virginia Police Department
Major Crimes Division Commander

EVIL DESIRE

Recollections of a Sex Crimes Detective

EVIL DESIRE

Recollections of a Sex Crimes Detective

Captain Dean T. Olson
(Retired)

Genius
Book Publishing

Los Angeles, California

Published By:
Genius Book Publishing
31858 Castaic Road
#154
Castaic, CA 91384
GeniusBookPublishing.com
Contact: publisher@geniusbookcompany.com

ISBN: 978-1-947521-12-4

190728

Table of Contents

Disclaimer
ix

About the Author
x

Acknowledgments
xi

Chapter One
Michael Cullen Series
The Cross-Dressing Rapist
1

Chapter Two
Sociopathy and Rape
32

Chapter Three
Michael Cullen Series
Conclusion
64

Chapter Four
The Child Killers
98

Chapter Five
Earl LaBelle Series
The Hot Prowler Rapist
125

Chapter Six
Mary Kay Harmer Rape-Murder
A Lamb Lured to a Wolf's Den
150

Chapter Seven
David Burdette Series
The Ten Most Eligible Women Rapist
176

Chapter Eight
Christina O'Day Rape-Murder
The Babysitter Killers
217

Chapter Nine
Henry Kamphaus Series
The Canyon Road Rapist
247

Chapter Ten
Conclusion
279

References
285

Disclaimer

Some names have been changed to protect the innocent. Composite personalities were created for some persons to protect their privacy.

About the Author

Captain Dean T. Olson is an award-winning criminal investigator. He commanded the Criminal Investigation Bureau of the Douglas County Sheriff's Department in Omaha, Nebraska, retiring in 2008 after 30 years of law enforcement service. Captain Olson earned a Bachelor of Science Degree in Criminal Justice and a Master's Degree in Public Administration from the University of Nebraska at Omaha. He also earned a Master of Arts Degree in Security Studies from the Naval Postgraduate School, Center for Homeland Defense and Security, in Monterey, CA. Olson is a graduate of the 193rd Session of the FBI National Academy and was formerly an adjunct professor of Criminal Justice for several Midwestern universities. Captain Olson's other books are: "Perfect Enemy: The Law Enforcement Manual of Islamist Terrorism," "Tactical Counterterrorism," and "The Omega Confluence: Examining the American Condition through the Lens of Faith."

Acknowledgments

This book is dedicated to the quiet professionals of the old Criminalistics Division of the Douglas County Sheriff's Department, forerunner of today's Forensic Science Division. You unflinchingly worked major crime scenes under the most arduous conditions imaginable from sub-freezing bitter cold to stifling triple digit heat. In spite of seldom receiving any recognition for the vital crime scene services you performed, the fact is that I couldn't have solved many of these cases without your excellent crime scene work. Sergeant Dave Krecklow' Deputy Ray "Raybo" Paulison (June 16, 1947-May 20, 1998); ID techs Bill Kaufhold, Dave Sobotka, and others too numerous to mention: *Et factum est in gloria.*

Also to Chief Deputy Tim Dempsey (December 7, 1943-December 16, 2016). You were my mentor as a young detective, as you were to many of my fellow detectives, during your long tenure as the captain of the Criminal Investigation Bureau. Detectives under your command channeled into action your dogged determination to eradicate the evil of the Hells Angels following the rape-murder of Mary Kay Harmer described in Chapter Six. Under your direction they succeeded in shutting down the Omaha Chapter twice and packing many of their members off to prison in 1981 and most notably again in 1990 during "Operation Rough Rider." No cop had been able to do that before. None has been able to do so since. The average citizen may not be aware, but Omaha is a safer place because of you. Every great mentor is hard to find, difficult to part with, and impossible to forget. Rest in peace.

To the memory of those
I couldn't protect
from the evil desire of
the human predators lurking in our midst.

Evil Desire

Chapter One
Michael Cullen Series
The Cross-Dressing Rapist

"…sexually violent predators are…a human plague…"
Florida Legislator Don Gaetz

A cop's view of evil is different from all others. The evil that psychiatrists, psychologists, and mental health professionals study in the detached comfort of an office interview, in medical school, during prison interviews, or from peer-reviewed journal articles is that which cops confront in person on a daily basis. For cops, evil has a human face. It ranges from the blood-drenched, snarling, maniacal rage of a meth addict who nearly decapitated his wife while cutting her throat because he thought she was a murderous space alien to the soulless, dead-eyed, apathetic gaze of a sociopath who raped an infant because he wanted to see how it felt. Name the depravity and if a cop has been on the job long enough, he or she has likely encountered evil's human expression.

For cops, evil is visceral, often life-threatening and ever-present. It permeates their environment and colors their world. It is a corrosive reality that seeks to penetrate even the stoutest emotional defenses. Like rust on the soul, unchecked evil seeks to devour those who are not prepared for its onslaught. It is insidious and unrelenting as it tries to pry cops loose from their moral tethers.

The sheer volume and variety of evil that cops see would stun those not accustomed to it. Evil's omnipresence forms the background hum of their lives. Its threat to society and the cop's role in countering it are acknowledged in the Bible in Romans 13:4. While God looks out for His protectors those who allow even the slightest space between His moral precepts and the manner in which they do their jobs invite dark forces to occupy the void.

Immersion in an environment laced with evil exacts a heavy toll. Nearly all cops wrestle with the impact of powerful psychological, emotional, and physical effects of evil. Alcoholism, drug abuse, divorce, marital infidelity, and destruction of families; life-threatening diseases like cancer, ulcers, diabetes, and heart disease; depression and suicide are evidence of evil's impact. Longevity studies show that cops die 10 years younger than the general population. The suicide rate for cops is 52 percent higher than most other professions.

Make no mistake: it is akin to hand-to-hand combat. Popular 1970s police author Joseph Wambaugh sums it up well, "Police work is not particularly dangerous physically, but it is the most dangerous job in the world emotionally." He goes on to describe what happens to cops working in an environment permeated with evil, "…the real danger is what it does to your emotions. You have experiences that take their toll on you, and one day you wake up and realize you're not the same person. You're cynical. You don't have the faith in people you used to have."

Of the varieties of evil cops encounter, rape ranks near the top of the scale. Criminality exists along an imaginary continuum from relatively minor innocuous petty crimes at the lower end to horrendous mass murder at the upper.

Rape is life-threatening violence only eclipsed by murder in the degree of evil. So it was when a woman named Jackie Brown crossed paths with rapist Michael Cullen. Like most of us, Brown had no idea men like Cullen even existed. She had a vague concept of evil but her frame of reference was stunted by a lack of firsthand knowledge of, and exposure to, the utter depravity and evil that stalks the innocent. In her world the evil that men like Cullen wrought was confined to nightmares that could be vanquished simply by waking up.

Jackie Brown was not complicit in the least for the violence that enveloped her. No victim is. Brown was simply a hard-working, salt-of-the-earth business professional who happened to fall under Cullen's rapacious gaze. Like all street predators, Cullen was constantly on the prowl for victims. His demons drove him relentlessly to seek out the defenseless and vulnerable on which to perpetrate his crimes. For Cullen, rape served a supremely selfish evil desire to compensate for his inadequacies by dominating and controlling someone less powerful than himself. By violently sexually debasing women he could exert the power and control that he felt was missing in his pathetic life.

It was just after 1:00 AM on Saturday, July 20, 1985 as Jackie Brown stumbled clumsily from the passenger side of the still rolling car. Although in her early fifties she was fit and looked and acted ten years younger. "Colin, you're ten feet from the curb," she screeched as her coworkers in the car laughed loudly. Someone in the backseat yelled to her, "You want me to walk you to the door?"

"No!" she shot back. "My door's right there." She pointed to her condo a few steps away while swaying drunkenly. As a successful single female executive she was, at that time in the late 1980s, among the rare women who shunned marriage and family to compete in the male-dominated boardrooms of corporate America. A lucrative promotion had brought her from Salt Lake City to Omaha. She had chosen the location on the 100 block of N 36th Street on a tree-lined street in midtown because it was only a few blocks from her job as an account executive at the headquarters of a large national insurance company.

"Well gang, we did it...we closed the deal today. Enjoy your weekend and I will see you all Monday," she said as she staggered up the steps to her front door.

At the time the midtown area was beginning to experience gentrification again. A hundred years before they were the homes of the upper middle class—examples of life on the upper rungs of the social ladder. In the intervening years the area was sucked backwards into the pit of poverty and despair that defines urban blight. The once grand monuments to upward mobility and success had fallen into disrepair and neglect. Many of the huge stately old homes had succumbed to urban blight. More and more had been acquired by slumlords who rubbed their greedy mitts together at the thought of buying up huge older homes at fire sale prices so they could wring from them maximum profits by dividing them into cramped warrens of multi-family apartments and flophouses.

As their profits soared and they refused to improve their properties the area became a magnet for the urban underclass and unfortunate illegal aliens who could afford nothing better. That underclass brought with them the trappings of their low lifestyle including noise, litter, decrepit cars—many without mufflers—vulgarity, violence, crime, drugs, and a ubiquitous, ominous "is this all there is to life" variety of despair. Jackie Brown's purchase of the condo was part of a trend that bucked the stubborn downward currents of decline. The influx of higher class residents fostered an uneasy tension stemming from the culture clash of two diametrically different worlds increasingly competing for the same real estate.

Brown fumbled with the door locks, hindered by her alcohol-fueled confusion. Finally able to get the door open she gestured to her coworkers still waiting curbside to be sure she got safely inside. "Have a great weekend guys" she waved as they roared off. Once inside she fumbled for the light switch and noticed that her cat Lily had not wandered out lazily to greet her as usual. Setting down her purse and keys she called out, trying to coax the cat from her probable location, the bed in the spare bedroom, "Lily, I'm home."

The cat still failed to appear as Brown walked toward the hallway to her bedroom. After turning on the hallway lights her attention was drawn to something lying on the floor just outside her partially open bedroom door. She walked closer and bent down to pick it up. It was a large lace pastel purple bra. Confused at first, she wondered if she had dropped it on her way to the laundry room at the back of the condo, but turning it over and over in her hands, she was baffled because she did not recognize it.

Awash in the fog of her alcohol-hampered mental state she struggled to make sense of the foreign bra on the floor and the failure of her cat to come out to greet her. At first a slight discomfort tugged at her consciousness. She acknowledged a growing sense of dread that something, although she was still not sure what, was not quite right. As she looked down the hallway towards the spare bedroom naked fear began to rise within her. It penetrated the mental haze that dulled her reasoning and slowed her responses, "Had someone been in her condo? Could they still be here?"

She tried to shrug it off even as it continued to nag her. "You're being ridiculous," she thought to herself as she turned to walk to the spare bedroom to find Lily. Still examining the bra, she paused halfway there as the nagging fear returned. She continued to try to push back against the fog of alcohol that blunted her survival instincts.

It was too late. To her horror, a monster from her worst nightmare burst out of the shadows of the spare bedroom into the glare of the hallway lights. Her breath was sucked out of her by a paralyzing jolt of fear at seeing him. She gasped loudly as the naked man moved quickly for her, a glint of light flashing from the large knife he held in his hand. He looked other-worldly and monstrous due to a nylon stocking pulled tightly over his head that hideously deformed his face.

Gripped by fear she turned to run away but it was too late. In a sudden burst of fury he bridged the gap between them in a couple of leaps and grabbed her roughly around the neck from behind. She tried to scream but it was as if the terrifying fear had throttled her voice. He clamped a hand over her mouth and pressed the blade of the knife against her neck. Hissing into her ear he threatened, "I will cut off your ear if you don't give me what I want. It's the only part of the human body that can't be sewed back on."

Brown's knees were close to buckling under the crippling terror that permeated every sinew of her body. A fear-induced near catatonic state paralyzed her. She was unable to move or speak as her body suffered waves of small tremors. She didn't know it at the time but she was suffering from Tonic Immobility, a little-understood phenomenon in which debilitating fear induces a temporary state of paralysis. The victim is literally frozen in fear as a result. Medical researchers believe that it occurs in as many as half of all rapes (Russo 2017).

Jackie struggled to speak through his hand clamped tightly against her mouth. Her muted pleas slipped from between his fingers still roughly pressing against her mouth. "Please, please don't hurt me," she muttered. "I will give you anything you want," she begged

He tightened his grip around her neck and pressed the knife blade ever harder against her throat. He breathed menacingly into her ear, "Shut up. Do what I want and shut up and I won't hurt you. Nod if you understand?"

His hands were coarse and unwashed and his breath was atrocious, reeking of cigarettes and beer. Brown nodded meekly and began to sob. She was living a woman's worst nightmare. "This way" he said as he forced her towards her bedroom. Pushing her through the partially open door she noticed that the room had been ransacked and her dresser drawers rifled. The floor and bed were littered with her panties and bras. Her high heeled shoes had been removed from their boxes in the closet and were scattered on the floor as if someone had discarded them haphazardly after frantically trying them on.

He pushed her face-down on the bed as he grabbed handfuls of bras and then panties from the floor. After throwing them on the bed next to her he began trying them on. Once he had selected an acceptable bra and panties to wear, he forced Brown to stand and undress in front of him. She hesitated and began to plead, "Please. Don't do this…."

"Take it all off or I'll cut it off," he snarled while ominously grabbing the knife from the nightstand. He tapped the blade against his hand and stared at her. "I'm waiting," he said.

As Brown disrobed he started to masturbate. "Ahhh, that's it," he said as he savored her naked body while slowly then vigorously stroking his erect penis while moaning loudly.

"You do it!" he ordered, motioning for her to take over masturbating him. She hesitated, but began to awkwardly stroke him as he lay back on the bed. "Ahhh…just right," he said as he reached down and began to penetrate her with his fingers until she recoiled in pain at his rough handling. "Please, please," she cried. "You're hurting me."

Agitated, he sat up abruptly and began to examine the bras and panties on the bed. After selecting a suitable set he threw them at her, "Put these on," he ordered.

He watched as she slipped into the panties and put on the bra. Apparently not content with those, he forced her to try on multiple sets of bras and panties. After trying on three different bra and panty combinations he was apparently satisfied. He stood up and grabbed her roughly and shoved her back onto the bed face-down. He then used pantyhose removed from her dresser to tie her hands and feet spread eagle to the four-poster bed. He ordered her not to look at him. He fashioned a hand towel he had apparently placed on the nightstand earlier into a blindfold and warned her again about staying quiet and not trying to escape. After blindfolding her he removed the nylon he had pulled over his head to distort his facial features.

In his haste he had placed the blindfold on her head slightly askew. Though she was face down on the bed, she was able to see out the bottom of the blindfold and caught glimpses of him from the chest down as he moved around the bedroom. Afraid to move her head too far, she was able to see as he removed the bra and panties he was wearing and tried on others. He also tried to put on several pairs of her high heels but his feet were too big.

The cross-dressing ritual continued for some time. She could see that he was masturbating while handling and sniffing her underwear. He stopped abruptly and returned to the bed. Unclasping her bra he reached under her to fondle her breasts. He squeezed them very hard, causing her to recoil in pain. "These are nice," he sneered as he began to rip off her panties.

By now Brown was sobbing uncontrollably. "Please don't hurt me. Take what you want. I have money in my purse...you...you can have it all...and...keys to my car in the garage...take them.... Please don't do this...."

"Shut up!" he barked as he began to subject Brown to three hours of hell by repeatedly raping her vaginally from behind.

℀

Rape is one of the most underreported crimes. Many researchers estimate that as many as half go unreported. Sexual assault ranges from stranger rape to acquaintance or date rape to statutory rape involving sexual relations between an adult and an underage person to child sexual exploitation. Crime statistics indicate that a rape is committed every six minutes in the U.S. Of reported rapes, Department of Justice statistics show that less than 40 percent result in an arrest. That is a far lower figure than for other violent crimes such as murder or aggravated assault. And when an arrest does occur, stubborn and deep-seated societal attitudes make rape uniquely difficult to prosecute. The stigma of rape makes victims ashamed or afraid to report it.

Rape also remains one of the most misunderstood crimes. Stubborn cultural myths persist that portray women as somehow deserving to be raped or that some women harbor a subconscious fantasy of being raped. Variations of these harmful myths hold that rape is merely part of the courting ritual between men and women. According to this pernicious fallacy, chaste women pretend to protest to protect their virtue, and rape allows women to enjoy sex without feeling guilty. None of these bogus and thoroughly debunked myths have any bearing on the brutal reality of rape.

Prosecutors can be reluctant to pursue rape cases. Rapes involving drugs and alcohol cloud the issue of guilt. Juries can struggle to determine whether a victim consented to sex, especially when the assailant is a friend or acquaintance.

Rapists are typically young, most under age 25. Many come from low socioeconomic backgrounds. The majority of perpetrators are racial-ethnic minorities. They tend to target victims of their own race. Rapists are often versatile criminals who engage in many different types of crime. Sexual offending reflects only one manifestation of an underlying antisocial bent. The psycho-sexual background of most rapists includes a history of conflict and other trouble with women often characterized by a marked inability to relate to women personally and sexually outside of force.

As many as 80 percent of all rapists are men their victims know and trust in what are called date or acquaintance rapes. (NY State Police 2016). They may be a friend, neighbor, colleague, fellow student or someone met at a party or club. However, it is the repeat rapists targeting strangers who grip a community in fear. They achieve notoriety with sensational news coverage and designer monikers like the Pillowcase Rapist, the Ski Mask Rapist, the Midtown Molester, and the Stocking Strangler. The typical serial rapist leads a Jckyll and Hyde existence undetected by neighbors, coworkers, even family. In the wake of a criminal career that can span a decade or more he may leave dozens or even hundreds of victims before he's caught, assuming he ever is.

In the early 1970s the FBI began to research rape in earnest (Hazelwood and Burgess 1987:16-24). The bureau's first major research involved 41 serial rapists doing hard time in state prisons. They were responsible for 837 reported or admitted rapes. That's an average of more than 20 sexual assaults per rapist. And those are just the ones known to police or admitted to by the rapists themselves. In my experience, rapists underreport their crimes for various reasons. They want to avoid further criminal liability or try to avoid the social stigma of having violently assaulted extremely vulnerable victims like the elderly or children. Perhaps they want to keep the "body count" low to avoid further stigma. And some are sociopaths who can't resist giving the cops the finger by lying about their crimes.

Rape has less to do with sexuality than it does with exercising power, control, and humiliation of the victim. The myth that rape is about sexual pleasure supports many of the harmful misconceptions about rape but was thoroughly debunked by the FBI research. As one of the eminent rape researchers described it, "Rape is the sexual expression of aggression, not the aggressive expression of sexuality."

Most of the rapists studied by the FBI stated that "rape is lousy sex." This factor explains why many rapists experience delayed ejaculation or inability to achieve orgasm. They often rape a victim repeatedly because of this. And contrary to the widespread myth that rapists commit their attacks because they are doing without, many of the rapists studied were married or involved in an intimate relationship when they committed their crimes. Most victims were chosen based on availability, vulnerability, and physical characteristics other than attractiveness or sexual allure.

From an investigative standpoint the FBI research yielded some interesting facts. Many of the rapists began their assaultive behavior as teenagers. Most had committed their first rape by age 16. Two-thirds engaged in nuisance sex offences such as voyeurism and exhibitionism beginning in their early teens. Voyeurism and exhibition are "paraphilias." Paraphilias involve aberrant sexual arousal and gratification using an object or engaging in activity that most people don't find arousing. Examples include voyeurism, which is obtaining sexual gratification by looking at sexual objects or acts, especially secretively, and exhibitionism, which is sexual gratification from the indecent exposure of one's genitals to others.

Harold Lamont "Walkin' Willie" Otey was an admitted serial rapist and the perpetrator of one of Omaha's most heinous lust murders. Legendary NYPD Bronx Homicide Commander Vernon Geberth defined lust murder in a 1998 article as "…homicides in which the offender stabs, cuts, pierces or mutilates the sexual regions or organs of the victim's body" (Geberth 1998:32). Otey was executed in the Nebraska electric chair for the 1977 gruesome mutilation rape-murder of college co-ed Jane McManus. He described his motivation for rape: "To me, the fun part wasn't the raping," Otey said in the taped confession to police after his arrest. "I got off on seeing the fear in their eyes." He said it was the same fear he saw in 13 other women he admitted to raping during his travels across the country.

❧

For nearly three hours Jackie Brown endured some of the cruelest and most dehumanizing abuse imaginable. At one point the rapist tried to force her to orally copulate him. She gagged and retched at the stench of his unwashed genitals. Brown apologized and said in desperation, "I am sorry...sorry, I just can't do that. Anything else, just not that."

At that her tormentor left the bedroom momentarily. When he returned he had a bottle of olive oil taken from the kitchen. While she was still face-down on the bed, he used it to lube her anus then sodomized her. He grew increasingly angry and profane at his inability to reach orgasm. He cursed her and began to violate her roughly by trying to insert the olive oil bottle into her rectum. After he was done abusing her, he demanded that she do the same to him, saying, "Use it on my ass." By this time Brown was in extreme pain and was sobbing hysterically. He realized that in her distraught state he was not going to be able to force compliance. He resorted to masturbating again until he ejaculated on her back.

After seemingly endless hours of savage rape and writhing around face-down on the bed, her blindfold had slipped enough to see a little more. In spite of her terror and pain she began to mentally record details about the rapist and the attack. She noticed that the alarm clock on the nightstand showed 2:50 AM. The rapist left the bedroom again and returned with her purse. "It's getting late," he said, pouring the contents onto the floor next to the bed. While he was focused on her purse she struggled to see what he looked like. Although unable to see his face clearly she was able to see that he had reddish-brown hair, and appeared to be in his mid-30s with three-day's growth of beard. She also noticed that he spoke with a slight accent that she was unable to pin down at the time.

He removed all of the cash from her wallet and took her driver's license and bank cards. He also took her checkbook, work ID, and the electronic access card to her office. He removed one of the pillowcases and stuffed several of her bras, panties, a couple pairs of her high heel shoes and the loot from her purse into it. He then went into the bathroom just off the bedroom and dressed. When he came out she could only see from the waist down. He was wearing jeans and brown work boots like construction laborers wear.

Picking up the pillowcase he told her, "Don't move until it's daylight." As he headed out the bedroom door he paused, "I know cops downtown. If you call the cops I'll know and I will come back." Before leaving by the back door he threw two one-dollar bills from her purse onto the bed next to her, saying, "This is all I pay for a whore." As the sound of his footsteps faded, Brown heard the back door open and then close. Fearing that he had not actually gone she was initially afraid to move. After listening intently and hearing nothing she began to struggle against the pantyhose that bound her.

cs

My phone rang shortly after 4:30 AM. I fumbled picking it up as I struggled to fight through the fog of sleep. On the other end was a patrol sergeant. "Sorry to bother you so early but there's a rape victim at Methodist ER. The night guy is tied up handling a cutting so I called the LT. He said you'd want to catch this one anyway. The vic says the perp threatened to cut off her ear if she didn't cooperate."

"Okay, I am on my way," I said as I sat upright to turn on the bedside lamp, careful not to awaken my wife. The sergeant's words resonated despite my sleep-enveloped mind, "Perp threatened to cut off her ear...." Those words struck a nerve. I was already working another rape case in which the suspect threatened the same thing to overcome his victim's resistance. It was much too early in the investigation to tell for sure, but it looked like a serial rapist was prowling our city's streets.

The patrol sergeant continued, "Some weird shit this one. Told my guys that she came home..." I interrupted her, "Okay, let me get it from her. Be there in half an hour and be sure one of your guys stays with her until I get there."

I pushed my unmarked car ever faster northbound on 72nd Street. I finally hit a red light at Grover. The early morning traffic was sparse so I slowed slightly and, after ensuring that there was no cross traffic, stood on the accelerator. I did not see the Omaha Police cruiser sitting in the shadows of the hotel parking lot on the east side of the street. It was a two-officer training car and the new guy was probably anxious to make a traffic stop. He squealed his tires leaving the lot and mashed the accelerator to catch up with me. I slowed slightly to ten or so miles per hour over the speed limit to allow him to get close enough to run my plates. Detective cars of the sheriff's department are licensed with regular passenger car plates but list the owner as the county. I was hoping that I could save time and avoid being pulled over if the cruiser got close enough to run the plates. The training officer would hopefully also recognize the small antenna for the police radio and the county registration as an unmarked detective car.

I imagined the recruit anxiously running the license plate hoping that in addition to a traffic scofflaw he also had a stolen car. After all, at 4:30 in the morning you're as likely to find a real criminal speeding as some traffic miscreant. Sure enough, he must have run the plates and when the dispatcher gave the registration the training officer probably told him "better luck next time" as they flashed a spotlight in my direction and then peeled off.

Walking into the Methodist Hospital Emergency Room on the night shift was like a homecoming. I knew most of the doctors and nurses from my years working patrol. I had spent many nights in the ER handling the aftermath of shootings, suicide attempts, stabbings, fights, domestic violence, child abuse, rapes, car wrecks, and the assorted mayhem that metropolitan hospitals collect.

As I entered the emergency room one of the younger nurses recognized me and grabbed me by the arm. She was one of the specially trained sexual assault nurses. She ushered me towards an interview room and closed the door.

"She's an older lady, not overly emotional, but she has been through hell," she said as she thumbed through her case file. "This guy really did a number on her, tore her rectum with an olive oil bottle. We're going to keep her for at least a day or so."

I nodded as she spoke, "She may be the second victim by the same guy," I said, pulling out my case folder. "Does she have anyone with her? Friend, relative..." I said as I scribbled some notes.

The nurse replied, "Yes, she has a female friend with her. If you like I can sit in with you during the interview."

I nodded again, "Yes, if she doesn't have a problem with that, I would appreciate it."

We made our way to an examination room off the emergency room complex where Jackie Brown waited. I released the patrol deputy standing outside. He appeared to be relieved to be cut loose.

Interviewing a rape victim is fraught with potential dangers. They must be asked highly intrusive questions that force them to relive an extraordinarily painful and frightening experience. To determine the motivation behind a rape it is imperative to determine the type and sequence of the acts and verbal activity of both the rapist and victim during the attack. A rapist reveals a good deal about himself and the motivation behind the assault through what he says to the victim and the type of sexual acts he performs during the assault. The rapist may also make her say certain words or phrases that enhance the rape for him.

The nurse knocked lightly several times before opening the door. Jackie Brown wore a hospital gown and was reclining in the bed. She was hooked to an IV and several monitors displayed her heart and respiration rates. Her friend stood next to the bed speaking softly to her. Jackie was remarkably composed considering the ordeal she had just survived. The nurse began by introducing me, "Jackie, this is Detective Olson. He is here to talk to you."

I stepped closer and extended my hand. "Hi Jackie," I said as she grasped my hand in a firm handshake. I was impressed as she looked me in the eye. I then turned towards her friend and introduced myself.

Turning back to Jackie, I continued, "I am very sorry this happened. I'm going to do my best to find the man who did this. But I need to ask you some questions first." After she nodded her head I continued, "Some of them will be uncomfortable but they are necessary. If you don't want to answer them now, they can wait. You might have answered some of them already for the patrol deputy. I apologize for that, but I need to ask you for as much information as you can give me. What might seem trivial or insignificant to you might be valuable to my investigation so please bear with me."

She nodded again, "I understand."

I glanced towards her friend, "Can your friend wait outside while we talk?" She nodded again. Rape victims normally hold back some information, especially if it is extremely embarrassing. The more degrading the violence perpetrated against them the greater the tendency to avoid revealing those aspects of the assault. Having another person present, even a close friend, can make it more difficult to share such information.

After the friend closed the door behind her, I began by asking Jackie to tell me everything she had done that evening leading up to her returning home. The focus of the questioning revolved around triggers such as things she remembered including anything she saw, heard, smelled, felt, tasted. She described her day at work and the night's celebration at a local bar afterwards. I spent the next forty-five minutes interviewing her about the rape. I asked her to try to remember any unusual things that had happened recently that at the time may have only caught her attention but now seemed more ominous. "Like what?" she replied.

"Feelings like someone watching you, being uncomfortable around a person or place, strange phone calls, hang-up phone calls, a delivery driver or maintenance guy who made you feel uneasy...."

I then asked her to describe her attacker. During the interview she struck me as an attractive, classy, well-educated and articulate woman. She impressed me with the detail she recalled—far more than most blindfolded victims. Even though she was not able to his face clearly she was able to give me a wealth of information about his apparent age, hair color, that he wielded the knife in his left hand and smoked, what he was wearing, a possible accent that she was still not able to pin down, as well as facts about possible employment given his work boots and rough hands.

"Do you remember if you locked your doors when you left last night?" I asked. The crime lab was still processing her condo. One troubling finding was that there was no sign of forced entry. There were no tool marks or pry marks on any of the doors or windows. If Brown was correct about locking her doors when she left, and having to unlock them again on her return, how did the rapist get in?

I spent a great deal of time probing about his paraphilic behaviors. This guy had several. The first was Sexual Masochism defined as the act of being humiliated, beaten, bound, or made to suffer. Brown's description of having to help him cross-dress mimicked the humiliation of forced cross-dressing. It was reinforced by her description of his insistence that she insert the olive oil bottle into his rectum.

His second paraphilia was Sexual Sadism. This includes acts that focus on psychological or physical suffering or humiliation. While it was evident by virtue of the victim herself, a non-consenting rape victim, other factors exhibited included humiliating her by inserting the olive oil bottle into her rectum while being forced to masturbate him, and throwing several dollars at her on the bed as he left, saying, "That's all I pay for a whore."

The third paraphilia evident was Transvestic Fetishism. It stemmed from her attacker's focus on cross-dressing. There is a related compulsion to collect female clothing that is used to cross-dress. It is often associated with Sexual Masochism as an associated feature of that paraphilia. In addition, cross-dressing may be an antidote to anxiety or depression. It was evident in the fact that he cross-dressed before initiating the rape and that he brought a bra he had collected or owned to the rape—the pastel purple bra she had found lying on the floor outside her bedroom door.

After finishing my questioning about his paraphilias I homed in on her impressions of the rapist. "Did you see anything about him that looked familiar, like the way he walked, the way he talked? He wore a mask which means he was obviously trying to protect his identity, or you may have seen him before. You mentioned that he had rough hands and wore work boots. Have you had work done on your house recently? Anything like carpentry, plumbing, any tradesmen working in or around your house?"

I was surprised by her response. "Yes, I have workers in and around my condo all the time. It is a newly renovated building and they are still working on some of the units." I made a note in my case file to look into tradesmen with access to keys to Brown's condo, or those who had been in her unit in the past.

As the interview wound down, I started to ask her to call me if she remembered more later. She interrupted me, "I've been trying to figure out why this happened. Who he is. I just can't think of anyone. And I don't recognize him, from what little I saw of his face."

"That's normal," I replied. "In the next few days things might get clearer and you may remember more."

I gave her one of my business cards again. "At this point in the investigation," I told her, "you might remember details while you sleep or when you are not thinking about what happened." Sometimes when the mind is free to wander thoughts that are not accessible at other times when we are preoccupied bubble up for recall. I told her that it could be her subconscious pointing out important details. I stressed that if it comes to mind while she is asleep, even though it may seem trivial, she should write it down immediately when she woke up so as not to forget it, then tell me about it the next chance she had.

❦

Rape victims suffer a multi-dimensional trauma that is deeper and more profound than mere physical injury. The emotional harm often creates more severe and longer lasting injury than other types of assaults. It manifests itself as feelings of intense fear, powerlessness, and hopelessness. They can overwhelm the strongest emotional coping mechanisms, leading to loss of a sense of control, connection, and meaning in a victim's life.

Rape trauma includes physical and emotional harm that can have a lifelong and severe impact on the course of a victim's life (Wolbert Burgess 1974). Rape victims are more than four times more likely than those who are not victims of crimes to contemplate suicide. They are thirteen times more likely to attempt suicide, three times more likely to suffer from depression, six times more likely to suffer from Post-Traumatic Stress Disorder, thirteen times more likely to abuse alcohol, and twenty-six times more likely to abuse drugs. The emotional trauma even has an official name: Rape Trauma Syndrome (RTS). The syndrome includes disruptions to normal physical, emotional, cognitive, and interpersonal behavior. It was first described by psychiatrist Ann Wolbert Burgess and sociologist Lynda Lytle Holmstrom in 1974 (Wolpert

Burgess 1974). The syndrome includes psychological and physical reactions common to most rape victims immediately following and for months or years after a rape.

The power of emotional injury to re-victimize includes triggers that remind victims of the assault. They may be auditory, visual, tactile, and/or olfactory links to something that occurred during the rape. For example, triggers might be a man's voice; a look of disgust by a family member; the smell of cologne, cigarettes, or beer; the sight of a beard; an unwanted touch; or hearing about someone sexually assaulted on the news or at the movies. At the sound, touch, sight, or smell of those cues, victims can experience the same surge of neuro-chemicals that were triggered during the actual assault. Their hearts may begin to race, blood pressure may spike, and breathing rate can increase. These fear reactions are not conscious choices nor overreactions. They are an automatic response triggered by traumatic memories. That is why it is crucial for detectives interviewing rape victims to gather information at a rate that does not overwhelm them.

The powerful neuro-chemicals that trigger the fight-flight-or-freeze response have far-reaching effects, including dramatic effects on the manner in which memories are recalled. Often, a traumatized person cannot generate the kind of narrative memory that normally follows an important experience. Their memories are often fragmented, out of sequence, and filled with gaps. They may recall very specific details from particular aspects of the assault and little or nothing about others. The fact that a victim recalls a detail that they did not remember earlier is not evidence of fabrication. Rather, it demonstrates a characteristic way in which traumatic memories are stored and recalled.

Examples of the pain and devastation of rape go back to the beginning of recorded history. The Bible provides insight into the emotional fallout of sexual assault in the rape of Tamar, the sister of Absalom and daughter of David in 2 Samuel 13. Scripture describes Tamar's pain following her attack by saying she "… put ashes on her head and tore the ornate robe she was wearing. She put her hands on her head and went away, weeping aloud as she went" (2 Samuel 13:19). Scripture also describes the long-term consequences: she "lived in her brother Absalom's house, a desolate woman" (2 Samuel 13:20).

Many women will only seek counseling after the emotional damage has caused their life to become unmanageable. This can occur years after the rape. I had a case in which a young woman reported a rape five years after it had occurred, well after the three-year statute of limitations had elapsed, making an arrest impossible. She had been 15 years old at the time and was walking on a jogging trail late at night trying to sneak home after staying out beyond her parents' curfew. She was taking the trail to save time when she was accosted by a rapist who walked past her going the other direction. He circled around behind her, pulled on a ski mask and blitzed her by knocking her down and dragging her in the brush. There he violated her with a knife before raping her vaginally and anally.

She had never reported the rape out of fear of being out past curfew and the stigma of what had happened. When I asked he why she had waited so long to report it she said that the latent emotional baggage had made her life unmanageable. She had become consumed with fear of being attacked again. It had started to affect her job and personal relations. She finally sought psychological counseling through her employee assistance program at work. As part of her treatment her counselor suggested that she make a police report on the rape. Finally overcome with the lingering debilitating effects of Post-Traumatic Stress Disorder, she was making a report as part of her therapy but did not want to actively pursue an investigation.

During my interview of Jackie Brown I homed in on the fact that her attacker knew her routine well enough to feel comfortable disrobing and lying in wait inside her condo. He had enough information about her to be reasonably sure he would not be interrupted before he could attack, that no man or others would accompany her into the condo and ruin his plans.

Disrobing to lie in wait is a very high-risk move. If Brown had varied from her routine and invited her coworkers into the condo her attacker would have had to flee naked or risk being captured by the several males accompanying her. That risk-taking behavior is significant because it indicated the strength of his fantasy-driven criminality. He was willing to risk being caught flat-footed and extremely vulnerable and exposed while naked instead of taking the more cautious and prudent approach of breaking in later to surprise her while she slept.

A key goal during the victim interview is to identify offender modus operandi, or MO, and his signature elements. The MO are the methods the perpetrator uses to commit the crime, make his escape afterwards and avoid capture. Examples include the type of restraints used, type of weapon used, tools used to gain entrance to the victim's home or location of the rape, efforts to avoid identification and arrest such as wearing a mask or disguise, wearing gloves to avoid leaving fingerprints, or using a condom to avoid leaving bodily fluids and DNA.

They are his method of doing things and are learned behaviors that develop over time and change as he gains experience, builds confidence, or learns from mistakes that got him arrested. Prisons are called graduate schools for crime because the convict learns from the mistakes that landed him behind bars while also comparing notes with similarly situated cons who teach him new, often more effective techniques to commit the crime without getting caught.

Signature behaviors differ from MO because they are actions or behaviors that go beyond those necessary to commit the crime. They are the products of the offender's fantasy and are committed to satisfy the emotional and psychological needs of the offender. They define the theme of a crime. In sex crimes the offender oftentimes subconsciously acts out sexually significant behaviors that reflect his underlying personality and lifestyle.

A signature is a trait an investigator recognizes as belonging to a single perpetrator. It does not change as the criminal gets better at his crimes. Torture, for example, is almost always signature. No matter what crime an offender is committing he doesn't need to torture a victim to pull it off. He does so because it feeds a sadistic emotional need. Of signature and MO, signature is the more important of the two to an investigation because it can identify the offender's personality and motives. The rapist's paraphilias in Jackie Brown's assault are examples of signature. Other examples include the level of injury to the victim, the location or sequence of the criminal acts, personal items or souvenirs taken from victim, and type of victim targeted such as occupation, age, race, or other physical characteristics.

Rape serves primarily non-sexual needs such as power and aggression expressed in unique and often complex sexual fantasies that have been described as a template or theme for serial rape. These fantasies serve a complex organizing function in the offender's behavior and commonly drive his verbal interactions with his victim, the sex acts he engages in and his overall pattern of behavior. Signature does not change dramatically because it is the manifestation of his fantasy served by the assault. In essence, it reflects the underlying motivation for committing the crime.

Human behavior, although often unpredictable, is also oftentimes repetitive. Research has indicated that certain actions engaged in at a rape scene by certain types of personalities will repeat themselves in other rape investigations. Understanding and recognizing both the modus operandi and the signature aspect of the crime can enable the detective to "link" crimes in a series. The common challenge in distinguishing MO from signature lies in the fact that certain offender actions may satisfy both MO and signature. Wearing a mask may serve MO by preventing a victim from identifying him while also serving signature aspects by heightening victim fear that satisfies the offender's Sadism paraphilia.

⁊

As I wrapped up the interview, I asked Jackie if she had any questions. "Do they ever come back?" she asked. I told her that it was common for rapists to return to the scenes of their crimes. Returns varied from simply driving past the scene to breaking in again to steal personal items from the victim to, in extreme cases, returning to try to rape the victim again. Brown's fragile composure evaporated at that point. It was obvious that she was deeply troubled at the prospect that her attacker might return. I asked her if she had someplace else to stay. She responded that she did, saying that her friend waiting outside would allow her to stay with her until she could move. She told me "...there is no way I will ever spend a night in that place again."

Before I left, I gave Jackie a copy of the Serial Offender Linkage Analysis (SOLA) questionnaire and asked her to complete it as soon as she felt up to doing so. The SOLA is an invaluable tool developed in cooperation with several metropolitan detectives working task forces targeting serial rapists. It was compiled based on the investigative experience of numerous detectives and includes facts learned from prior cases. The universe of investigative experience and knowledge they possessed was invaluable in solving what can be difficult crimes by cataloging rapist MO and signature aspects, such as what type of victim they targeted, how they were selected, where and at what time the rape occurred, what happened during each assault, how the rapist gained entry to the victim's apartment, what restraints were used, if any, and other details.

The SOLA includes approximately 50 questions asking the victim about activities they participate in and locations and businesses they frequent, such as recent deliveries the victim received including from and by whom; what gym they belong to; what dry cleaner, bars, restaurants and grocery stores they frequent; the hair salon they use; even where they buy gas and have their car serviced. It also asks about unusual events that have occurred recently such as hang-up phone calls; anonymous notes left on their windshield, car, or home, or mail tampered with; feelings of being followed or being watched; strange or troubling comments made by others including friends, coworkers and casual acquaintances;

missing or stolen items; and any recent awards, publicity, or honors they have received.

The goal is to find connections between victims who are strangers to each other to narrow the universe of suspects by focusing on linkages between victims and potential suspects associated with the links. For example, if two women received deliveries from the same company the rapist might work for the company. The linkage of the delivery company with the victims provides detectives with an investigative lead that might otherwise be missed.

Another key investigative tool we now have is to be able to categorize rapes into four types. These categories come from the research of a small band of criminologists, psychologists, FBI behaviorists, and police officers who made it their life's work to find out who rapists are and what makes them tick. Their body of knowledge evolved to include elaborate psychological profiles. The profiles are valuable to detectives to identify suspects and to attempt to elicit confessions after their apprehension.

A pioneer in that research was Dr. A. Nicholas Groth, a clinical psychologist who has worked extensively with rapists in prison. His pioneering research led him to train FBI agents and led to their ability to profile the offenders. Groth underscores the importance such profiles play in solving serial rapes, "…understanding the mind of a rapist can be key to solving the case." Groth's work, expanded upon and refined by the FBI, classifies rapists into four categories (Groth 1977: 400-406).

When discussing rapist categories, it is important to recall that sexual assault it not about sex. Rape is about anger, domination, and control. Sex is merely the weapon. And not all rapists are alike. There are differences in their motives, characteristics, and techniques. Many times, rapists exhibit characteristics from more than one category but taken as a whole their rapes fit one category more closely than others. Identifying rapist type is important because details such as frequency of assault, location, victim type, and unique offender characteristics are commonly associated with each type. Knowing rapist type can help predict future offender behavior including where the rapist might strike next and when, as well as other factors that may help identify him.

The Power Reassurance Rapist (PRR) is the most common type of serial rapist (Groth 1979:44-45). It is estimated that 21 percent (up to 44 percent in some estimates) of all rapists fit this category. The PRR is the least violent and has been referred to by some observers as the "gentleman" rapist. He is socially inept and suffers from very low self-esteem. His psychosocial background will usually include a single parent home, a 10th grade educational level or less, and a menial job. He's quiet, passive, and may live with an aggressive, controlling mother or alone. He often has no close friends and may not have a girlfriend. The cross-dressing and highly fetishistic rapes of Jackie Brown described in this chapter and the rape of Sara Beth Donnelly in Chapter Three highlight the nature and actions of this type of attacker.

The Power Assertive Rapist (PAR) operates on the assumption that women owe him sex. Estimates vary but it is believed that 12 to 24 percent of all rapists are PARs. They view people as prey objects, and use trickery, manipulation, head games, intimidation, verbal abuse, and isolation to gain access to their victims. For these rapists the sexual assault is about dominating and controlling their victims by possessing them sexually. Power over his victim's sexuality is this rapist's means of expressing his mastery, strength, control, authority, and identity.

The PAR has an extreme sense of superiority and entitlement. He rapes women to validate his masculinity. In his view that is what men do. They take what they want including sex. He is usually athletic, exercises often, a flashy dresser and may drive a muscle car. He enjoys the macho image and can be loud and boisterous. The rapes by Hells Angel Thomas "Red" Nesbitt, culminating in the rape-murder of Mary Kay Harmer, described in Chapter Six, is a clear example of this type of rapist.

The Anger Retaliatory Rapist (ARR) is estimated to represent less than 30 percent of all rapists. This rapist is angry at the world and often at a particular woman, or at women in general. A perceived wrong ignites an attack that usually follows within 24 hours. Unlike the power-reassurance rapist whose crimes are often premeditated, the ARR commonly acts on impulse often using debilitating force. Once his rage is spent the ARR may never rape again or at least not until stresses reach a boiling point and his evil desire erupts again.

David Burdette, one of the most notorious serial rapists in Omaha history with his targeting of the Ten Most Eligible Women of the city, described in Chapter Seven, is a prime example of this type or rapist as are the rapes of Earl LaBelle described in Chapter Five.

The Anger Excitation Rapist (AER) is the rarest and most dangerous category of rapist, accounting for less than five percent of all rapists. The attacks are often excessively violent and often result in the death of the victims. In spite of its rarity, rapes committed by AERs often generate sensational headlines because of the bizarre and extremely savage nature of the attacks.

The AER uses ritualism, bondage, spanking, or other acts of sexual sadism to humiliate, frighten and demean his victims. He gets excitement and sexual arousal from watching their suffering. The assaults of Canyon Road rapist Henry Kamphaus described in Chapter Nine illuminate the crimes of this category of rapist.

 confidence

A key goal of the initial victim interview is to determine what type of rapist committed the attack. As I dictated my reports for typing by the Criminal Investigative Bureau (CIB) transcriptionists describing my interview of Jackie Brown and the facts of my investigation to that point, I was confused about what category her rapist most closely aligned with. I realized that many rapists were sociopaths but elaborating on that information by accurately categorizing the rape was imperative. Knowing what type of rapist I was dealing with would give me insight into his background, what drove him to rape and, more importantly, where he might strike next and what type of woman his next victim might be. Narrowing the universe of suspects is the most important product of successfully typing the rapist. When combined with insight into where he preferred to prowl in search of victims, this would enable me to close the net around him and hasten his arrest.

His next victim would leave no doubt about what type of rapist I was hunting. Tracking him down would hinge on the never-give-up work ethic of legendary football coach Vince Lombardi. My investigation would ultimately lead me halfway across the country to an internationally famous seaside resort area frequented by the rich and famous. It would culminate in the arrest and conviction of one of the most intriguing serial rapists I ever investigated.

Chapter Two
Sociopathy and Rape

> You can't "re" habilitate someone who
> has never been habilitated.
> **Dr. Stanton Samenow**

Many of the rapists I arrested were sociopaths. Criminologists, psychologists and psychiatrists have recognized the existence of traits now associated with sociopathy since the early 19th century. In the 1940s, psychiatrist Hervey Cleckley wrote "The Mask of Sanity," widely considered the most influential clinical description of the disorder. The term "mask of sanity" stemmed from Cleckley's belief that a sociopath can appear normal but the mask conceals the sociopath's true nature, allowing him to prey on the unsuspecting.

The sociopath has a pervasive disregard for the rights of others beginning in childhood or early adolescence and continuing into adulthood. They manipulate people by using them as objects to satisfy their own needs and desires. Using Cleckley's mask analogy, they operate behind a superficial charm that obscures their covert hostility. They perceive others as aggressors, competitors, and instruments to be used to get their way.

The evil among us prowl like wolves among sheep. They inflict massive physical, emotional, and financial harm on their unsuspecting victims. To them, their victims are nothing more than flotsam bobbing in the wake of their narcissistic and massively destructive machinations. It is difficult for people not familiar with evil to grasp how pervasive it is and its capacity to harm.

It is important to note that not all sociopaths are criminals. Sociopathic behavior is not confined to prisons or socially underprivileged settings. It manifests itself in society anywhere antisocial traits have survival value including business, law, medicine, and politics.

Sociopaths think radically differently than people who are basically responsible and law-abiding. They see themselves like the hub of a wheel around which everything must revolve. They view the world as their personal chess board with people and objects as pawns to serve their supremely selfish evil desire. They live their daily lives trying to control others. Their self-esteem depends upon it. Some are obvious in that they bully and threaten. Others are more clandestine, insinuating themselves into the lives of others while maneuvering and probing those around them for vulnerabilities. They cleverly and expertly conceal their motives. When they spot weakness, or what they perceive as weakness, such as kindness, they pounce without regard to the damage done to others.

The trauma of victimization can have a profound and devastating impact. It can alter the victim's view of the world as a just place and leave them with new and difficult feelings and reactions that they may not understand. The consequences of crime can affect victims on multiple levels, psychologically, financially, physically, and spiritually.

The evil they perpetrate has a ripple effect that washes over many others. Their primary victims are those directly harmed by their evil, such as a rape victim. Secondary victims include those not directly touched by the violence but who may suffer because they are emotionally and psychologically attached to the victim. This includes parents, spouses or significant others, siblings, children, grandparents, and close friends. Research shows, for example, that each homicide victim leaves behind at least three secondary victims who sustain significant loss and suffering as a result of the murder.

Crime has an impact not only on primary and secondary victims but also the entire community. High-profile major crimes can have a wide effect by fostering community-wide fear. Most people fail to consider the impact high profile violent crime has on a community and its quality of life. It can include flight from the community as worried citizens move to what they perceive as safer areas, declining property values, and reduction in the creation of new retail and personal service businesses.

Depending on the severity of the crime, some victims will experience Post-Traumatic Stress Disorder (PTSD), a mental health condition triggered by a terrifying event. Symptoms may include flashbacks, nightmares and severe anxiety, as well as uncontrollable thoughts about the event. The phrase "time heals all" does not apply to many crime victims with PTSD. They do not spontaneously recover without treatment. Some experience PTSD years after they were victimized.

As seen in Jackie's case, the biggest fear many rape victims have is that their attacker will come back. A victim of David Burdette's 1982 Omaha's Most Eligible Women rape spree, described in Chapter Seven, feared for her safety when she learned that her attacker had served his prison sentence and was back on the streets after 15 years. Old fears came back to haunt her and she had trouble sleeping. Every night she double-checked the locks on her doors and windows. "I was afraid he could track us down," she said. "You lose your sense of trust and your sense of security."

Dr. Stanton Samenow, noted criminologist, describes the allure of crime evident in statements criminals have made to him in his over 40 years of working with them: "Take my crime away, and you take my world away," one criminal asserted. Another commented, "Crime is like ice cream; it's delicious."

He explains, "The offender fantasizes, schemes, and develops a modus operandi. There is excitement in every phase—before, during, and after the act. In a bank robbery, he selects his target. He makes a series of choices as to how he will carry out the crime. There is excitement enroute to the scene, in committing the crime, in the getaway, and in the self-buildup after the offense. Gaining publicity and eluding the police enhance the excitement. Even if he is apprehended there is the challenge of dealing with the police, his attorney, and others who hold him accountable. If the perpetrator ends up in jail or prison the excitement may not end even there. For many criminals, prison is simply the streets brought indoors with more opportunities for intrigues, con games, and conquests" (Samenow 2011).

Building on Cleckley's work, mentioned above, Canadian psychologist Robert Hare developed the Psychopathy Check List (PCL) in the 1970s. Psychopathy was the term for sociopathy at that time. They are essentially interchangeable terms but today psychology prefers the term sociopathy. Hare's PCL was based partly on his work with male prison inmates in Vancouver, B.C. Hare's checklist is a diagnostic tool used to rate a person's psychopathic—now referred to as sociopathic, or antisocial—tendencies. It measures symptoms of sociopathy including lack of a conscience or sense of guilt, lack of empathy, egocentricity, pathological lying, repeated violations of social norms, disregard for the law, shallow emotions, and a history of victimizing others, among other factors.

One percent of the U.S. population are sociopaths but it is estimated that as many as twenty-five percent of incarcerated individuals are. They account for fifty percent of the most serious crimes committed including half of all serial rapes (Kiehl 2011:357). A disproportionately high number of cop-killers are sociopaths. Unlike many people, sociopaths lack any symptoms of worry or depression. They are supremely selfish and have a marked inability to love others or give true affection. Sociopaths lack a moral compass which deprives them of any remorse or guilt. They lack the capacity to see themselves as others do.

Sociopaths are pathological liars who are highly cunning, unreliable, irresponsible, and impulsive. They suffer from profound pathological stimulation seeking (Quay 1965). Research indicates that they have an excessive neurological need for thrills and excitement. The biological basis of that need is not fully understood but sociopaths suffer a higher number of traumatic brain injuries than the rest of the population, most likely from pathological stimulation seeking that blocks inhibitions to danger. That biological condition may also be related to the fact that small amounts of alcohol usually cause them to become vulgar, domineering, loud, boisterous, and reckless.

Several sociopathic traits impact on serial rape. First is their marked inability to accept blame. Albert DeSalvo, the infamous Boston Strangler of the 1960s, blamed his rapes and murders of 13 women between the ages of 19 and 85 in the Boston area on his wife's sexual hang-ups. Similarly, it is common for cop killers to blame the officer for some perceived offense that they claim precipitated the killing, like writing the sociopath a traffic citation. Rapists blame the victim for dressing provocatively, drinking heavily or being at a singles bar, "She asked for it by being at that meat market."

Other significant traits of sociopaths include callousness and sadism—deriving pleasure, especially sexual gratification, from inflicting pain, suffering, or humiliation on others. They possess a remarkable ability to disregard the pain and suffering they cause to others. Sociopaths may rape a bank teller during a standoff with police without any regard to others present just to see what it is like. The sadistic nature of many serial rapists is traceable to their sociopathic tendencies. That explains why violence committed by sociopaths is often especially callous and cold-blooded.

There is no known treatment for sociopathy.

One of the most revealing encounters I had with a sociopath occurred early in my career when I was a young patrol deputy. It was July 1981 and I was working the "A" or overnight shift that spanned the 11 PM to 7 AM hours. I loved working that shift because you were more likely to encounter hardcore criminals than at any other time. After all, most honest people work for a living and they are in bed during those hours. In contrast, criminals often use the hours of darkness to obscure their illegal acts. The lack of honest citizen activity at that hour translates to fewer witnesses to their crimes.

It was a fairly busy Friday night and I was assigned to cover three western patrol districts. It was a lot of territory on the edges of the suburbs with some smaller towns scattered throughout, but much of it was farmland. After the radio calls fell off after bar closing at 1:00 AM I was able to do some patrolling instead of running from call to call.

In 1981, there was a trailer park at 174th and W. Dodge Road near the eastern boundary of my patrol districts. It was called Regency Park but there was little of a regal nature about it. The place was crammed with ramshackle single-wide trailer homes.

Dodge Street is one of the main streets in Omaha and handles a lot of traffic. As Dodge Street makes its way westward it changes to West Dodge Road at about 84th Street. In those days it narrowed to two lanes as it left the density of the city behind.

I had just finished going through the trailer park with my car blacked out looking for suspicious activity. Patrolling while blacked out refers to turning off headlights and brake lights which can be seen from long distances at night, tipping off suspects that I am approaching. I was sitting at the only entrance to the complex in the parking lot of an RV repair company adjacent to it. The street lights ended just west of the trailer park where I sat watching, listening, and ready to pounce. The spot I chose partially hid my cruiser behind a travel trailer parked in the lot. I liked to sit in a strategic location with everything turned off and the police radio turned down. Sound travels farther at night because it is usually cooler and the air is denser. Also, suspicious sounds—like breaking glass, a door being pried open, or a woman screaming—are easier to hear at night because there is less background noise to obscure or confuse the sound.

As I sat there waiting I spotted a faded blue '64 Impala as it turned off West Dodge Road into the trailer park. It was nearly 3:00 AM and the car didn't have a front license plate. I lost sight of the Impala as it drove down the hill towards the east end of the complex. As I watched it reappeared near the top of the hill on an adjacent street. The driver slowly crept along as if looking for something or someone.

I continued to watch and wait, straining to listen for anything out of the ordinary as the Impala prowled the trailer park. After navigating all five streets in the complex, apparently without stopping to engage in any mischief, the Impala reappeared as it headed towards the entrance and back onto the highway. It turned westwards and continued to creep along in spite of a 55 mph speed limit. The driver spotted me as I left the parking lot and turned to follow him. Pulling up behind him I saw that the rear license plate was a Colorado plate. It was also covered with bug splatter. Bug splatter could only get on the rear plate if the impossible had happened; the car had been driven in reverse at high speed over a long distance.

It was a fairly common mistake made by thieves. In their hurry to steal license plates and get them affixed to a stolen car they overlook the bug splatter, perhaps because they were also operating in the dark to avoid detection and hadn't noticed it. I wanted to know if the car was stolen or not, which was likely, even though I was going to exercise extreme caution due to the suspicious nature of the driver. I notified the dispatcher that I was making a stop, giving the license plate and location. I also asked for wants and warrants and the registration for the plate before initiating the stop. Because it was an out of state plate the dispatcher had to query the National Crime Information Center (NCIC) along with the Colorado system for the registration. It was all automated but took longer than computer checks on local vehicles.

I also asked for a backup unit. Being a busy Friday night/early Saturday morning no backup was readily available. My closest backup was handling a bad traffic accident that would tie them up for hours. Dispatch had to send a unit from several districts farther away.

As I followed the slowly moving car at a safe distance the dispatcher came back after less than a minute to advise me that the license plate registration was not on file. That didn't mean the plate was not stolen, it could mean either the plate had not been reported stolen yet or there was a glitch in the computer system that temporarily blocked all queries related to the plate. In those days all NCIC inquiries made a near-the-speed-of-light cross-country round trip from the computer terminal in our dispatch center via a dedicated telephone line to the computers at the State Capitol in Lincoln. From there they streaked to a data hub in Arizona and from there on to the central database in Clarksburg, West Virginia and back. In spite of the distance covered, NCIC inquiries averaged only 90 seconds, unless there were network problems or slowdowns. The system wasn't foolproof and, at that time, there were more than occasional glitches.

You often see NCIC mentioned in cop movies. The real NCIC was launched in 1967 with only 356,000 records identifying fugitives, missing persons, and stolen property. Today, it is such an indispensable law enforcement tool that it contains over 12 million records and averages a staggering 12.6 million transactions each day.

I wasn't focused on any of that at the time. My attention was on the suspicious car creeping slowly along in front of me. I could see the driver's shoulder dip, indicating that he might be hiding something...or reaching for a weapon. Because my backup was so far away I wanted to try to stop the hump while he was under the street lights. Instead of closing with him I maintained my distance and asked dispatch the ETA of my backup. They responded that my backup had collided with another car and was unable to continue. I found out later that the deputy had been broadsided at an intersection by a drunk driver. (The deputy was injured and off work for months but was eventually able to return to duty.)

One of the dangers of working the overnight shift is the prevalence of drunk drivers and the risk they pose to officers. This stems from not only being hit by drunks running red lights or stop signs, but also those who strike deputies standing outside their cars conducting traffic or field interrogation stops. Four out of ten cops killed in the line of duty die in traffic accidents or from injuries sustained in traffic accidents (Wolfe 2015:460). Most of those deaths occur during high speed pursuits or responding to emergency calls while driving at high speed, but a fair number occur when cops are struck by drunk drivers.

As a last resort I asked dispatch if there were any state troopers available. After a moment they replied that all troopers were out of service handling calls. I was now on my own and there was no way I was letting this hump escape my grasp. As we continued to creep along we got farther and farther away from the security of the street lights and into the darkness beyond. Since I was on my own it wasn't necessary to delay initiating the stop, waiting for backup to get closer, so I activated my overhead red lights and the driver immediately pulled onto the shoulder of the road.

I placed my cruiser offset from the Impala, extending into the traffic lane about four feet to give me a space to stand that was shielded from traffic approaching from behind. I then turned on my takedown lights on the overhead bar. They were a pair of incredibly bright aircraft landing lights that created a wall between the bad guy and me. I could see him clearly but all he could see was a blinding curtain of light that obscured me. As soon as I turned them on the driver started adjusting his rearview and side mirrors to keep the piercing light out of his eyes.

I stepped out of my cruiser while simultaneously drawing my Smith and Wesson Model 66 revolver. I was intently focused on the driver and what he was doing. The gun and my hand controlling it rested slightly behind the holster alongside my leg in what is called a "low profile carry." I wanted my gun out in case it was needed quickly, following the officer survival adage, "Better to have it out and not need it than need it and not have it out." In that way it was barely noticeable by the driver but would be ready much more quickly than if it had remained holstered.

Instead of approaching right away, I slowed things down. I closed my door softly so as not to give away my precise location while I remained obscured behind the glare of the takedown lights. I never took my eyes off the driver and what he was doing before moving to the back of my cruiser. Once there I leaned over my trunk to watch him through the rear window of my cruiser. Not only was I cautious about his suspicious actions but a familiar reassuring presence or state of mind was pulling me towards caution. It wasn't a voice warning me so much as it was a nagging sense that real danger lurked in that car. I had never conducted a traffic stop in that manner before. For those lacking faith, that nagging sense might be considered a sixth sense. For me, I knew it was the presence of Jesus at my side.

The feeling of danger was reinforced when the driver started waving what appeared to be a vehicle registration and perhaps insurance or other vehicle identification papers out the window with his left hand. It was as if they were a lure to attract me to approach and to distract me once at the driver's door. He was doing everything he could to make sure that I approached on that side of the car just as he expected.

Watching the driver wave the papers out the window led me to continue to do the unexpected. I decided to approach on the passenger side where he wouldn't be watching for me. I had never done a passenger side approach before. It wasn't a tactic being taught in the academy at the time.

I moved cautiously and slowly alongside the passenger side of my car towards the Impala. I never took my eyes off the driver as I inched ahead, trying not to make any noise that would give away my presence. The closer I got the more I could see of his upper body. It hinted that he was holding something close to his chest in his right hand. As I moved closer the driver twisted in his seat to look backward out the driver side window to see if I was coming. He had no clue that I was about to derail his plan and that he was looking in the wrong direction. I continued to move forward slowly until I was just behind his passenger side door. I could now see that he was holding something up to his chest in his right hand. He continued to wave the papers out the window while twisting to that side to see where I was. I stepped forward a little more where I could see clearly that he held a revolver in his right hand. I raised my Smith and Wesson Model 66 and pointed it at his head and yelled, "Don't move, asshole. Drop the gun!" He was stunned. The gun remained glued to his chest while his head jerked from looking over his left shoulder to the right to look at me. He was staring straight down the barrel of my gun.

"Drop it or I'll spray your brains all over the car!" I yelled. He paused for a moment as if weighing his options. "Let the gun fall from your hand. DO IT NOW!" I ordered.

"Look man, I thought you was my girlfriend's husband…." he stammered while still clutching the gun. The hammer was coming back on my gun as my finger began to squeeze the trigger. The hump was dangerously close to dying and he must have sensed it.

"All right, all right," he said, his voice strangely calm and emotionless as he cast a sideways glance at me. "Like I said, man, I thought you was…" he tried to continue.

I interrupted him abruptly, "Shut up, asshole! Drop the gun NOW!"

Cunning, street savvy predators know that if they can get an adversary to respond to their banter they gain an advantage because it slows down reaction time. It's called the reaction gap and it stems from the mental process necessary to initiate a physical response to a threat—in this case movement of the weapon towards me. Contrary to conventional wisdom, reacting to the threat is not instantaneous because there is a delay in responding due to the mental steps necessary to respond (Olson 1996:4).

Reacting is more than physically responding by pulling the trigger. The physical response is predicated on a four-step mental process that must precede it. It begins with perceiving the threatening action—in this case seeing the movement of the gun—followed by evaluating the information to confirm it is a threat, then formulating a response, and finally initiating a motor action or physical response such as firing my weapon.

These steps take mere milliseconds, but they must occur each and every time as part of the mental process necessary to initiate a physical response to a threat. After all four steps the process culminates in your brain telling your finger to pull the trigger. Since the bad guy goes through the same mental process the moment he begins to move his gun he is already literally three steps ahead of you. That slight delay reinforces the training adage "action is always faster than reaction," giving a slight edge to the bad guy. That is why a determined thug who is not directly pointing a weapon at an officer can bring his gun to bear and fire at least one shot before or simultaneously with the officer responding by firing his or her sidearm even though it is drawn and pointed at the bad guy.

Apex predators like this guy don't have to know the science behind the reaction gap. Their experience with street violence has exposed them to its reality. This was borne out later when this hardcore sociopath admitted to involvement in at least one gunfight with police. I also did not know it at the time but additional realities about sociopaths were at play with this guy too. Their inability to understand emotions like fear, including the fear of death or serious bodily injury, fails to deter them from trying to kill a cop.

When their impulsivity is combined with their pathological need for stimulation and thrill-seeking, and their possessing a grandiose sense of self-worth that fuels extreme over confidence, it is little wonder they are not hesitant to take on cops. In an early 1990s study the FBI found that 44 percent of cop killers were sociopaths even though they comprise only one percent of the U.S. population (Babiak 2012:3).

I wasn't concerned with any of that at the moment. My street survival instincts were in overdrive as I sensed what he was up to. He hesitated momentarily then let the gun drop from his hand as directed. It fell onto the floor in front of the driver's seat. "Keep your palms up!" I ordered as he turned to look at me.

"You was gonna kill me, weren't you?" he asked.

"Shut up and listen," I ordered. "Look away from me. Move very slowly and do exactly what I tell you."

"Okay, man, Okay. No need to panic…" he said as he sat frozen with his palms facing upwards.

"Shut up or I'll put a bullet in your brain," I replied. "Slide over here, slowly," I ordered while stepping back from the car a few feet. He started to drop his hands before moving.

"Uh, uh! Keep those hands palms up where I can see them." I commanded. He complied as he slid slowly, deliberately across the bench seat.

"Open it. From the outside. S-l-o-w-l-y," I said as he moved ever closer to the door. He kept watching me out of the corner of his eyes intently sizing me up like a cat measuring his prey. He showed no sign of fear in spite of staring down the muzzle of my gun. It was as if I could see his mind turning, searching for an opening to turn the tables on me.

As he climbed out of the car, I ordered him to turn away from me and to kneel. He immediately began to try to con me again by stalling, "Come on, man. It was a mistake. I meant no harm. Like I said, I thought you was…"

I cut him off abruptly, "Shut up, asshole. On your knees," I commanded. I wanted him to know that I knew what he was all about.

He began to turn slowly towards me with his hands up. "Man, why you treatin' me like this?" he said before I cut him off again.

"KNEEL!" I ordered as he paused.

In that instant I remembered the words of one of my academy instructors during street survival training: "When you find a gun on a suspect always assume he has another one." I moved back one step to create distance and give me reaction time if he tried to rush me as I braced myself to fire. I could feel the hammer beginning to come back ever so slightly as my finger began to squeeze the trigger again. At that point he seemed to realize that I couldn't be conned into dropping my guard. He slowly turned away from me and dropped to his knees.

Once he was kneeling on the ground I ordered him to lace his fingers together behind his head and to place one foot over the other. After he had grudgingly done that I ordered him to sit back on his feet. In that position it is impossible to get up quickly and the longer he sits that way the more his legs begin to go to sleep.

"You was gonna kill me, weren't you?" he asked. "I could tell it in your voice."

"I may kill you yet if you don't shut up," I barked.

I moved in cautiously to handcuff him by ordering him to place his right hand in the small of his back, palm out and thumb up. I then holstered my weapon. The last thing you want is a gun flopping around and accessible to the suspect if you have to go hands-on with a resisting bad guy. After stepping firmly onto his overlapped feet to keep him from standing up I quickly grasped his upturned palm and smoothly clamped the right cuff on his wrist with my right hand. If he tried to attack me now all I had to do was drag him over backwards by his cuffed right hand and use the cuff to inflict debilitating pain to nerves in his wrist to control him. It's called an iron wristlock and it is very effective at controlling a resisting suspect. But using it meant trying to prone him out for control. Given his extremely dangerous predatory antics so far I was more inclined to use Plan B and simply shove him onto his face while disengaging by stepping back to redraw my weapon. That way I could minimize the risk of getting tangled up with him. I was under no illusions about how dangerous this guy was.

He was totally compliant as I brought his left hand down to complete the handcuffing. Before letting him stand up I double locked the cuffs with the oversized cuff key I kept clipped to the pen opening of my uniform shirt pocket. Now that he was temporarily restrained I began to study him closely. He was lean and sinewy, about 5'8" and 155 pounds. He looked to be about 50 years old. His long gray hair was pulled back in a ponytail that framed his weathered, deeply creased face in a manner that reminded me of Willie Nelson. Unlike Nelson he spoke with a slight Chicago accent.

I didn't know it at the time but he was among my first encounters with a stone cold sociopath—a guy who would have killed me without a second's hesitation. That became clear when I secured him in the front seat of my cruiser after locking my shotgun rack and seat-belting him in. On the drive to booking he revealed a little about himself, half bragging and half conning while looking for any opportunity to get the better of me. Like all sociopaths he was constantly manipulating those around him. Prying, probing, searching for kindness, weakness or confusion that he could exploit.

"No offense, man, but I would've shot you in the face back there," he said. "See, I know you guys all wear bullet proof vests. So gotta go for the head, make sure you don't shoot back," he continued while he let slip a muffled chuckle.

"Is that right?" I replied.

"Yep, nothing personal. Just been down that road before," was his reply. He then told me how he had jumped parole from a prison in another state and stole the Impala and the license plate from a truck stop. He claimed his name was Edward Henry (Hank) Leggett. Like many career criminals he used several aliases to hide his true identity. He'd spent a few days breaking into houses looking for cash and valuables before heading for a small airstrip in search of a gun. Leggett knew that some small planes had survival kits that contained a gun. At that time, airport hangars were notorious for being poorly secured. The first plane he broke into had a kit from which he stole a Smith and Wesson Model 34 survival "kit gun." In addition to the eight-shot .22 revolver he also stole a box of ammo for it.

Leggett claimed he was looking for an old girlfriend at the trailer park when I spotted him. He also told me that he had been in a shootout with two Indiana State Troopers in the early 1950s after a botched bank robbery in Gary, Indiana. One of the troopers was hurt pretty badly but survived. The other trooper brought Leggett down with two rounds that put him in a jail hospital for six months with wounds to his abdomen. He had been convicted of robbery and attempted murder of the troopers and sentenced to 50 years. He sought and was granted a transfer to serve the remainder of his sentence in another state claiming that he had "worked with" prison authorities in Indiana to bust corrupt guards. He claimed his life was in danger in Indiana so he had to be moved to another prison out of state.

Sociopaths are pathological liars. They lie when it is easier to tell the truth. Leggett was no exception. He could spin a believable fraud as quickly and effortlessly as honest people breathe. Instinctively I knew that nearly everything he was telling me was a lie or he was twisting the facts so badly that the truth was unrecognizable. He was so fundamentally crooked that if he ate a nail he would crap a corkscrew. His "coming clean" by admitting that he had intended to kill me, even though he repeatedly reminded me that it wasn't personal, was part of his well-honed sociopath hustle. He played everyone, trying to generate good will through fake honesty to exploit later when the target of his hustle let their guard down. He was among a handful of the most dangerous thugs I encountered in my career.

When I asked him why he jumped parole he claimed that his parole officer (PO) "had it in for me," and was "setting me up for a fall." According to Leggett, violating his parole and fleeing were purely defensive measures to protect him from going back to prison at the hands of a crooked PO and then being subject to abuse by equally corrupt prison guards.

In his warped sense of morality my stopping him that night was also wrong because it interfered with his right to "not be hassled by cops" and his desire to not return to prison. If he had allowed me to stop him peaceably, he would have been equally guilty, along with the crooked PO, and by extension me, for landing him back in prison. "How could I go along with that?" was his reply. It simply made no sense to a sociopath like Leggett. The world revolved around him and his needs. No others were even close to that level of importance. In true sociopath form he believed that he was simply doing to others what they would do to him if they got the chance.

Years later, when I was assigned to the Intelligence Unit working organized crime involving outlaw motorcycle gangs I ran into another high-order sociopath who was an informant for a deputy on my team. He had been involved in a horrendous bike accident in another state that landed him in the hospital off and on for eight months.

Like many sociopaths he was attracted to the outlaw biker culture because it focused on hedonism and indulged his unbridled lust for consequence-free immediate gratification. It was a counter-culture that eschewed social norms under the pretense of its members being social mavericks. Like all sociopaths they are supremely selfish with no ability or interest to empathize with those they chew up and spit out.

One night he was drinking heavily and snorting meth in a local biker bar when he decided to go for a thrill ride. While high, drunk, and racing around town he was spotted by the city cops who tried to pull him over. He sped off at high speed, leading them on a chase for several miles until he approached a red light at a heavily travelled four lane highway. Instead of stopping, he rolled the dice figuring that if he made it through the intersection he would lose the cops who would be unable to continue the chase due to the heavy cross traffic present.

He gunned the motorcycle, hitting speeds up to 60 mph, and ran the light. He made it halfway through the intersection when his luck ran out. He struck the driver's side door of a small car proceeding through the intersection. The force of the collision propelled him up and over the handlebars and eighty feet beyond the intersection where he landed in the gutter after toppling over and over like a rag doll in a clothes dryer. He broke many of the major bones in his body and sustained a grocery list of severe, nearly fatal internal injuries including a torn liver, fractured vertebra, skull fracture, broken ribs and a collapsed lung. Miraculously, he survived albeit with a severe limp and more pins and bolts in his extremities than in a hardware store.

The unfortunate driver of the car he hit was not so lucky. The force of the crash propelled the motorcycle into and nearly halfway through the car, killing him instantly. A split second of wanton recklessness by a morally bankrupt sociopath had snuffed out the life of an honest, hardworking father of four. The balance scales of life were knocked off their mount that night. They would be left adrift like so much flotsam in the destructive wake of a sociopath's supremely selfish evil desire. Their inconceivable suffering and loss were inconsequential to the sociopath and his biker buddies who rallied around their fellow gang member. There was no such outpouring of comfort and support for the innocent secondary victims of his predatory antics.

When later describing the crash to another biker who was unaware of the circumstances, the informant was asked if anyone else got hurt in the crash. His emotionless reply was stunning in its callousness. "Nope," he replied nonchalantly. In his morally stunted mind, as in the mind of all sociopaths to one degree or another, the pain, suffering, even the senseless death of another human being due to his wanton recklessness failed to trigger the slightest trace of empathy or remorse. In fact, I am sure that in his twisted morality, or lack thereof, the other guy was to blame because if he hadn't been driving that night he wouldn't have been in the path of the motorcycle.

In another example of the thorough moral rot of this guy, he grudgingly agreed to watch his girlfriend's four-year-old son one summer afternoon while she worked as a manicurist at one of the nail salons owned by the gang. Cash-intensive businesses like nail salons are often used to launder money from drug pushing and other crimes. It was one of three jobs she worked to support the shiftless leech so he could pal around with other bikers unhindered by gainful employment. After all, nothing throttled the unbridled hedonism of the biker lifestyle more than having a regular job and legitimately earning your way in life. Like many sociopaths he moved from one parasitic relationship after another. His girlfriend sacrificed and slaved away for money to pay the bills so he could hang out, booze it up, and do dope while plotting crimes with his fellow gang members.

That day, the biker was using a pneumatic nail gun in the garage to build a workbench while the child played in the driveway. Soon one of his biker buddies showed up asking him to go riding and "get a few beers." The biker had to find a way to leave the child unattended. As in the death of the motorist, the biker's solution was as stunning in its callousness as it was shocking in its immorality. He fastened the child to the side of the garage using the pneumatic nailer to nail through the edges of the sobbing child's pant legs so he couldn't wander off. By the time the girlfriend returned home hours later the child was sunburned, dehydrated and terrified. He had soiled himself repeatedly and cried himself hoarse.

Two more stunning examples of the callous, cold-blooded, wantonly depraved violence sociopaths are capable of involve other outlaw motorcycle gang members. As detailed in the rape-murder of Mary Kay Harmer, described in Chapter Six, the sociopathic violence of gang members often extends beyond the orbit of the gang. When it does it can engulf the most innocent and vulnerable among us resulting in staggering, heartrending evil.

The first example began in early 1976 when Margo Compton had had enough of the abuse from her biker husband Doug Compton, a gang associate. In desperation she turned to Odis "Buck" Garrett for help escaping from her marriage. Garrett was the president of the Hells Angels Nomad chapter in Vallejo, CA. Typical of many women attracted to the outlaw biker lifestyle, Compton's childhood was a hardscrabble upbringing as one of ten children in a poverty-stricken, broken home in Benicia, CA (Fagan 1995).

According to her younger sister, Lynne Spieckerman, while growing up they had little parental supervision and often ran with a bad crowd. Typical of the low lifestyle, most of Margo's life had been a tumultuous flight from crisis to crisis with the exception of the birth of her twin daughters with Doug Compton. Typical of the predatory sociopaths populating outlaw biker gangs, Garrett capitalized on her vulnerability and desperation and began conditioning her to work as a hooker at a sleazy nude encounter studio run by the gang in San Francisco. Called "The Love Nest," it was nothing more than a filthy brothel. After giving her a "sex test" to prove her proficiency at oral copulation he gave her a room in a house he kept for hookers and put her to work (Doe 2002).

She lasted seven weeks before going to the police after a customer beat and raped her and after Garrett refused to let her quit, claiming she owed $4,800 for protection from her husband and for her weekly issue of methamphetamine. She told police that she and four other Love Nest women had to return forty percent of the money they earned to the Angels. The operation also allegedly had the protection of two San Francisco vice officers who were paid off in cash and sexual favors. To make her pay and ensure her return to hooking, Garrett held her twin daughters at his Bay Area home as ransom (Fagan 1995).

Compton was now dating a Bay Area auto salesman and with his help she got a team of Contra Costa County sheriff's detectives to retrieve the children. Still furious, she agreed to cooperate with police trying to shut down The Love Nest by testifying against Garrett.

When she testified against him at a preliminary hearing in a pimping trial her fate was sealed. In the unwritten code of the outlaw biker everyone knows that "snitches wind up in ditches." But Garrett wanted more than just Margo Compton (Valdemar 2009). He wanted to make an example of her to other would-be informants. In an uncommon streak of vicious evil he demanded that the twins be murdered in front of Compton before she was killed.

In 1976, after testifying, Compton was moved for her safety into a small house under the ponderosas in Laurelwood, a sleepy little town small town about 25 miles from Portland, Oregon. Her then six-year-old twin daughters, Sylvia and Sandra, were living with her. It was a fresh start. Neighbors described Compton as a sad-eyed woman carrying a soul-sapping variety of life's weariness well beyond her years. They noted that she appeared to be working intently inside the house and rarely left except to drive her two six-year-old girls to and from school each day. The family kept to themselves.

Unknown to her neighbors Compton was writing a book—an autobiography of her life back in California with the Hells Angels. It was a story with names and places. How the Angels had forced her into prostitution, kept her on drugs, brutalized her. How she finally had escaped from them and turned state's evidence. She was under no illusion about the danger she faced. Convinced that Garrett would try to seek her out, Compton and her new boyfriend hid a half-dozen guns throughout the house: by the bed, under the couch, anywhere they could be hidden and retrieved quickly (Fagan 1995).

Compton had been corresponding with relatives in Vallejo. She was unaware that the Angels had intercepted a letter with her Oregon address. Garrett put a plot into motion, hiring a Hells Angel prospect named Robert "Bug Eye Bob" McClure and gang associate Benjamin "Psycho" Silva to perform the hit. McClure was in debt to Garrett for drugs. For murdering Compton and her daughters he would earn his "cuts" and become a full Hells Angel member, repay his debt and have two pounds of meth waiting for him when he returned. Garrett provided them with two guns for the contract: a .357 Magnum for Silva and a .22 caliber for McClure.

On August 7, 1977 the gunmen struck. A third gang associate drove the team to Laurelwood and waited for them to complete the murders before returning them to Vallejo. The wheelman bragged later, "We know how to take care of people like that."

Unknown to the gunmen before they arrived, Gary Seslar, the 19-year-old son of Compton's boyfriend, was present at the house. Detectives theorize that Seslar was shot in the head by Silva as he rose to fight off the hitmen. As he lay dying on the floor they forced Compton and her daughters into the girls' bedroom where the sobbing and terrified twins were forced to lay face-down on their bed. Silva placed a teddy bear under each child and wrapped their arms around it. He then pinned the distraught Compton against the door and forced her to watch as McClure placed the muzzle of the .22 behind the left ear of each girl before pulling the trigger. McClure then finished Compton off with three shots to the head. The gunmen threw their weapons into the Klamath River outside of Weed, CA 350 miles south before returning to Vallejo.

In a letter to her parents a week before she was murdered, Compton wrote, "I have been through hell and it's not over yet. My life, I suppose (to other people), has been a series of unbelievable events." With no fingerprints, no murder weapons and no witnesses the case quickly went cold. Years after the quadruple murder, Bug Eye Bob McClure was sent to prison on an unrelated charge. Now a full-patched Hells Angel he openly bragged to other inmates about the shooting of the twins. His inability keep his mouth shut would be his undoing (Fagan 1995).

The case was at a standstill until the early 1980s when tips began to filter up to an investigator in Oregon still working the cold case. They came from California prison officials who said informants behind bars were starting to talk about a quadruple hit in Oregon. In the mid-1980s investigators got the break they needed when Michael "Iron Mike" Thompson, a former leader of the hyper-violent Aryan Brotherhood prison gang, gave prison intelligence officials a detailed account of conversations with Garrett. Garrett was then in prison on methamphetamine distribution charges. Thompson claimed that Garrett confessed the hits to him in Folsom Prison.

Other inmates said that McClure boasted of the murders while incarcerated in San Quentin. They said they heard him brag about the 1977 killings of Compton, her daughters and a friend, and describe how the children's heads were shattered by his bullets. One prisoner testified that McClure had bragged about making Compton watch as he shot her daughters first and that they had died clutching their teddy bears (Fagan 1995).

Eighteen years after the murders, Aryan Brotherhood members Mike Thompson and Clifford Smith, along with other California prison inmates, testified against the murderer of Margo Compton, her twin six-year-old daughters Sylvia and Sandra, and the family friend. Bug

Eye Bob McClure was convicted and sentenced to four consecutive life terms for the quadruple murders.

Benjamin Silva was already in San Quentin for a grisly double murder. He was never charged in the Compton case. Prosecutors said it wasn't worth the expense and effort because he was already on death row for the 1981 kidnapping, rape, and torture slayings of two college students in Lassen County, CA (Fagan 1995).

The summer after McClure's conviction, Garrett stood trial for the quadruple homicides. Like McClure before him, Garrett was convicted of four counts of murder and sentenced to four consecutive life sentences. A one-time millionaire dealer of "crank," or methamphetamine, Garrett was at one time considered by the DEA to be one of the biggest meth distributors in the nation. He was already serving a life term in Lompoc federal prison in California on a narcotics conviction when his Oregon trial began (Fagan 1995).

Sometimes the evil that sociopaths perpetrate is so reprehensible that it offends the sensibilities of even the most hardcore con. The killers' downfall, Thompson and his fellow informants agreed, is they didn't understand that even the most calloused inmates don't respect people who kill children, no matter what the motive. The inmate witnesses said they decided to testify at McClure's trial because he broke a cardinal rule among biker and prison gangs: "snitches" should be killed but their innocent children should not be harmed. Even cons have a code of ethics.

A second example also involved the stunningly cold-blooded murder of a child at the hands of outlaw bikers again associated with the Hells Angels in Vallejo, CA. On Sunday, October 5th, 1986 evil perpetrated by sociopaths descended upon the normally tranquil community of

Fort Bragg, CA. Headlines would later read that Fort Bragg had suffered one of the "worst mass murders in Mendocino County history" as a result.

Former Hells Angel Billy Grondalski had moved to Fort Bragg to escape his past and give his family a new start by leaving the outlaw biker lifestyle behind. Less than a week before, the club had declared Billy was no longer a welcomed member of the Hells Angels Motorcycle Club (HAMC). He had quit in bad standing. However, Grondalski possessed two pieces of club property: $600 worth of HAMC support decals and a club tattoo worn on his left arm that read, "In 84, Out 86" commemorating his time in the club. To the Angels those constituted unfinished business (Doe 2002).

A couple of hours inland from Fort Bragg sits the tiny riverfront community of Guerneville. On that Sunday the Vallejo chapter was hosting its annual motorcycle rally there. The weekend campout was attended by hundreds of bikers and their supporters. Two people present at the bike-run were chapter president Gerald "Butch" Lesterand vice president Charles "Chuck" Diaz. Lester and Diaz were assigned to get the decals back and cover up or forcefully remove Grondalski's tattoo.

On that Sunday, Grondalski's 5-year old daughter Dallas, her mother Patty, and her 17-year old stepbrother, Jerami Vandagriff, were home. Lester and Diaz arrived in Fort Bragg around noon, shortly after Billy Grondalski arrived home. The two bikers entered the house and confronted Billy in the living room. Words were exchanged and the situation deteriorated rapidly as Billy's family watched in horror.

Lester pulled out a .45 caliber pistol from his waistband and shoved it into Billy's face. Later he claimed that the gun went off accidentally. The bullet entered

Grondalski's mouth and lodged in his brain. He was dead before he hit the floor. Five-year old Dallas, horrified at the sight of her father's murder, ran into her bedroom. Grondalski's murder in front of witnesses meant that all present had to be eliminated. As Dallas fled the horror in the front room, Lester yelled at Diaz to "Take care of that one!" (Doe 2002).

As Diaz pursued the terrified child, Lester turned his attention to Jerami Vandagriff, shooting him below the left eye and killing him instantly. In the murderous chaos, Patty Grondalski made a desperate dash for the door. Lester grabbed her by the hair and thrust the .45 into her face. She tried to shield herself with her forearm but Lester fired a single round through her arm and into her forehead, inflicting a fatal wound. In a matter of seconds three people had been murdered. One witness remained—the most vulnerable and innocent among them.

In the next room Diaz was having difficulty killing the 5-year-old with his knife because the knife was dull. By the time Lester entered the room Diaz had slashed the defenseless child five times across the throat from ear to ear, nearly decapitating her. One of the cuts was so savage that her spinal cord was severed. To satiate his bloodlust, Lester contributed to the child's slaughter by firing one round from his .45 into her chest. It was clearly a case of overkill because her death certificate revealed that she died of multiple stab wounds (Doe 2002).

The killers then went to Billy Grondalski's body and sliced off his tattoo, using the same knife used to murder little Dallas. The severed piece of flesh was placed in a paper bag. The killers then fled the crime scene and returned to the Guerneville run. Once there, Lester used the toilet of a friend's motor home to flush the severed tattoo into its black water tank where the chemicals inside would dissolve the hunk of flesh.

He ordered that a fresh pot of coffee be brewed and then took the coffee to a sink and washed his hands in it. Coffee is often used by outlaw bikers to cover up the telltale mess and potential forensic evidence, like gunshot residue and blood or body tissue associated with a bloody murder. Later that day the .45 was melted down with a torch and the slag was scattered over several northern California counties. The knife and sheath used by Diaz were also tossed.

The next day, Monday, October 6th, 1986, Diaz went to his job as usual as a civilian employee with a DOD security clearance at the Mare Island Naval Shipyard in Vallejo. Lester, on the other hand, was concerned about incriminating evidence left behind at the murder scene. Later that afternoon he recruited the help of fellow Hells Angel Charles "Francis" Haas. Both men returned to Fort Bragg with a couple of cans of gas to torch the Grondalski home and destroy physical evidence. They arrived in town about the same time Monday Night Football was playing on TV. The Angels entered the Grondalski home, doused the corpses in gasoline and lit a time-delay fuse. They went to a nearby café to drink coffee while they waited for the fire trucks to pass by to verify that the fire had done its job (Doe 2002).

At 9:33 PM fire trucks started rolling down Highway 1 towards the Grondalski home. Both men gulped down their now tepid coffee and fled Fort Bragg. In their rearview mirror they could see flames illuminating the cold night sky in the distance. When the bodies were discovered and Billy Grondalski's past came to light investigators labeled the murders a typical Hells Angel hit, difficult to investigate and impossible to find witnesses for. Instant suspicion fell upon the Vallejo chapter but due to lack of evidence and witnesses no arrests were made. The case went cold and remained unsolved for eight years (Fagan 1995).

On March 31st, 1994, Charles Haas was arrested on federal drug charges for his role in a large-scale meth ring. People react to the prospects of a long prison sentence in many ways. Two of the more common are finding Jesus or becoming a snitch by using knowledge of other crimes as a bargaining chip to negotiate a more lenient resolution to their legal troubles. Haas was facing 30 years behind bars. He knew who killed the Grondalskis and he had personally participated in the cover-up. He became a government informant by fingering Lester and Diaz after ensuring that he got immunity for his part in the cover-up. It was the break cops needed. On May 5th, 1995, Diaz was arrested in Vallejo and Lester was arrested in Fort Smith, Arkansas (Fagan 1995).

After two mistrials, Lester was convicted on November 6th, 1997 and sentenced to four life terms at California's notorious Pelican Bay maximum security prison. Diaz was convicted later in a separate trial and sentenced to 29 years to life in prison. As in the case of the Compton murders, some of the members of the Vallejo Angels chapter were shocked and disgusted by the murder of five-year-old Dallas Grondalski. Former FBI agent Tim McKinley, an expert on the Hells Angels, described gang reactions to the murders, "…the killing of Dallas hit a lot of Hells Angels wrong. The [homicides] were over the top and hit their gag reflex a little bit too hard" (People v. Diaz 2007).Yet their code of silence and loyalty to their fellow patch brothers prevented them from coming forward.

A sociopath's inability to see others as human allows them to view everyone around them as targets and opportunities. My partner Dave Vencalek described the nature of a sociopath's relationships with those around him. "Instead of friends they have victims and accomplices who end up as victims." To a sociopath the end always justifies the means and they let nothing stand in their way. Completely indifferent about destroying the lives of others they are supremely oblivious to the devastation, heartbreak, misery, and sorrow they cause.

My partner in the Intelligence Unit once remarked about outlaw bikers, "They're just bigger punks." He was only partly right. Sociopathy boosts them to the level of apex predators. Unfortunately for the rest of us they are not confined to the margins of society amid the ranks of outlaw biker gangs.

As the examples above show, in the mind of a sociopath the comfort and safety of a vulnerable child take a backseat to the supremely selfish evil desire for immediate gratification, or in this case, avoiding consequences. No more horrific examples exist than the Compton murders-for-hire involving the cold-blooded savagery of killing twin six-year-olds in front of their mother and the butchering of five-year-old Dallas Grondalski during another quadruple murder. I would go on to confront a lot more sociopathy in my thirty years on the job, much of it concentrated among the predators that prowled the streets in search of women to rape.

Chapter Three
Michael Cullen Series: Conclusion

> By its very nature, rape displays a
> total contempt for the personal integrity
> and autonomy of the victim;
> short of homicide, [it is] the ultimate violation of self.
> **Coker v. Georgia.**

Shortly before 2:00 AM, Saturday, February 22, 1986, Dr. Willard Norman was asleep in his ground floor apartment on South 87th Plaza in the Wentworth Apartment complex. Norman had just moved in following a divorce. While he slept Michael Cullen was prowling looking for his next victim. He chose the sprawling Wentworth complex because he was intimately familiar with it, having lived there a few years earlier. Cullen probably felt comfortable with huge apartment complexes because he knew they were filled with strangers who neither knew their neighbors nor were overly concerned seeing people they didn't recognize in and around their homes. A bonus attraction is that such complexes often have high concentrations of young, single females living there. All of these factors made the sprawling Wentworth a rich hunting ground.

Like many sexual predators, Cullen likely had several potential rape victims in his crosshairs at any given time. In the case of the Norman burglary he may have been seeking the former tenant to rape. Her departure may have prevented her from becoming his next victim. For many serial rapists, burglary is the most common non-sexual offense in their background. Some of their crimes are actually "bonus rapes," the result of opportunistically encountering a vulnerable woman during a burglary. Their expertise at breaking and entering makes gaining access to their victims easy.

Like most Power Reassurance Rapists (PARs), Cullen's inferiority complex and inadequacy with women was a fundamental aspect of his desire to rape. Like many PARs he may have felt that he was a loser. He was relentlessly buffeted by low self-esteem and intense feelings of insecurity and self-doubt. This is not atypical of narcissism. They often feel inadequate and seek to rectify this by acting and doing anything necessary to make themselves feel important. Cullen struggled to suppress warring factions within his psyche that told him that he was capable of being everything he was not while simultaneously reminding him of how utterly pathetic and inadequate his life was. Those feelings combined with a plethora of deviant sexual desires and paraphilias and serious emotional problems may have been the reason he attempted suicide on several occasions.

Mental instability was likely a key precipitator of Cullen's rapes. Like other PARs he may have raped to restore self-confidence and as confirmation of his manhood. By dominating and controlling a woman less powerful than himself he sought to increase his self-esteem and gain control that he felt he lacked elsewhere in his life. Rape served to assuage his deep-seated doubts about himself and was both sexually and emotionally reassuring. When the insecurities and self-doubt that fueled his evil desire attained critical mass he lashed out, fueled by a combination of psycho-emotional needs and fantasies that were constantly brewing beneath the surface, often for years before he acted on them.

Often, Cullen lashed out as a result of some perceived personal affront or loss of face, usually at the hands of a woman. Almost any loss of face can trigger the PAR's need to prove his worth. For him, rape offers the illusion of complete control obtained either by a weapon, physical or verbal intimidation, or drugging. He prowls and window-peeps in familiar neighborhoods, often selecting and surprising his victims at random and targeting those who seem weak or vulnerable.

The parking lot outside of Norman's apartment was quiet at 2:00 AM. Cullen probably parked in an adjacent lot and watched the buildings and the surrounding area to be sure he would not be seen as he made his approach. He slipped out of his truck, possibly leaving it unlocked so he could get back in it quickly if he had to flee. He may have closed the door softly to minimize the sound, and surreptitiously crept across the parking lot between cars and across the grass to the ground level patio door of Apartment 3. He likely glanced around again to be sure no one was watching before slipping into the shadows of the patio. There he pulled a screwdriver out of his pocket and pried open the pot-metal lock of the sliding door.

It is likely that Cullen slid the door cautiously to the side and paused to listen and look into the darkened interior. When nothing stirred, he opened door fully and slipped inside. He made his way through the darkness as subdued illumination from the parking lot lights filtered through the partially open window blinds. He made his way to the single bedroom where he was surprised to find a middle-age man snoring loudly in bed instead of his intended victim.

He spotted a watch, wallet, checkbook and a small amount of cash on the dresser and grabbed them before retreating to the kitchen to examine his haul. The watch was old and well-worn but expensive. He put it in his front pants pocket. He placed the checkbook in a back pocket and removed credit cards, cash, and an ATM card from the wallet. As he examined the ATM card in the dim light he congratulated himself because Dr. Norman had written his personal identification number on it. It was like a blank check that Cullen couldn't wait to cash.

Because there were only two break-ins in the Wentworth Apartment complex that night it can be assumed that they were not random. Cullen may have been frustrated that a rape victim had eluded him by moving out of the apartment Norman had moved into, so he changed to Plan B. He left his truck parked in the overflow lot near Dr. Norman's apartment building and walked to Sara Beth Donnelly's apartment building several blocks away. Her apartment was on the second floor, but the wooden deck/patio area of her unit was barely five feet off the ground. The first floor was built partially as a basement set halfway into the ground. Cullen had an easy time jumping up to grab the wooden railing and hoisting himself onto the patio. He pressed his forehead against the door glass and framed his forehead with his hands to peer inside the darkened apartment. Satisfied that no one was up and moving around he pulled out his screwdriver once again and began to work on the sliding door lock. In less than a minute he had popped it free from its latch.

Sara Donnelly was a 22-year-old high school girls' basketball coach. It was her first teaching job following college and she was well liked by the students and other staff members. Donnelly was trusting, outgoing, friendly, and very personable. She exuded a quiet, unobtrusive personal strength that was noticeable on first meeting her. Her peers were very impressed with her skills in handling all types of students in their urban, inner city public high school.

Donnelly was new to an urban lifestyle having attended a small private college not far from Omaha. She had lived most of her life in a small town in the eastern part of the state not far from the college. She was close to her parents and her father was concerned for her safety when she moved to the city. Both of her parents were involved in helping her find a suitable apartment and they inspected the apartment, the complex, the surrounding area, and spoke with the management about crime and safety.

Because she lived alone her father had specifically asked her to make sure she locked her doors and windows every night, drew her curtains, and requested that she not live in a ground floor apartment. Her apartment was on the second floor facing west. At the time Donnelly's building was on the perimeter of the complex with the back of the building overlooking what was then an undeveloped tract of commercial property. The front faced other buildings in the complex and overlooked a series of interconnected parking lots.

Donnelly was not dating anyone at the time of the assault but had several close male friends she described as "platonic." Most were also teachers at the same high school or were college friends. She seldom drank and never went to bars alone. When she did drink it was usually because she had been invited to join others on a special occasion such as a birthday. Sara Donnelly was the quintessential low-risk victim.

Donnelly had retired at 11:30 PM on Friday, February 21, 1986. As was her custom she locked all her doors and windows and dressed in a t-shirt and underwear for bed. She was awakened by Cullen at 3:00 AM when he climbed into her bed while wearing one of her bras and a pair of her white bikini panties. The bra cups were stuffed with tissues, indicating that he had been modeling it for himself. After climbing into bed with her he held a knife in his left hand and pulled on her right ear threatening to cut it off if she refused to cooperate. He used the same MO tactic that he had to control Jackie Brown, including saying that "the ear is the only part of the human body that can't be sewed back on." He then stated, "We are going to have sex. Right? Right?" Donnelly recognized the knife as one of her kitchen knives.

Donnelly stalled Cullen by telling him that she would have sex with him if she could go to the bathroom and insert her diaphragm. He allowed her to do so after ordering her to remove all of her clothing first. He removed her shirt and panties himself. After entering the bathroom and locking the door behind her, Donnelly observed Cullen's clothes piled on the floor. She spotted a checkbook in the back pocket of his jeans. Assuming that it was Cullen's and would later lead to his identity she tore off a check from the middle of the book and hid it in the bathroom. Fearing that any attempts to scream or to attract attention would result in Cullen breaking down the bathroom door and using the knife on her, Donnelly returned to the bedroom telling him that she could not find her diaphragm and that she did not want to get pregnant.

Cullen ordered her to lie on the bed and then attempted to force vaginal intercourse as Donnelly resisted. During this resistance his mood changed abruptly and he stated firmly, "You are going to do it my way." She told me during the interview the next day that "they rolled around a bit" and he began to kiss her. He eventually performed oral copulation on her, stating, "I'll do anything to please you, what do you want me to do?" He fondled her breasts and vaginal area and continued to make statements such as, "You can fulfill my fantasies," "Oh, you are very nice" and "You make me feel very nice."

As she continued to resist his attempt at vaginal intercourse, he asked her if she wanted to get dressed and she said yes. He then told her that they should get dressed into "something different." They got out of bed and he began trying on her lingerie and pantyhose. He specifically asked for "something sexy" to wear and Donnelly gave him a bra, slip, and pantyhose that he put on. He then put on one of her dress blouses and asked for a pair of her shoes. She pulled out several pairs and he selected a pair of dress heels, forcing his feet with great difficulty into her size-eight shoes. As Donnelly helped him get dressed, she stated that his demeanor was that of a "little boy."

After dressing he suggested that they go into the living room because he wanted to drink beer, smoke, dance and "undress each other and make love." While in the living room he noticed that Donnelly was shivering. He let her go unescorted into the bedroom to put on socks and a pair of sweatpants. When she returned to the living room he began to talk about his life and how he came to be in her apartment. He claimed that he originally came to the apartment complex looking for an "old girlfriend." When he couldn't find her, he broke into Donnelly's place "looking for some excitement." He told Donnelly that he picked her apartment at random and that he had never seen her before. He talked about growing up in Connecticut and attending grade school in New York.

As he continued to talk, he revealed more about himself. He stated that he had run away from home at 14 years of age and had been sent to a reform school.

He bragged about "living life in the fast lane" in Los Angeles, having a brother in Newport Beach, California and selling trailer homes in Albuquerque, New Mexico. In between talking about himself he kept talking about having sex, but Donnelly was able to change the topic as he continued to talk about his personal life. Eventually he told her, "I'll make a deal with you and let you go if you give me head."

About two and a half hours had elapsed and it was nearly 5:50 AM. Donnelly told Cullen that she had to get ready to go to a basketball game in the morning, prompting her attacker to ask what she did for a living. She told him she coached basketball at a high school in Omaha. He responded that he knew a track coach at Papillion High School, a suburb of Omaha. Donnelly tried to get up from the couch where they were seated and mentioned that he should probably go because her boyfriend would be over soon. In response he pointed to the east and said they would not be able to see the sunrise because the balcony faces west. He then wrestled her to the living room floor and attempted to perform vaginal intercourse again after removing her sweatpants and fondling her. When she again resisted, he stopped and asked her to fix him breakfast. He told her that if she would do that for him, he would leave. The suspect's mood then abruptly changed, and he led her to the bedroom, stating, "We have 10 minutes and there is no one in bed."

In the bedroom he started talking about having sex again and asked her if she had inserted her diaphragm. Donnelly reminded him that it was at her boyfriend's house and that she was afraid of becoming pregnant if they had intercourse. He forced her into bed and once again attempted to mount her to perform vaginal intercourse. When she protested and resisted more vigorously, he compromised by saying "You'll have to give me something else then," telling her that she would have to "give him head." She was then forced to perform oral sex on him. He ejaculated a short time later, in her mouth and on her chest.

Donnelly had some semen on her hand that she wiped on his chest, causing him to say, "That was rude, why don't you use a towel?" She picked up one of her shirts from the floor and wiped the semen out of her mouth and off his chest. He then told her to get up and make some coffee while he got dressed. He asked if he could use her hairbrush and she agreed. After combing his hair and dressing he offered to fix the patio door he broke to get in using one of Donnelly's screwdrivers. When she said that it was not necessary, he replied "This place doesn't fix anything." He then left by the front door, apologizing to her and thanking her. As he was leaving, he paused and asked sarcastically, "How does it feel to be raped?" He then stated that he was really embarrassed by the incident and had too much to drink prior to "coming over." Before leaving for good he told Donnelly that this was the only time that he had done this and reassured her that he would never do it again. Donnelly later noticed that her purse had been dumped out on the living room chair and that her attacker had sorted her charge cards but had not apparently taken anything. She later found three one-dollar bills left by him on the kitchen counter mirroring his comments to Brown just before leaving when he said, "That's all I pay for a whore."

His modus operandi required a surprise approach (Hazelwood 1990:11). Most power reassurance rapists rely on a surprise approach by sneaking up on a single, often sleeping woman. Since it involves the assailant lying in wait for the victim or approaching her after she is asleep, it presupposes that the rapist has targeted or preselected his victim through surreptitious observation and knowledge of when the victim would be alone. They usually stalk their victims for a time, first learning their habits, especially when they go to sleep, and by watching for the presence of a man in the victim's life, ensuring that they will be alone when attacked. Threats and/or the presence of a weapon are often associated with this type of approach. However, there is usually no injurious force applied during the attack.

Other rapists use a con or a blitz approach (Hazelwood 1990:12). In a con approach the rapist approaches his victim using a ruse. He might pose as an authority figure, a police officer for example, or use another ploy to openly approach the victim and request or offer some type of assistance or direction. As described in greater detail in Chapter Six, Hells Angel Thomas "Red" Nesbitt used a con approach to grab dancer Michele McKesson before raping her. He lulled her into a false sense of security by complimenting her dancing and then inviting her to accompany him to a party nearby. To continue to inch ever closer without alarming her, he claimed he was from out of town and asked for directions. This allowed him to continue to maneuver his pickup truck nearer to her as she walked to her car in a parking lot. When he had worked his way in close enough he jumped out and grabbed her before she could flee or cry out for help.

Serial murderer Ted Bundy used a clever con to lure his victims into a trap (Keppel 2005:3-6). He often wore his arm in a sling or in a fake cast. He would ask his victims to help him carry things to his car or help load or unload things. Once the victims got in his car or were leaning in he would strike them over the head with a crowbar or pipe. Once rendered unconscious he would handcuff them to immobilize them. He was also known to impersonate authority figures such as police officers and firefighters.

Bundy was a charming, good-looking man and many of his victims did not fear or question him because he did not appear to be a stereotypical "monster" and was charismatic and socially adept. He preyed on college campuses, first in Washington, later in Utah and Colorado, and finally in Florida. His victims were women who looked much like a young woman who had broken off her relationship with him though this may have been a coincidence because many women at the time had straight hair parted in the middle, as his former girlfriend did. Bundy raped and murdered scores of women, strangling and mutilating them. He displayed their lopped off heads in his apartment and slept with and had sex with their corpses until decomposition made it unbearable. Bundy was finally sentenced to death and died in the electric chair in Florida in 1989. At the time of his execution he had confessed to 30 murders, though there were certainly more. The actual number remains unknown.

A variation of the con approach involves an incapacitating drug, often referred to as a "date rape" drug, because it is slipped into an unsuspecting girl's drink at parties, bars, and other social settings. After ingesting the laced drink the victim is incapacitated and raped. The three most common are Rohypnol, also known as "roofies"; gamma hydroxybutyric acid (GHB), also called "liquid ecstasy"; and Ketamine, also called "Special K." All three come in pill, liquid, or powder forms (Bechtel 2007:502). They are colorless, odorless and tasteless. Date rape drugs can also cause seizures and even death especially if administered in too large a dose.

In a blitz approach the rapist uses a direct injurious physical assault which subdues and physically injures the victim. His goal is to violently attack her to stun her, keep her off balance and control her while simultaneously striking out against a symbolic victim. A symbolic victim is a surrogate for the actual target of his rage who could be an ex-girlfriend, boss, or wife. The symbolic victim may share the same age, physical description, hair color or style, mannerisms, manner of dress, or in some other way remind the rapist of the true target of his rage. The attacker may use pepper spray, mace, or an incapacitating gas like ether or formaldehyde. He makes use of his ability to physically overpower his victim. Even though it is used less often than the con approach, the blitz approach usually results in more extensive physical injury and inhibits certain fantasy components of the rape that may be arousing to some rapists.

In one case typical of this type of attack a twenty-six-year-old woman was awakened at 2:00 AM when the offender smashed his fist through the glass door of her apartment building. He reached in and unlocked the door as she came out into the hallway to investigate the noise. He grabbed her around the neck, put a knife to her throat, and dragged her into his car. When in the car he warned her that if she moved he would "chop her up" with the knife. When they arrived at an abandoned building he forced her to undress, dance in the nude, and utter obscenities about women while dancing. He grabbed her breasts and buttocks and her hair and slapped her face, all while ordering her to repeat more obscenities about women over and over again. He sodomized her, performed cunnilingus, forced her to perform fellatio, and finally had intercourse with her. Throughout the assault he told her to keep swearing, saying that he liked to hear it. Eventually he got back into his car and drove off, leaving the victim to walk five miles to the nearest house.

Cullen's approach in the Donnelly case was contingent upon finding a sleeping woman that he could surprise by climbing into bed with her, pressing a knife against her neck, grabbing an ear with his other hand and threatening to cut it off if she resisted. His paraphilias demanded a surprise approach so he could rummage through his sleeping victim's bras, panties and high heel shoes and have enough time to try them on before crawling into bed to startle his victim awake. Later, he would indulge in his other paraphilias during the rape with the victim's coerced assistance.

The Donnelly rape is classified by the FBI as a Secondary Felony Rape (Douglas 1997:319), where the "secondary felony" refers to another crime committed at the same time. The primary intent of the offender is sexual assault but a second felony, such as burglary, is also planned. This implies that the offender knows or assumes that a person will be present for two crimes to occur. In the Donnelly case, the suspect's skill in breaking into the victim's apartment indicated that he was an experienced burglar. However, the selection of lone female victims, the serial nature of his assaults, the physical similarity of the victims, bringing female undergarments and a knife with him to be used during at least one rape, and statements made by him indicate that his primary motivation for these crimes was rape, with burglary as the secondary felony.

This rapist's signature expressed during these assaults represents a constant theme in which he inserts his personality into the crimes, in unique and often complex sex fantasies that have been described as a form of "template" for serial rape. According to legendary FBI profiler Roy Hazelwood, rapes serve a complex organizing function in the offender's behavior and commonly drive his verbal interactions with his victim, the sex acts he engages in, and his overall pattern of behavior (Kocis 2006:92). According to Hazelwood's research, the rapist's signature does not change substantially because it is the manifestation of his fantasy served by the assault. In essence it reflects the underlying motivation for committing the crime.

The following analysis of Cullen's rapes of Donnelly and Brown is based on a psychological profile I completed as part of my graduate-level training in Forensic Psychology while attending the FBI National Academy in Quantico, VA (Olson 1998:n.p.). Power Reassurance Rapists, like Donnelly's attacker, rape to reassure themselves of their masculinity through exercising power over women. They lack confidence in their ability to interact socially and sexually with women. Typical of this category of rapist, the suspect engages in pseudo-unselfish verbal and sexual behavior and relies on minimal to moderate levels of force. Attacks generally occur in late evening or early morning hours and the victim is often alone or in the company of small children. Following the assault, and consistent with pseudo-unselfish behavior, this type of rapist may apologize, ask for forgiveness or, in the case of Donnelly's attacker, offer to repair the lock on a door damaged when he broke in to commit the attack.

At several points in the rape Cullen was dissuaded from vaginally raping Donnelly by her resistance. Bespeaking her courage, she told me during my interview of her that she consistently resisted vaginal intercourse "because he was not going to take that from me." When confronted with her resistance he attempted to bargain with her. This type of rapist will avoid using more aggressive tactics if a victim vigorously resists because using force to overcome the resistance would destroy the fantasy of the rape being a consensual encounter.

In both of these assaults the rapist used a surprise approach by sneaking up on his victims as they slept, or in the case of Brown, hiding to surprise her after she came home. He used threats, minimal force, and a weapon to subdue both victims. The force level varied in each case in response to the different resistance of the victims. Both victims resisted passively, verbally and physically. However, Jackie Brown was brutalized more severely than Sara Donnelly because she tended to resign herself to her fate by telling her attacker to "do what you have to do" after refusing to perform oral copulation. In effect, Brown's resignation and subsequent passivity from that point on may have left her attacker free to indulge more of his fantasies, resulting in more brutal and varied sexual aggression in the fulfillment of his paraphilias.

Cullen's verbal activity in the Donnelly rape included inquiries about her personal life and occupation. He also made revelations about his life, most of which were verified during the course of the investigation. He paid her compliments, made apologies for the rape, and expressed a faux concern for her welfare such as offering to fix the patio door he pried to gain entry.

The pseudo-unselfish behavior demonstrated during the Donnelly assault indicates low self esteem and reflects the rapist's belief that his displays of "concern" for the victim's comfort and welfare will win her over in the hope that she will "realize" he is not a bad person. Cullen attempted to "seduce" Donnelly to be a willing participant in the act, sexually and verbally, and thus fuel his fantasy that she was enjoying his presence. The PAR will normally do what the victim allows him to do so long as she does not aggressively resist his acts or demands.

Cullen's behavior does not indicate a desire to harm his victims physically like other rapist types who, in addition to the sexual assault, physically beat their victims or force them to engage in acts they resist. Depending on the individual rapist, this may be due to a lack of confidence or, as mentioned before, because the use of force would destroy the fantasy that the victim has become a willing partner. If the victim puts up any kind of resistance, as in the Donnelly case, this type of rapist may attempt to compromise, threaten or leave. His comment to Donnelly, "I'll make a deal with you and let you go if you give me head" is an obvious compromise in response to the victim's repeated resistance to vaginal intercourse.

I asked the FBI Behavioral Science Unit in Quantico to prepare a psychological profile on the Brown and Donnelly rapes. It indicated that a motivating factor for the rapes might be the unavailability of a consenting partner with which the rapist could engage in his fantasy and indulge his paraphilias. In the course of my investigation I found out that he was recently divorced at the time of these assaults and his wife had filed a sexual assault report listing him as her assailant. Immediately following the assault, his wife left the state and filed for divorce. It is impossible to determine if the sexual assault of his wife and their divorce were due to his aberrant sexual practices. However, the psychological pressures involving a critical, disapproving partner who refuses to indulge the fantasies of his multiple paraphilias, coupled with marriage dissolution, could have provided at least a partial trigger for these rapes.

It is obvious that the rapist was a skilled burglar at the time of these assaults. It is equally apparent that he lacked experience as a rapist and was unfamiliar with police forensic processes because he casually left hair, serology, and fingerprint evidence at both scenes.

&

After her attacker departed, Donnelly tried to regain her composure. She was confused and terrified. She wanted to notify the police by calling 911 immediately but remembered her rapist's warning. Instead, she called a close friend, a male basketball coach from another school, and asked him to come over right away. In spite of her remarkable composure during her ordeal, once her friend arrived she broke down as she told him what had happened. After discussing her options they both decided it was time they called the police.

A patrol deputy responded and took the initial crime report. Because of the nature of the rape, and especially the perp's threat to cut off Donnelly's ear if she refused to comply with his demands, he notified investigators after recalling a CIB bulletin describing the Brown rape and its unique MO. He also called out the crime lab to process the scene.

Detective Craig Madden was the on-call investigator. He interviewed Donnelly, who was an outstanding witness. The combination of her courage during the assault and Madden's investigative skills yielded a lot of information that helped eventually lead to the rapist's identification and arrest. Madden was able to get from Donnelly a complete detailed description of exactly what had transpired during the rape as well as the specific phrases spoken by her attacker. Her quick thinking on seeing the checkbook in the perp's pants pocket and tearing off a blank check proved to be a crucial link to the Norman burglary.

About the time Donnelly was speaking to the patrol deputy, Dr. Norman noticed several items, including his wallet and checkbook, missing from his apartment. He also found the broken patio door lock. Because Norman's wallet contained a bank card he called his bank and informed bank personnel of the theft. He learned that a transaction had been recorded on his account that morning. Norman then reported the burglary to the sheriff's department.

At first Madden thought Norman might be a suspect in the Donnelly rape when she provided him the blank check removed from Cullen's jeans. However, after learning of the Norman burglary, and more importantly that his stolen bank card had been used at an ATM, I contacted the bank and arranged with security officers to view the video loop from the ATM. It showed that a suspect had used the stolen card within two hours of leaving Donnelly's apartment. Later that day a blonde woman, who was subsequently identified in the course of my investigation as the rapist's live-in girlfriend, tried to use the ATM card again. She was not successful because the bank had already flagged the card as stolen. The machine kept the card as well as recording the image of the female accomplice. I had the Criminalistics Division prepare a six-photo lineup including the photo from the ATM and showed it to Donnelly. She positively identified the man using the stolen ATM card as her rapist. I now had a picture of the rapist. I hoped that the picture would make it relatively easy to identify him once I arranged to broadcast it on local TV stations and in the newspaper. Unfortunately, I was wrong.

As I reviewed Madden's reports and re-interviewed Donnelly, a large amount of information about the rapist came into focus. I knew from his comments to Donnelly that the suspect was originally from "out east," had been in reform school in Connecticut and attended school in New York. He was a troubled youth who, while in a juvenile reform school there, had followed his favorite counselor from the school to Omaha. He told Donnelly that the counselor had taken a job as a track coach for Papillion High School. He also claimed to have been "living life in the fast lane" in the Los Angeles area with a brother living in Newport Beach, CA. His comments after offering to repair the patio door lock about "This place doesn't fix anything around here" indicated that he may have previously lived in the Wentworth complex. Most serial predators prefer to operate within areas they feel comfortable in, such as their own neighborhoods, apartment complexes they formerly lived in, locations near where they work, and other geographic areas they are intimately familiar with. This further narrowed the suspect pool.

Over the next nine months I ran down every lead in the case. I showed the picture from the ATM surveillance loop to the Wentworth apartment complex managers but they were not able to identify him. Turnover in those jobs is high so the odds of finding a manager who was working for the complex if and when the rapist lived there were slim. And the sheer number of tenants they deal with made identification unlikely, unless the guy stood out somehow, perhaps because he had been a royal pain in the ass or was in some other way easily remembered. I also interviewed the Papillion High School athletic coaches without success.

I shared the picture of the rapist from the ATM surveillance loop on TV and in the newspaper and received more than 20 leads. I ran each of them to ground and eliminated the suspects named in them. I also showed the suspect picture to the developer of Jackie Brown's condo to see if he could ID the suspect as one of the tradesmen who had worked on the condo. Neither he nor his staff was able to do so. I later discovered that Cullen had been a temporary laborer working for a subcontractor on the building. He was not known to the developer even though he had spent a considerable amount of time working in and around Jackie Brown's unit.

I was troubled that no reported rapes had occurred following the Donnelly case. And I was bothered by a significant change in MO between the Brown and Donnelly cases. He wore a mask and used a blindfold during the Brown rape but made no such efforts to conceal himself from Donnelly. Rapists choose not to use a disguise or blindfold their victim for multiple reasons. They may lack criminal experience and underestimate the ability of a rape victim to identify them after an attack by providing police with a physical description sufficient to prepare a composite drawing or by perusing mug-shot books. A particular attack may have been spontaneous, leaving the suspect unprepared to adequately protect their identity. Sometimes they are too intoxicated to disguise themselves. Research varies, but some estimates hold that as many as three out of four rapists are under the influence of alcohol at the time of the attack. Or a rapist might not wear a disguise or blindfold his victim because he plans on leaving the area soon after the rape. I later learned that this rapist fit the last category. He left the Omaha area for Massachusetts within days of the rape.

Shortly after the rape I placed a BOLO ("be on the lookout") in the Nebraska State Patrol (NSP) statewide law enforcement bulletin with a picture from the ATM surveillance loop, details of the rapes, and a suspect description. I received no response. Nine months later, after all leads had been exhausted, I reluctantly considered classifying the investigation as a cold case and placing it in the inactive file. As distasteful as that decision was, there really was no other option, although I was reminded of the words of Vince Lombardi, legendary coach of the Green Bay Packers football team. In a now classic 1968 motivational training film, Lombardi described his personal philosophy as "The Second Effort." Lombardi taught that if you fail at first you don't give up. You pick yourself up, dust yourself off, and try again until you succeed.

Before giving up, I decided to run the BOLO again. This time I got a hit from a female sergeant with the NSP. She had been on vacation when the first BOLO was issued and missed it. She called me saying that the surveillance picture looked like the boyfriend of her husband's daughter from a prior marriage who was currently living in Massachusetts. Her ex-husband was the sheriff of a rural county about 90 miles from Omaha. She named my suspect as Michael W. Cullen and gave me his approximate age. The trooper believed that he was currently house-sitting at a home on Cape Cod in Barnstable, MA.

It was the break I needed. Coach Lombardi not only excelled at football coaching, his work ethic indirectly helped solve a difficult serial rape case in Omaha. I located Cullen in the county's computerized criminal history database. One of his old addresses was in the Wentworth complex. I also found a pickup truck registered to Cullen in Douglas County.

A "Triple I" search on the NCIC system confirmed more of the comments Cullen made to Donnelly. The

Triple I, which stands for Interstate Identification Index, produces a nationwide criminal history of all felony arrests of the person being queried. Cullen told Donnelly that he had been "living life in the fast lane" in the Los Angeles area before coming to Omaha. The Triple I revealed he had been arrested in Newport Beach, CA, a place he claimed to Donnelly that his brother lived, for sniping passersby with a pellet gun while hiding on his patio. It also showed that he had attempted suicide on several occasions.

I was contacted again by the NSP trooper who told me that they had received an update indicating that Cullen had moved to Oak Bluffs on Martha's Vineyard where he was again house-sitting over the winter. The protocol for interstate criminal investigations is to contact a counterpart law enforcement agency in the jurisdiction where the offender is located. In this case, Martha's Vineyard is in Dukes County, MA. A check of the sheriff's department there indicated that the Dukes County sheriff's office did not have a law enforcement division that could assist me. They managed law enforcement support services including the county jail and the Communication Center, as well as handling process service. The five other police departments on the island were small and unlikely to be able to assist me with such a major investigation. Luckily, there was a state trooper barracks on the Island.

The Massachusetts State Police was established in 1865. When the Massachusetts Commonwealth created the statewide force, its creation was unprecedented in this country. It is the largest law enforcement agency in New England with nearly 1,500 sworn troopers. Troop D includes the southeastern section of the commonwealth with its headquarters located in Middleborough on Cape Cod. Its D-5 barracks are located in Oak Bluffs on Martha's Vineyard (Powers 1998:3-5). I contacted the barracks on the island and asked to speak to an investigator. I was told that there were no investigators but that any trooper could help me so I asked them to verify that Cullen was at the address provided by the NSP trooper. I gave them the Nebraska plates and truck description. They drove by the home several times but did not see the truck.

I called back multiple times and there was still no sign of the truck. Not being investigators they were at a loss as to how to proceed without being seen by Cullen if they continued to drive by in their marked cruisers. I asked them to contact the post office to see if Cullen was receiving mail at the address. The postmaster said that Cullen and his girlfriend were getting mail so I was sure that Cullen was in Oak Bluffs.

I settled in to wait for additional confirmation that he was at the residence. I asked the troopers to watch the ferry from the mainland and drive by the residence occasionally looking for Cullen's pickup. It came several days later when a trooper called to tell me that he had driven by the house and saw Cullen's pickup parked outside bearing the Nebraska plates.

In the meantime, I had prepared an affidavit for an arrest warrant for Cullen based on my investigation. I presented it to prosecutor Tom McKenney of the Douglas County Attorney's Office who prepared the warrant for a judge's signature. While it is not necessary or even common practice to have the prosecutor prepare a search warrant in Douglas County, arrest warrants are different. An arrest warrant must be prosecuted by the County Attorney's office, so it is necessary to present an affidavit to a prosecutor who will take the case to court after the suspect's arrest.

I flew to Boston several weeks before Christmas. The weather was stormy and the connecting flight to the island of Martha's Vineyard was delayed for hours. While the flight would take me over Cape Cod, most of the flight would be over water from Logan International Airport on Boston Harbor in Massachusetts Bay to Cape Cod Bay and on to the airport on Martha's Vineyard, which is surrounded on three sides by the Manuel F. Correllus State Forest. The barracks on the island is an old two-story former residence in Oak Bluffs.

The troopers on the island treated me like gold. They were consummate professionals and bent over backwards to help me. They more than facilitated my obtaining a search warrant for Cullen's residence and interrogating him after his arrest.

Much of effective interrogation is theater. Using the tried and true Reid Interrogation Method, I wanted to not be associated with Cullen's collar. The Reid Technique is a widely used method of questioning suspects developed by criminal investigation consultant and polygraph expert John E. Reid. It relies on a nine step process designed to elicit a confession from a resistant suspect. A key step is to offer the suspect a face-saving theme that he can accept to explain why he committed the crime. Once the theme is accepted the interrogation is maneuvered to elicit a full confession (Jayne 1999:23).

I set the stage for the arrest after dark on December 13th, 1986 by waiting at the barracks as the troopers executed the search and arrest warrants. They transported Cullen to the barracks where I waited to introduce myself and set the psychological stage for his interrogation.

I had choreographed with the troopers exactly what I wanted to happen with his arrest, presentation to me at the barracks, and the interrogation. I wanted them to be intentionally vague on the charges and who they were taking him to meet. They told him only that he was being arrested on a felony warrant from Nebraska. When they brought him in I was seated in the shadows of the first floor assembly room adjacent to the barracks base station radio. I had my feet up on the desk when they ushered Cullen in wearing handcuffs. He was psychologically off-balance, subdued, and thoroughly cowed. It was obvious that he was visibly shaken and appeared to be ripe for an interrogation. They halted midway into the room and stood silently waiting for me to speak as we had rehearsed. Speaking from the shadows, I said in the best melodrama I could muster, "Hi Mike. I'm a detective from Omaha. I've been looking for you for a long time."

Pausing to let my words sink in, I turned on the light on the desk next to where I sat. It brought me into full illumination. I was wearing a sport coat and tie. You could see Cullen was shocked as he realized he was now being arrested for rapes he thought he had gotten away with. He swallowed hard and stared at the floor as his body began to shake. The troopers said nothing as they escorted him to the back room I had arranged into an interrogation room by removing all police symbols such as pictures, insignia, news clippings of significant arrests and other police-related memorabilia. I wanted a sterile environment that wouldn't intimidate Cullen and remind him that he was in custody in a police facility. I even rearranged the furniture, setting the stage for his psychological capitulation. The troopers sat him in a hardback chair and left the room, closing the door after themselves. They left his handcuffs on as I had instructed.

I waited for a few minutes to let his predicament sink in and then entered the room carrying nothing but a file folder containing my investigative notes. I said nothing as I took a seat across the desk from him. He was seated with his back against the wall. The room had two doors, one that led to the assembly room at the front of the barracks and another that led to the only bathroom in the building. I purposely situated Cullen's chair so that his back was to both doors. That way he had no psychological lifeline by seeing an avenue of psychological escape that would bolster his effort to resist my interrogation.

I stepped forward and unlocked his handcuffs. He rubbed his wrists and began to plead, "I don't know why..." before I cut him off. I wanted him to remain silent and listen to my well-rehearsed interrogation strategy. It was predicated in large part on keeping Cullen from denying the rape because once denied it is that much harder to subsequently confess. I didn't look at him directly, instead leafing slowly through my case file, appearing to read various reports in it. Cullen shifted uncomfortably in his chair, clearing his throat and anxiously waiting for an opportunity to deny his guilt. He started in again, "I can probably explain..." before I cut him off again by saying, "Mike, I'll be with you in a moment," and continuing to thumb through the file.

Before asking Cullen incriminating questions I had to advise him of his Miranda warnings. I read each of them from a Miranda card I carried in my wallet. I wanted to minimize its impact on him by reading from the card rather than using a Miranda form and asking him to initial each advisement signifying that he waived each of his rights against self-incrimination and his right to a lawyer if he wanted legal counsel.

Cullen was so nervous that his knees were shaking and he was shivering. After some time I closed the file and placed it on the desk. I looked into his eyes and began, "Mike, I am here because three women in Omaha reported being raped. I have spent the last nine months working on those cases. The results of my investigation are contained in this file. Twenty different suspects were investigated and subsequently cleared."

Cullen tried to interrupt to claim his innocence but as before I cut him off, saying, "Mike, let me explain what is going on. You can tell me what you want to say later." I pulled out the picture taken from the ATM and placed it face-down on the desk. I continued, "The results of my investigation indicate that you are the guy who raped those women."

Cullen stiffened and began to shake even harder. I thought I heard his teeth chattering. He started to protest his innocence again before I cut him off. "Let me finish," I said. I summarized my investigation and how I'd identified him as the man responsible. I then turned over the picture of him using Dr. Norman's ATM card and pushed it towards him.

"You made some mistakes, Mike. The most serious was using the stolen ATM card and getting your picture taken. It led me to you because your girlfriend's family recognized you after I placed this picture in a statewide bulletin to law enforcement officers. Your girlfriend's dad, a sheriff in a county outside Omaha, and his wife, a state trooper, saw the picture and identified you. They also told me where you were here on Martha's Vineyard."

Cullen's shoulders slumped and the color drained from his face. He began, "I can explain all of this…it isn't what you think…" before I cut him off again.

"Mike, let me continue," I said. "I think there is an explanation for what happened. You and I both know that there are two sides to every story. I think that is what is going on here."

Desperate to regain control over the situation he mistook that comment for a potential lifeline as I had intended. He shook his head in agreement, "Yes, I think so, too."

I slid my chair around the side of the desk closer to him. I was now seated directly in front of him. I continued to dangle the faux lifeline in front of him like bait before a hungry fish patiently biding my time until I could sink in the hook. "Mike I've been doing this for a long time. I learned a long time ago that things aren't always what they appear to be. Sometimes a woman says she was raped when what happened wasn't rape at all. Perhaps more a misunderstanding."

He nodded slightly, "Yes, you're right. A misunderstanding." He had swallowed the bait hook, line and sinker.

As I inched my chair closer to him he tried to slide his chair away from me to resist my interrogation, but the back of his chair was against the wall so there was no way for him to psychologically distance himself from me and what I was saying. Once he realized that he couldn't move away from my encroachment the psychological surrender began.

I continued expanding on the theme that the rapes were a misunderstanding. The psychological lifeline initially minimized his guilt and allowed him to grasp at a face-saving version of what he had done. I pressed the misunderstanding theme home saying, "I think what happened is that you met Sara Donnelly in a bar. You were both drinking a lot. We both know how these things go."

With that he looked at me, "Yes, we were having drinks…she came onto me. We both had too much to drink."

Now that he had accepted the theme I wanted to get him to admit that he had sex with Donnelly. While he could claim it was consensual and think that he was talking his way out of charges, in fact he would be admitting to a significant element of the crime, penetration of the victim. In the case of the Donnelly rape, vaginal penetration had not occurred, but oral penetration had. Under Nebraska law when Cullen forced her to fellate him he had penetrated her. Similarly, when he orally copulated her he penetrated her and committed First Degree Sexual Assault. At trial the victim would destroy his assertions that it was consensual and no jury would believe Cullen's protestations otherwise. But I wasn't done. Once he admitted having sex with Donnelly I would maneuver him to admit the truth that it wasn't consensual at all. From there I would introduce the Brown rape and expand his confession to completion.

I continued working the theme, "You know how women are. They want it as much as we do but sometimes they're embarrassed afterwards. They try to protect their reputations by claiming it was not consensual after all."

Cullen glanced up from staring at the floor, "Yes, yes, that's right."

Now that he had accepted the theme of a misunderstanding he was not likely to continue to try to deny it. It was time to ask him to tell his side of it knowing that he would fold in the theme as at least a partial justification for what had happened.

I moved my chair even closer, "Mike, am I right? It was a misunderstanding?"

"Yes," he replied, looking back down at the floor.

"Tell me about it," I said as he continued to look at the floor to avoid my gaze.

"We met in a bar…had some drinks…we went back to her place," he said.

I interrupted, "What bar, Mike?"

"Uh, it was Strawberries, you know it? It's on 84th just North of L Street."

"Yeah, I know the place, not far from her apartment," I replied.

"Yes, just up the road. We had drinks and we were probably both drunk or near drunk and you know how it goes. We went to her place afterwards and..."

Just then there was a knock on the door to the room. Cullen sat upright in his chair at the sound. It was bad timing because it broke his mental surrender and his embrace of my theme as the lead-up to a full confession.

I responded to the knock by saying forcefully, "Not now!"

On the other side of the door a trooper spoke through the closed door, "It's his girlfriend. She has to use the bathroom."

Upon hearing that his girlfriend was just outside the door Cullen sat up and began to straighten out his clothing while brushing back his hair. It was over. He had been thrown a substantial psychological lifeline by that door knock and the realization that his girlfriend was on the other side. I tried to get the trooper to take her to another bathroom but he told me that it was the only bathroom and access to it was through my interrogation room.

I was beyond pissed. I had Cullen admitting to sex with a rape victim and he was on the verge of a full admission. Ten or fifteen minutes later and I would have had my confession. I opened the door and stepped outside. I quietly asked the trooper why he let the girlfriend in to the barracks. He seemed to be overly concerned with trying to explain to her what was going on. It wasn't necessary. She had no right to be there. I have no doubt that she was a full blown sociopath like

Cullen, or more likely a co-dependent sociopath and her panic to find out what was going on at the barracks after the arrest led her to con her way in so she could run interference for Cullen. The inexperienced trooper had played into her hands and ruined my interrogation. If he had done his job and turned her away I would have had my confession.

As she walked through the room, ostensibly to use the only bathroom in the place, I tried to position myself between her and Cullen. In spite of that their eyes met and they exchanged knowing glances. "Love you babe," she said. Cullen took a deep, breath as the color returned to his face. That type of psychological and emotional reinforcement destroyed my chances of continuing the interrogation.

After she came back through the room I closed the door again and tried to resume the interrogation. Cullen wasn't having any of it. He sat up in his chair and said, "Maybe I should talk to an attorney before saying anything more." I told him that he could have an attorney anytime he wished and asked him to continue explaining what had happened. He then said, "No, as much as I would like to, I want to talk to an attorney first." At that point my interrogation had to stop.

During the search of Cullen's residence several items were found that matched items worn during the Donnelly rape. Among the items seized were a shirt, a coat and a pair of boots later identified by Donnelly as those worn by her assailant. The troopers also found a resume Cullen created when he lived in Omaha. He claimed to be a lead carpenter for a real estate development company in town. On a hunch I visited the company when I got back to Omaha. They verified that Cullen worked as a temporary laborer on a construction crew that was involved in the renovation of Jackie Brown's building. He was not a finish carpenter as he claimed. Unknown to me before Cullen's arrest, that subcontractor was a secondary co-developer of the condominium project. If I had known that others were involved in the renovation I might have learned of Cullen's identity months earlier. Unfortunately, the primary developer failed to inform me that other companies were involved.

The manager of the subcontractor confirmed a hunch I had about how Cullen got into Brown's condo; he had access to master keys for the entire building. Cullen's job also explained why he wore a nylon mask during the Brown rape. He was afraid that she could identify him because she might have seen him at various times while he worked in and around her building. And it explained why he targeted Brown: he had seen her while working there. A third rape victim also lived in a building managed by the real estate company. Like the Brown case, her apartment showed no signs of forced entry, suggesting that the real estate company's master keys may have been used. This victim refused to participate in the investigation, demanded anonymity, broke her apartment lease, and hurriedly left Omaha for the Southwest just before the Donnelly rape. Such reactions are not unusual. They are the unfortunate byproduct of the severe psycho-emotional trauma of rape victimization. It was not possible to identity the perpetrator of this rape; Michael Cullen was not charged with this crime.

Cullen was booked into the Dukes County jail on December 15th, 1986. He was extradited back to Nebraska in May, 1987 and stood trial that October. He was convicted and sentenced to not less than 10 or more than 20 years imprisonment. For using a knife in his attacks he received an additional year to run consecutively to the rape convictions. In the burglary of the Norman apartment, which was separately docketed but tried with the other charges, Cullen was sentenced to 5 years imprisonment to run concurrently with the other sentences. He entered prison on February 4, 1988 and was released on November 8, 1999 after serving 11 years and 9 months in the maximum security Nebraska Penal and Correctional Complex in Lincoln, NE. Thanks to Megan's Law, described in Chapter Seven, as a convicted rapist he has to register as a sex offender and be monitored by law enforcement no matter what state he lives in.

Jackie Brown asked for and was granted a transfer by her company and left Omaha not long after Cullen's conviction. In the succeeding years I lost track of her. Sara Beth Donnelly left high school coaching. She returned to college, graduated law school and got a job with the U.S. Department of Justice as a trial attorney for the Voting Section of the Civil Rights Division in Washington, DC. She maintained her Nebraska roots by becoming a booster for her college and served on a board developing and implementing a planned giving program for its foundation. She was appointed chairperson in 2010. In 2013, in recognition of her work for the college, she was named grand marshal at the college's 93rd Annual Homecoming Parade.

In true sociopath form Cullen has run afoul of the law on at least two occasions since his release from prison. In February, 2014 he was pinched in Park Hill, Oklahoma (Newton 2014). A deputy sheriff was investigating the theft of medications from a local man who told officers where they might find the suspect. The deputy went to the address and saw a female shooting up the drugs in her leg. Cullen was sitting on the couch playing a guitar at the time.

After arresting the female and escorting her outside, the deputy returned and found that a needle and spoon used by the female had disappeared. Cullen denied knowing where the drug paraphernalia was but the deputy found the needle behind a door and the spoon among ashes in the fireplace. Other drug paraphernalia was also found including scales, pill bottles, and a piece of tinfoil with a white, powdery substance. Cullen initially claimed his last name was Collins but the deputy found his driver's license with his true identity on it. He was arrested for obstruction, destruction of evidence, and possession of a controlled dangerous substance.

In August, 2018 an arrest warrant was issued for Cullen by Frederick County, Maryland authorities (Arias 2018). He had violated Maryland sex-offender requirements by failing to register as a high-risk sex offender. He was believed to have fled to Massachusetts. At this writing he is a fugitive and is being searched for by sheriff's deputies and the FBI.

Chapter Four
The Child Killers

There is no **safety** *for honest men*
except by believing **all possible evil of evil men**.
Edmund Burke

Lt. Bob Tramp rushed out of his cubicle at the rear of the detective bay. He stood next to my desk anxiously waiting for me to finish a phone call. As I hung up the phone he said, "Dean get out to 168th and Ida. A farmer found a body." It was Monday, March 31, 1986, the day after Easter. Tramp's words triggered simultaneous emotions. If the body was Ricky Chadek's, I was saddened that any hopes 11-year-old Ricky was still alive were now gone. I felt sorry for his family. The only positive was that we would now have a crime scene and evidence that could be used to find his killer.

Ricky had been reported missing on Sunday, March 23, 1986 as he rode his bike in the parking lot of a bank at 42nd and Valley Street two blocks from his home. It was the first time his mother had allowed him to ride his bike alone to a friend's house. Plans were made of the route he would take to get back home and for him to make a phone call before leaving, letting her know when to expect his return. Ricky was keenly interested in ATM receipts and was attracted to the bank where he would go through the ATM trash container to examine the slips of paper. It is believed that he was looking for the receipts the day when witnesses said an old blue truck with blue wooden sideboards pulled into the parking lot behind him. Witnesses weren't sure, but the driver might have picked up Ricky.

When Ricky didn't return home on time, his mother searched the area and found his bike in the parking lot near a dumpster. It was standing upright with the kickstand down, indicating that he might not have been taken by force. Witnesses described the man driving the truck as white, 45 to 50, with a ruddy complexion. The truck was described as a medium blue 1968 to 1972 Chevrolet or GMC pickup with sideboards of the same color on each side of the truck bed. A forensic artist prepared a composite drawing of the suspect along with a rendering of the truck. It was widely distributed and shown on local TV newscasts and in the newspaper.

A task force had been hurriedly put together to find Ricky. It was being run by Omaha Police Lt. Tony Mohatt out of a Joint Operations Center (JOC) housed in Omaha Police Headquarters at 15th and Howard Street downtown. Detectives were under no illusions about how urgent the case was. They knew that in a little under half of child abduction cases the children are murdered within 1 hour of being abducted, three quarters are dead within 3 hours, and nine out of ten are often killed within 24 hours (Geberth 2010:523).

I wasn't among the nearly 60 detectives from nine local and federal agencies working 12 to 16 hour shifts running down leads in the disappearance of Ricky Chadek. My involvement was sporadic and dependent on the level of tips coming into the JOC. In any child abduction the ebb and flow of tips can peak depending on news reporting. Ricky's disappearance was no different. When a news report resulted in an avalanche of tips, the task force prioritized them. What appeared to be priority tips were assigned to the six teams of lead investigators while lesser priority ones were funneled to back-up detectives like me.

Local news organizations frantically worked their sources within the various law enforcement agencies, trying to peel back the shroud of secrecy surrounding the investigation. Some of that secrecy was essential. Keeping a lid on sensitive information, like the identity of a potential suspect who was not in custody, prevented the guilty from learning they had been identified and were wanted, leading them to flee or destroy evidence. "Hold back" information, such as the details of the cause of death, is crucial to distinguish a real suspect from a false confessor. In any high-profile case, nut jobs crawl out of the woodwork and plague detectives. They are generally the mentally unstable types who falsely confess because they crave attention or have some masochistic need for punishment. Then there are the well-meaning but flimsy tips like "My neighbor must be the kidnapper because he yelled at my kid for riding his bike in the street," or "The guy down the block should be checked out because he never waives to anyone, has no kids, and is seldom outside."

Time is a limited commodity in these cases. The time wasted on false confessors and flimsy tips reduces our ability to identify the real perpetrator by tying up detectives who could be doing more productive things. But in case any tip may lead to a suspect, detectives must run many of the flimsy ones to ground, especially during the initial phase of an investigation before the case gets fleshed out with detail and a better understanding of what transpired has been developed. My partner, Dave

Vencalek, was also running down non-priority leads. His frustration with them was evident one day in a phone conversation I overheard. He was talking to a supposed psychic, the fourth who had called the task force by then, who was providing tips on where to look for the then still missing boy. It contained the usual nonsensical and general-to-point-of-being-useless gibberish such as "I see him near water. I also see a church nearby, and trees, and a street sign on a two-lane road." Dave finally had enough and said, "Next time you're seeing through the eyes of the dead get a friggin' address or a street name," before slamming down the phone.

When the call about the body came in, I happened to be the closest available detective to the crime scene, having returned to my office in West Omaha to get my phone messages and dictate reports. I grabbed Vencalek and we headed out to Ida Street. The location of the body was on the edge of what was then a rolling farm field next to a line of scrub trees on the west side of 168th Street. The farmer was visibly shaken by what he had seen. He stood by his pickup truck on the edge of the road with a patrol deputy. As we walked up he blurted out, "I knew it was that little boy. My God, it's awful. That poor little boy."

I asked the patrol deputy if either he or the farmer had touched anything and to show me where they had walked to approach the body. He said he saw signs of lividity indicating death so he never got closer than ten feet to where the body lay. Lividity is a purplish red discoloration of the skin that occurs postmortem as blood pools in the lowest portions of the body after the heart stops beating. He pointed out the path he had taken from the roadway along the line of scrub trees to where the body lay. He said it was the same path the farmer had taken out of the field when he rushed back to his truck to drive home to call 911. The deputy did the right thing by trying to walk in the farmer's footprints to avoid contaminating the scene. Unlike many homicide scenes this one was pristine because neither the farmer nor the deputy had disturbed the body or trampled the area immediately surrounding it.

Vencalek and I said nothing as we slowly and methodically walked in the deputy's and farmer's tracks to get to the body, looking for possible evidence along the way. Like them, we approached, observed lividity and stopped. There was no rush now because the presence of lividity indicated that the child was dead. We wanted to get the crime scene experts of the Criminalistics Division there to begin the painstaking and laborious steps required to process the scene and the area around it before we could approach and examine the body, remove it and have it transported to the morgue for an autopsy.

The autopsy revealed that Ricky died of traumatic asphyxia caused by strangulation or smothering. Because the case remains unsolved the exact mechanism of death is confidential hold-back information. The autopsy revealed that he had been dead for approximately 12 hours. He had been kept alive for six or seven days after the abduction and cared for because his clothes were clean, he appeared clean and later we found out that were signs that he had eaten a meal not long before death based the contents of his stomach. There were no signs of abuse such as bruises, cuts or scratches. And he had not been sexually assaulted in any obvious way such as bruising or tearing of the anus or abrasions to the penis, inner thigh, or buttocks areas. However, there is often a sexual aspect to child abductions resulting in murder (Geberth 2010:539). The perpetrator may not sexually assault the victim in an obvious way, instead revealing the sexual motive by masturbating later as, for example, serial killer John Joubert admitted to doing after murdering two of his three victims (Pettit 2013:21-22):

Back in his own world, John Joubert lay naked on the bed (in his room on base). Over and over again, he relived the crime. Once more he saw the mostly undressed paperboy lying bound in the high grass, listened to his pleas for mercy, felt the knife cutting into the young flesh...the feeling of power was arousing....Slowly he began to masturbate. He could still hear the paperboy begging for his life. "Please don't kill me! Please don't kill me! Please!" The words echoed inside Joubert's head....In only a few minutes, he brought himself to a violent climax.... Masturbating had become a ritual. Sometimes he did it three times a day, always after glancing through his stack of true-crime magazines. But this morning he had taken his fantasies a step further [by killing Danny Joe Eberle], and he found that he liked the feeling of power it gave him.

Seeing Ricky's lifeless body dumped in that field like so much garbage angered me. He was the same age as my son at the time. The functional stoicism I depended on to push through such emotions to remain detached, focused, and functioning so I could do my job was sorely taxed that day. I wanted this killer; I wanted him badly. More important than personal vengeance I wanted little Ricky's killer behind bars so he no longer posed a threat to other kids. To this day, I have yet to see that happen.

The task force ultimately checked out and cleared more than 1,000 trucks in Nebraska and Iowa as well as dozens of potential suspects. Investigators traveled as far as 300 miles to run down leads. Hundreds of other tips were also checked, ultimately to no avail. As of this writing Ricky Chadek's killer has not been identified and remains at large. Because there is no statute of limitations on homicides, it remains an active but cold case.

In 2011, the case was transferred to the Douglas County Sheriff's Department because the body had been found outside Omaha city limits. Sheriff's detectives immediately reviewed the voluminous case file, called a "homicide book" or more accurately in a case this size, "homicide books," and began to work the case anew. They had no better luck than the original task force in 1986. However, the Douglas County Sheriff Forensic Science Division (FSD) examined the physical evidence again. DNA had just been coming into widespread use in criminal investigations in 1986. Advances in DNA techniques, such as "touch DNA," enable crime scene investigators to recover much smaller traces of DNA than they could in the mid-1980s. The homicide books revealed that none of the evidence had been processed recently for DNA. The scientists of the FSD found and successfully recovered DNA evidence. The exact nature of that recovery is also hold-back information. Because the person who left the DNA on the Chadek evidence is not known, the DNA is referred to as "from an unknown contributor."

Ricky's mother, Theresa Grooms, moved to Texas after the kidnapping. She returned to Omaha after the DNA had been recovered to give detectives a reference DNA sample. Her mother also provided a sample. Their DNA samples, and samples from other blood relatives, were used to rule out any DNA found by FSD personnel that came from a family member. Family members are not considered suspects in this case. The unknown contributor sample was then submitted to CODIS, the Combined DNA Index System, which is the basic term used to describe the FBI's program of support for national criminal justice DNA databases (FBI n.d.). In the case of a sexual assault where an evidence kit is collected from the victim, a DNA profile of the unknown contributor is developed from the swabs in the kit. The forensic DNA profile attributed to the unknown contributor is searched against all state databases of convicted offender and arrestee profiles through CODIS.

As of the date of this writing no match between the unknown contributor and an existing profile on file in CODIS has been found. That could mean that the perpetrator doesn't have a criminal history that would have led to his DNA profile being submitted. It is also possible that the perpetrator might have been arrested and incarcerated prior to the CODIS operational date in 1998. In that case, his DNA would not have been collected, or if it had been collected it might not have been submitted, resulting in no profile on file.

New forensic procedures now exist to match unknown contributor DNA to the profiles in commercially available DNA databases used for genealogy services and similar resources. While not as accurate and convenient as CODIS for criminal cases, commercial databases have been used to trace familial DNA to narrow the universe of potential suspects (Waltz 2018). Detectives are hopeful that eventually the unknown contributor in the Chadek case will be identified, perhaps using commercial DNA databases, or if he is arrested in the future for a crime that requires his DNA be submitted to CODIS.

❧

Ricky Chadek's murder occurred not long after the worst serial child murder case in Omaha history. The murders terrified the city for months until the killer was caught. Referring to that time and how it changed the city, Douglas County Sheriff Tim Dunning said, "Having back-to-back child homicides like that. People had a tendency... to take kids to school rather than let them walk no matter how...(close they lived)" (Fry, 2016). On September 18, 1983, approximately two and a half years before Ricky Chadek disappeared, 13-year-old Danny Jo Eberle disappeared while delivering newspapers near his home in Bellevue, NE, a suburb south of Omaha. Danny Joe's brother, who also delivered newspapers, had not seen him since they left the house together earlier but remembered being followed by a white male in a tan car on previous days.

"Eberle's parents realized something was wrong when they started getting phone calls from people who hadn't received their papers. They notified police who began to look for Danny Joe. Eberle had only delivered 3 of the 70 newspapers on his route. His bicycle was discovered at his fourth delivery along with the rest of the newspapers. There were no signs of a struggle. While searching for the boy, the police theorized that he might have run away. As time passed they began to fear that Danny Joe had been abducted." Officers from the Sarpy County Sheriff's Department, Bellevue Police Department and the FBI formed a task force (Pettit 2013:31). The task force had swollen to 130 officers after they announced that they were seeking law enforcement volunteers to help search for Danny Joe. Succumbing to the growing belief that he had been abducted, they wanted to avoid media coverage and untrained civilian volunteers finding what they assumed would be Danny Joe's remains at a crime scene, if only to preserve the scene for its evidence.

After three days of searching, the boy's body was discovered on the secluded Base Lake Road about four miles from where his bike was found. He had been stripped to his underwear, his feet and hands bound with a unique type of rope, and his mouth taped with surgical tape. After Danny Joe's body had been found, the task force shifted from finding and recovering the victim to the investigation to find his killer. What appeared to be a major break in the case came one week after the Eberle murder. Police had picked up an eighteen-year-old man for allegedly molesting two young boys. He had reportedly tied them up then sexually assaulted them. The suspect denied any connection to Danny Joe's murder and task force commanders were not convinced he was involved despite giving a false alibi and failing the first of two polygraph examinations. The task force commanders' instincts were correct. It was not him, and he was not charged for the Eberle murder.

The man eventually arrested for Danny Joe's murder, along with the murder of another Nebraska child and a third child from Maine, was John Joubert, an airman stationed at Offutt Air Force Base in Bellevue, 10 miles south of Omaha. He would describe to investigators, and later to a news reporter while on death row awaiting execution, how he had approached Eberle in the pre-dawn darkness, drew a knife and grabbed the boy. "Joubert clamped a hand over Danny Joe's mouth. Slowly he drew the thin blade from its sheath, with the whispering sound of metal against leather. He held the knife up so the boy could see. Danny Joe's eyes widened. Now he was clearly frightened. 'Don't make any sounds,' Joubert said. 'Come with me.' After checking for traffic and seeing none, he picked up the boy and placed him in his trunk" (Pettit 2013:12). Joubert then drove him to a secluded area near a small lake in the Offutt Air Force Base Lake Recreation Area east of the base where Joubert was stationed. Joubert's cold-blooded description of the murder is revealing (Pettit 2013:14):

"Please don't kill me," [Danny Joe] pleaded. Suddenly, Joubert plunged the knife into the boy's back. The teenager gasped at the red-hot streamer of pain that lanced through his body. "Please!" he begged. "Just take me to the hospital. I won't tell!" Four more times he plunged the knife into Danny Joe. He then turned the boy and slammed the knife four times into the child's chest. To make sure that the boy was dead he slashed the back of his neck. Still not satisfied, he bit the boy's body, fulfilling the cannibalistic fantasies he had harbored since childhood. The bites were random: once on the upper back side of the boy's left leg, twice on his upper left shoulder. Then Joubert picked up the knife again. Where he had bitten the boy's leg, he carved a star-like design. His fantasy now completed, John Joubert stood up and looked at what he had done. In one way, he felt proud; in another way, ashamed.... [Shortly afterwards Joubert] ate "a hearty breakfast" at McDonald's in Bellevue.

According to Dr. Blaine Roffman, the pathologist who conducted the autopsy on Danny Joe, his death resulted from loss of blood caused by one or more of nine antemortem stab wounds. Two additional wounds, one a deep wound to the left thigh and one a deep wound to the left shoulder, were inflicted postmortem (State v. Joubert 1986). Postmortem stab wounds often indicate picquerism because the victim is dead so the need to continue stabbing him to cause death no longer exists. Picquerism is a paraphilia defined as a sexual interest in penetrating the skin of another person with sharp objects such as pins, razors, or knives. Picquerism is also a form of the paraphilia sadism defined as deriving sexual gratification from inflicting pain, suffering, or humiliation on others. The penetration in picquerism can also include biting the victim (Griffiths 2015). Dr. Roffman reported that he found additional bite marks on Danny Joe's body including the one on his leg that the killer had cut a design on top of.

I believe that the carving of a design on the bite mark on Danny Joe's leg was an example of both signature and MO. It was a signature trait because it satisfied Joubert's picquerism paraphilia. It is simultaneously MO because it served to obliterate the unique characteristics of the bite mark that could be used to identify him. In an interview on death row with Mark Pettit, a local TV Newscaster at the time, Joubert admitted that he had "used a knife to try to hide the [bite] mark on Eberle's left thigh by cutting it or carving it" (State v. Joubert 1992). Many serial killers read "true detective" magazines, including Ted Bundy, Dennis Rader, Melvin Rees, Jr., and Robert Rhoades, among others (Ramsland 2017). Joubert also was an avid reader of those types of magazines. In an interview with FBI Agent Robert Ressler shortly after his arrest, Joubert said that he wasn't just inspired by detective magazines, they also taught him how to avoid being caught (Ramsland 2017). It isn't known for sure, but Joubert might have learned about forensic odontology from the many detective magazines he'd read. Forensic odontology is a branch of forensic science that employs dental science to identify criminal suspects from the unique characteristics of their bite marks. His attempts to obliterate the bite marks on Danny Joe's body might have been learned from what he read in detective magazines.

During the search for the killer, task force detectives discovered a large number of perverts with various attractions to children. The information they gathered and the tips they received led them to create a "pervert" list. One man reportedly paid a youngster eight hundred dollars to urinate on him and had offered to give another a new car if he would do the same (Sheriff Pat Thomas, personal communication, 2001). The tips snowballed so massively that the task force formed a separate "Pervert Squad" to handle them. Each person questioned would lead police to four or five others just like him. The list would eventually grow to an astonishing 2,800 names, many not known to police before formation of the task force. It was the anonymity shrouding the actions of child molesters that eventually led to Sex Offender Registry laws throughout the nation. Forcing convicted sex offenders to register and making that information available to the public deprives them of the anonymity they need to operate.

༄

Despite exhaustive efforts, investigators turned up nothing that would help them solve the Eberle case. Seventy-nine days had now passed since Danny Joe's disappearance and the community had begun to relax. Some task force members started to think that the killer might have left the area, been arrested, or in some other way prevented from committing more crimes. Others were not so sure. An ominous pall had settled over the task force. On December 2, 1983, fears were confirmed when 12-year-old Christopher Walden disappeared while on his way to school. The location of the abduction was about eight miles from where Eberle's body had been found. This time there were witnesses to the kidnapping.

That morning, Joubert got off work from his part time job delivering pizzas for Domino's. He had the day off from his duties on base so he cruised the pre-dawn streets with his rope, tape, and knife. But every time he spotted a potential victim something prevented him from pouncing. One boy had stepped under a streetlight before Joubert could reach him. On another occasion the young girl he was stalking had turned a corner where there was too much traffic for him to feel comfortable proceeding (Pettit 2013:129-130). Later that day witnesses saw a white man in a tan car parked near the intersection of 48th and Margo not far from Pawnee Elementary School (State v. Joubert 1986). It was John Joubert on the prowl for victims. The area around an elementary school made for a rich hunting ground. Joubert spotted Christopher Walden walking to school alone. He got out of the car and called out to him, "Hey, wait a minute. Can you give me directions?" Like many kids in those days, Danny Joe Eberle and Christopher Walden were taught to be polite to adults, even those they did not know. That gave Joubert the opportunity to move in close before his victims could react.

Christopher stopped as Joubert approached. Joubert placed a hand on the boy's shoulder. With the other hand, he touched the sheath on his belt. "Come with me, and you won't get hurt," he told the boy. A witness driving by came over the hill so Joubert put his arm around Chris's shoulders to control him and camouflage his lethal intentions (Pettit 2013:138). It worked because witnesses said later that they assumed that the young man walking with his arm around the child was an older brother or relative of the child. They were unable to provide any more descriptive information such as the license plate of the tan car or a specific make and model.

Joubert ordered the boy to get in the car and lie down on the floor. Chris did as he was told. The terrified boy began to cry as Joubert drove him to a secluded location he had selected days earlier. It was perfect for what he had in mind. The sparsely travelled location was a lightly wooded tract on 108th Street where railroad tracks crossed near Giles Road. Joubert led the boy into a patch of trees along the tracks not far off the road where he ordered Chris to strip to his underwear and to lie down (Ramsland 2009:67). Chris removed his coat and outer clothing but refused to lie down. After a brief but intense struggle Joubert overpowered the child by violently choking him and forcing him onto the ground. He next stabbed Christopher in the back multiple times then cut his throat to be sure he was dead (Pettit 2013:143). Dr. Jerry Jones, the pathologist who conducted the autopsy on Christopher Walden, stated that the boy was stabbed seven times (State v. Joubert 1986).

Many in Omaha were frightened when Danny Joe Eberle was murdered, especially when the killer eluded apprehension. When news broke that another child was missing, many in the city were terrified. I was assigned to the patrol division at the time. Christopher Walden was abducted two blocks from my home while on his way to the same elementary school my kids attended. My son was four years younger than Christopher but he was similar in appearance to both Danny Joe and Christopher. The city was changed forever. No longer were kids allowed outside without an adult watching their every move. Kids no longer walked to school alone. The parking lot in front of Pawnee School was so clogged with traffic from parents dropping off kids that police had to be called to direct the massive flow of cars into and out of the small parking lot in front of the building.

When Christopher Walden failed to arrive at school that morning no one at the school was alarmed. It wasn't unusual for kids to miss school for sickness or other reasons. His parents had no idea he hadn't shown up until he failed to return home after school. In a panic, Christopher's mother began to search the neighborhood when she saw a friend of his. When she asked him if he had seen Christopher at school, the boy told her Christopher hadn't been in school that day. She told her husband who called police and the task force was notified.

One of the changes that occurred in society in the advent of the Joubert case was the requirement that school officials notify parents when a child without pre-approved permission fails to arrive at school.

Just that morning, the Eberle task force had been cut back because of dwindling leads in the case. Now it had happened again. The task force quickly swelled to at least one hundred officers as the efforts to find Christopher Walden kicked into high gear. Along with Christopher Walden, the relatively crime-free innocence Omaha had known before vanished that day. Christopher Walden's abduction, following that of Danny Joe, demanded drastic action. A child killer was prowling city streets and the public was scared for their children like they had never been scared before. So were many cops.

Sometimes the actions were desperate as law enforcement worked to assuage the public's fears. When Uniform Services Bureau Captain Jim Wintle showed up to talk to every roll call, we in the patrol division knew something was up. It was highly unusual for the bureau commander to appear at the patrol division's midnight shift roll call. He was there to announce implementation of an unprecedented region-wide Metro Area Response (MAR) plan that would be activated the minute police learned of an abduction. He started out his presentation saying, "I have never seen people this scared and I've lived in this town all my life. We all have kids so pay attention to the plan I am going to describe and let's see if we can help the task force find this bastard."

The ambitious plan detailed the immediate flooding of the area around the site of an abduction with every available law enforcement officer in the region. A ring of containment would be established at ever widening circles outwards from the abduction point. Checkpoints would be set up on every street into and out of the area, and officers would stop and search every car. The plan was only marginally workable due to the logistics involved in shutting down and controlling the flow of traffic into and out of a relatively large geographical footprint in a metropolitan area. It was implemented only once, albeit only partially, for an incident that turned out to be unfounded. Ultimately it was abandoned when the murders stopped after Joubert's arrest.

Searchers combed the area around the Walden home all night. A helicopter was brought in to use its searchlight to penetrate the darkness. All of the local TV stations broadcast Christopher Walden's picture, asking for the public's help in finding him. The next morning, Christopher's parents, Steve and Sue Walden, made an impassioned and heart-rending appeal on TV for the return of their child. Christopher Walden's body was found in the snow by hunters two days later. The autopsy revealed a grisly detail: the killer had not only stabbed the child multiple times and cut his throat, he had also carved what appeared to be a design into the boy's chest. When word leaked out about the chest design it heightened the sinister nature of the fear that gripped the city. It also linked the crimes via the signature of the carving.

Task force leaders met the next morning to discuss the killer's actions in carving Chris Walden's chest.

Sheriff Pat Thomas believed it looked like some kind of leaf, perhaps a marijuana leaf. FBI agent Chuck Kempf thought it could be the insignia from a Boy Scout badge (Pettit 2013:164). Because of its crude nature, all agreed that they couldn't be sure what the design represented, if it represented a design at all. It is not clear why Joubert carved the design into Christopher Walden's chest. That detail has since been lost in the minutia of the huge volume of information generated by the task force. I believe it was simply more and varied picquerism on Joubert's part as he indulged that paraphilia while also biting, stabbing, and cutting Christopher. Its fear-enhancing effect wasn't limited to the public. Many of the seasoned cops working the task force were trying to visualize the kind of monster who could do such things to a child. I remember hearing from detectives on the task force that a common image floating around over water cooler gossip was of an ominous, hulking brute, perhaps with a huge scar running down the side of his face; someone who made women cower and children cry at the sight of him. The truth would turn out to be far different.

A month went by and task force detectives still had no viable suspects. Sheriff Thomas was sure the killer was following the investigation in the media. He proposed broadcasting an appeal to the killer's manhood to get him to respond and hopefully make a mistake that would lead to his capture. The FBI was vehemently against that tactic, and felt that it would be ineffective and even counterproductive, possibly leading to another murder that an angry public could blame on the broadcast, and by extension the entire task force. They brought to bear the considerable weight of their reputation as the gold-standard experts in these types of cases to lobby against it. Some of the other taskforce commanders agreed with them, but the sheriff was not to be dissuaded. In his deep baritone voice he reminded them that they weren't making much headway finding the killer by continuing to do the things they were already doing (Sheriff Pat Thomas, personal communication, 2001). Against the wishes of some task force commanders, and especially the FBI, the sheriff made a televised appeal to the killer. In it he asked the killer to turn himself in, if not to the sheriff then to a priest or a minister. He ratcheted up the rhetoric by referring to him as a "coward who could only kill children." He added, "If he were a real man he would stop picking on children and start picking on someone his own size" (Pettit 2013:199).

Much to everyone's—except the Sheriff's—surprise, it worked. The veteran lawman's instincts were spot on. On January 11, 1984, John Joubert's car was in the shop and he desperately needed cash. That didn't bother him nearly as much as hearing Sheriff Pat Thomas refer to him on TV as a "coward who could only kill children" and not being a "real man." The sheriff's final taunt, about "stop picking on children and pick on someone his own size" riled Joubert. So much so that he decided to prove to Sheriff Thomas that he was not a coward (Pettit 2013:201).

John Joubert made the mistake Pat Thomas was hoping for. He was prowling the neighborhood near Aldersgate Church on 36th Street near Greene Avenue in Bellevue, driving a loaner car from the shop repairing his car. It was little more than a mile from where he had abducted Christopher Walden. In anticipation of attacking a woman he had slipped the knife up his sleeve where he could reach it in a hurry. The rope lay beside him on the seat. As he pulled into the driveway of the preschool attached to the church he saw a woman sitting near the window inside. Barbara Weaver had seen the Chevy Citation pass the church twice. With the killer at large she, like many people in the area of the abductions, was anxious and hyper-vigilant about anything that looked out of the ordinary. When the car turned in and pulled up to the door, she looked at its license plate, 59-L5154, and repeated it over and over to herself to remember it (Pettit 2013:202).

When the suspicious man stopped at the window and motioned for her to go to the door, she was scared. She refused to open it fully when the man asked for directions. She said his voice was "soft and quivering" and he appeared to be trembling and near tears. She focused on his face, burning the image into her mind. When he asked to use the phone she lied and told him there was no phone inside. Suddenly, he grabbed for the door. "Get back inside or I'll kill you!" he said in that same quivering voice. Barbara Weaver acted on impulse. She pulled the door fully open and pushed past the man to get out of the building. She scrambled through the parking lot as she bolted along the gravel drive to run to the parsonage a block away. She burst into the parsonage winded and terrified. After blurting out that she had been attacked by a man she believed to be the child killer, church employees called the police (Pettit 2013:210).

Joubert fled the scene in a panic, returning to his room on base where he eventually fell asleep. Responding deputies traced the car to the repair shop where they found Joubert's Chevy Nova. It fit the description witnesses had given in the abductions. They obtained a search warrant and went through the car. Inside they found the same type of distinctive rope as had been used to bind Danny Joe Eberle. From the repair shop and vehicle registration on the Nova, they got Joubert's address. They proceeded to the base where they met with Air Force Office of Special Investigations agents and the base commander and went to Joubert's room. He was roused from his sleep and arrested. While searching his room they found more of the distinctive rope used to bind Danny Joe.

Joubert was taken to the cramped task force headquarters at the Bellevue Police Department for interrogation. By then the place was abuzz with the news. Everyone knew who was coming through the back door to the station. They all stopped what they were doing and looked up in unison as Joubert was ushered in wearing handcuffs. I was told by task force members who were present at the time that many were almost disappointed. To instill such pervasive and suffocating fear in a community the suspect they had worked so long and hard to find would have to be a monster. Instead a short, harmless-looking kid had walked through the door. They had a hard time wrapping their heads around the notion that he was capable of the horrific violence he had inflicted on Danny Joe Eberle and Christopher Walden. When I consider the reactions of the task force detectives to the diminutive Joubert, I am reminded of philosopher Hannah Arendt's "banality of evil" which holds that huge evils are often perpetrated by seemingly ordinary people. For the time being it was all so anticlimactic. That would change.

Joubert was taken to a captain's office at the back of the Bellevue Police Station. Three task force members were chosen to interrogate him, including its commander Lt. Jim Sanderson of the Sarpy County Sheriff's Department. The veteran investigators showed Joubert the rope they'd removed from his room and car, noting that it was extremely rare. He resisted this at first, but soon admitted that he'd gotten it from the scoutmaster he assisted in a local scout troop. He said the scoutmaster had brought it back from Korea. He seemed taken aback that it could place him at a crime scene (Pettit 2013:214). It was the opening Sanderson had intended.

While Joubert was off balance, Sanderson employed the Reid Interrogation Technique to obtain a confession (Jayne 1999:23). Sanderson shrewdly used a theme that would allow Joubert to make an admission without committing himself to a full confession. It was an incremental process designed to overcome Joubert's instinctive resistance to admitting his guilt. Sanderson talked with Joubert about his "bad" side, the part of him that compelled the good part to do something he knew to be wrong. It wasn't long before Joubert was ready to admit to everything (Blogger dg 1952:2008). Joubert admitted that he had killed Eberle and Walden and told the detectives that he would likely kill again. He seemed relieved that they had stopped him. On January 12th, Joubert was charged with two counts of murder and held for trial. On July 3rd, on the advice of his court-appointed attorney, Joubert changed his original plea and pled guilty to both counts.

Other facts that emerged during the extensive post-arrest interrogation of Joubert, as well as during psychiatric evaluations during subsequent court proceedings, were jaw-dropping. The likelihood of an officer or detective investigating a serial killer is as uncommon as unicorn fur. Estimates vary, but data from 2015 indicate that there are 30 serial killers active in the U.S. at any given time (Aamodt 2016:7). Most cops will never work such cases because of their rarity. Many task force detectives were unprepared for the utter depravity the diminutive young killer revealed about his motives and actions. He described having increasingly violent sadistic fantasies beginning as young as age six according to three psychological reports prepared on him following his arrest. The fantasies revolved around murdering and cannibalizing a neighborhood girl who babysat him. He told one psychiatrist that he had nothing personal against the girl, she was "just someone to kill" (Clendenning 1996).

His violent fantasies progressed to the point where he contemplated killing strangers on the street, including tying and gagging those who resisted him. Soon he was acting on his homicidal impulses. At 4:05 PM on Dec. 12, 1979, six-year-old Sarah Canty dropped a football outside her house at Oakdale and Dartmouth streets in Portland, Maine. As she bent to pick it up, Joubert rode up behind her on his green, 10-speed bicycle and stabbed her in the back with a pencil. Then he rode on, according to police reports. Crying, Sarah ran inside her house. Underneath her jacket, shirt and undershirt was a quarter-inch puncture wound (Clendenning 1996).

About six weeks later, on January 24, 1980, 27-year-old Vicky Goff was walking on Deering Avenue in Portland at 7:15 PM, heading to a creative writing class at the University of Southern Maine. Joubert walked past her going in the opposite direction. Goff said "Hi" to him as he passed. Moments later she felt a hand clamped over her mouth from behind. Goff said she then felt like she'd been punched in the side. She recalled falling down, standing up and yelling, "Why'd you do that?" to Joubert as he ran away. Goff saw blood and realized she had been stabbed with a knife. She had surgery for a punctured kidney at Maine Medical Center and spent a week recovering in the hospital (Clendenning 1996).

The next day, Joubert took a razor blade and slashed another girl as he biked past her. Joubert later admitted to choking an eight-year-old boy named Chris Day when he was 16, nearly killing him. The violence continued to escalate with each attack (Ramsland 2009:64). On March 24th, two months to the day after Goff was stabbed, a third-grade student was walking on Deering Avenue in Portland when Joubert, again on his 10-speed bicycle, beckoned the boy to come closer. He asked nine-year-old Michael Witham who he was and where he was going. When Witham looked away for a moment, Joubert slashed him across the throat with an X-ACTO knife. Michael ran home bleeding. It took 12 stiches to close the two-inch wound (Clendenning 1996).

Joubert's escalating violence culminated in murder on August 23, 1982. Eleven-year-old Richard "Ricky" Stetson was jogging on Back Cove Trail in Portland, Maine. When he had not returned by dark, his parents called the police. The next day a passerby found the boy's body under a pedestrian foot bridge over Interstate 295 (Pettit 2013:114). The attacker appeared to have attempted to undress him and then stabbed and strangled him. As he had done in both the Eberle and Walden murders, Joubert indulged his picquerism paraphilia by stabbing and biting Ricky Stetson postmortem. Not long after Stetson's body had been discovered, a suspect was arrested for the murder. He was eventually released after detectives determined that his teeth did not match the bite mark on Stetson's body. With no witnesses, no leads and no suspects, the Ricky Stetson murder case went cold.

Special Agent Robert K. Ressler, the FBI's head profiler at the time, had prepared a psychological profile of Danny Joe Eberle's killer shortly after the task force in Bellevue had been formed. It was generic to the point of being useless and was wrong on several key assumptions, including that Danny Joe might have been kept alive by his killer for several days before being killed (Pettit 2013:64). Ressler revised the profile after the Walden murder but it didn't add much of value to the original and played no role in Joubert's arrest. Ressler's work was not in vain. In 1984, while he was presenting the Joubert case to a training class at the FBI Academy at Quantico, a police officer from Portland, Maine noted the similarities to the Ricky Stetson murder in his jurisdiction. Hair samples and bite impressions were obtained from Joubert on Nebraska's death row in February 1985. He was indicted in Ricky Stetson's murder in January 1986 and convicted on October 15, 1990. The Maine court sentenced Joubert to life in prison without the possibility of parole (State v. Joubert 1992). Even though Maine didn't have the death penalty, an agreement between the states of Maine and Nebraska was hammered out before Joubert's transfer to Maine to stand trial in the Stetson case. Joubert was transferred back to Nebraska to have his death sentence imposed.

Ressler and detectives in Maine came to believe that Joubert joined the Air Force to get away from Maine after the murder of the Stetson boy (Ressler 1992:93-112). Witnesses had reported seeing a young man riding a green ten-speed bike following Ricky Stetson on the day of the murder. Several days after that, Joubert had been detained while riding his bike near the murder scene. A patrol officer asked him if he had been in the area on the day of the murder and if he knew anything about it. Joubert kept his composure and told the officer "No." He was allowed to continue on his way (Pettit 2013:112). Further investigation in Maine revealed two previously unknown crimes between the pencil-stabbing of six-year-old Sarah Canty in 1979 and the murder of Ricky

Stetson in 1982. Ressler's investigation revealed that, in 1980, Joubert had slashed a mid-20s male teacher who "had been cut rather badly, and...(was) lucky to be alive" (Ressler 1992:93-112).

In 1995, Joubert appealed his death sentence in the murders of Danny Joe Eberle and Christopher Walden. His lawyers argued that the aggravating factor of "exceptional depravity" that was required for the death penalty to be imposed was unconstitutionally vague. The court agreed (Joubert v. Hopkins 1996). The state of Nebraska appealed to the United States District Court for the District of Nebraska, which overturned the appeal, saying that he had shown sadistic behavior by torturing Eberle and Walden. Joubert was executed in the Nebraska electric chair on July 17, 1996 (UPI 1996).

In 2001, I was teaching as an adjunct professor at a local university, instructing an undergraduate course on Forensic Psychology that dealt with profiling serial offenders, including John Joubert. I called Sheriff Pat Thomas to ask him to speak to my class when we got to the Joubert case. He had a scheduling conflict that prevented him from appearing but he graciously agreed to send Captain John Kucer in his stead. Kucer was very knowledgeable about the case and many of the little known details of the task force investigation. My students found his presentation fascinating and informative. Even though the sheriff could not appear, he talked to me by phone about the case. I already knew many of the details of what had transpired during the investigation, having talked to detectives from my department who had assisted the task force, but it was enlightening to speak to the man who was at the center of it all. He told me that he talked to Joubert after he pleaded guilty to the Eberle and Walden murders. The sheriff asked Joubert if he would kill again if he was released. Joubert considered the question for a moment then replied, "Yes, I couldn't stop myself" (Sheriff Pat Thomas, personal communication, 2001).

Sheriff Pat Thomas passed away unexpectedly on September 21, 2010 at the age of 70. He had retired five years earlier. He was among the last of a dying breed; a plain-speaking, old-school lawman who is considered by some to be a legend in local law enforcement. Many of those posting comments to his obituary page thanked him for his work in the Eberle-Walden murders. A grateful community remembered his pivotal role in arresting John Joubert, an arrest that ended a terrible saga and helped a grieving community begin the healing process.

Perhaps no single member of the task force can be credited with solving the John Joubert serial murder case. It was a team effort. But I believe two things are certain: If not for Pat Thomas' steadfast insistence on taunting the killer on TV it is unlikely that John Joubert would have been arrested as quickly as he was. And as long as he remained at large, Joubert posed a lethal threat to children in the area. I am convinced that Pat Thomas' actions saved the life of at least one child—a child who would have become Joubert's next victim had Joubert not been arrested so soon following the sheriff's unconventional but effective investigative tactic.

Chapter Five
Earl LaBelle Series
The Hot Prowler Rapist

"I'm not certain there's any such thing as
a non-serial rapist... I think what happens is that
some of these individuals get caught
before they become serial rapists."
Dr. Stanton Samenow

In the spring of 1985 I earned my first award for
rape investigations. Various civic and professional
organizations in the metropolitan area took turns hosting
an annual "Law Enforcement Officer of the Year" award
for local cops. That year it was the Insurance Women of
Omaha group's turn. They hosted a huge banquet with
the notables of the criminal justice system in attendance
including judges, prosecutors, mayors, chiefs of police,
and sheriffs.

Also around that time a series of hot-prowling
burglaries occurred in large apartment complexes near
84th and Q Street in southwest Omaha. A hot prowl
burglary normally occurs at night when an offender
enters a building or residence while occupants are inside.
The intent of the burglary ranges from theft, robbery,
sexual assault, to murder. They are considered especially
dangerous because of the potential for a violent altercation
between the occupant and the offender. About 11:00
PM, Wednesday, June 12, 1985, Bill and Maggie Cross
went to bed in their second floor apartment in the Citadel

Apartment complex at 85th Ohern Street. As he did every night before crawling into bed, Bill took off his watch and wedding band and set them on the dresser across from the foot of their bed. Even though the Citadel area was relatively crime free the couple was usually careful to lock their front door and double check the sliding door on their patio before retiring for the night. That night they forgot to lock the front door.

When he wasn't lugging beef at his overnight job in a packing plant near 132nd and Q Street, Earl LaBelle and his girlfriend prowled large apartment complexes in the area. LaBelle's girlfriend drove the car while Earl scoped out likely victims for theft…and more. Seeing a building that held potential for his thievery he would tell her to drop him off and circle the area until he came back out.

Two types of women gravitate to sociopaths like LaBelle. They are both enablers who do the bidding of the sociopath but for different reasons. The first and most common are the weak-willed perpetual victims who latch onto him and endure his abuse out of some twisted masochistic need for acceptance. The second are fellow sociopaths who mirror their pathology and willingly participate in their predations. LaBelle's girlfriend was of the first type. Like a long-suffering beaten dog she willingly did what was asked no matter how extreme or bizarre in order to lick the hand of her abuser.

About 3:00 AM the pair arrived at the Citadel complex. They stopped in front of the Cross building as LaBelle told his girlfriend that he was going to "find a poker game." As he stepped out of the car and into the hot humid summer night he tucked a pair of the mesh gloves he used to lug beef around the freezers at work into his back pocket. She didn't ask any questions before dutifully driving around the area waiting for him to reappear.

LaBelle made his way around to the back where he skulked in and out of the shadows of the sleeping complex. He tried several patio doors but none were unlocked so he headed around to the front of the building. Once inside he tried every door on the first floor. They were all locked. He made his way to the second floor where he continued trying doors. At the Cross apartment he found what he was looking for. Their front door was unlocked. After pulling on his gloves he carefully, slowly and ever so quietly pushed the door open and slipped inside. The apartment was deathly still as he paused to let his eyes adjust to the darkness. The only light came from the outside security lights that shone through the partially open patio door curtains.

He made out a purse on the kitchen table and headed for it. Because of the darkness he carried the purse near the patio door where he dumped it out on the floor. Positioning the pile in the filtered light of the patio door he rummaged through its scattered contents looking for cash, credit cards and anything else of value. He ignored bulkier items nearby like the TV and VCR. His take was restricted to cash, jewelry, credit cards and any small easily concealed items that he could secret on his person.

After finishing with the purse he crept slowly and cautiously through the apartment. He made his way down the hallway towards the bedroom. The door was open so he stepped forward and peered into the darkened room. The only light filtered around the edges of the closed drapes. It was just enough to allow him to see his way around without stumbling into things.

In the shadows of the darkened room he watched the couple sleeping from the foot of their bed. He tiptoed to the side of the bed next to the woman. Appraising her sexually from head to foot as her chest rhythmically rose and fell he savored her form beneath the sheets. He was disappointed that she was not alone as he leaned down and placed his hands near her face. Her husband sleeping next to her saved Maggie Cross from being another one of LaBelle's rape victims.

Like most Anger Retaliatory Rapists (ARRs) LaBelle was angry at the world and often at a particular woman or women in general. Because anger and displaced aggression are the key to the assault ARRs are often too angry to achieve orgasm. Their attacks may include profanity-laced vulgarities and no amount of pleading will cause them to stop. Rage-based rapists are difficult to profile and catch because their attacks are stress-based. Their unpredictable attack cycles are triggered by a relationship ending or job loss that leads to a spontaneous eruption of violence.

A perceived wrong, often idiosyncratic to the rapist, ignites an attack that usually occurs within 24 hours of the sleight. LaBelle's desire to rape stemmed from anger at women he wished to strike back at. He had a lengthy criminal history that dated from his early teens. Like many serial rapists his criminal versatility complemented his sexual predations by granting him easy access to vulnerable victims.

In LaBelle's case his perpetual hot prowling served often simultaneous and complementary urges. He was an accomplished burglar who supplemented his income and satiated his antisocial urges through theft. And when the right buttons had been pushed by a female in his life or a work situation he also hot prowled in search of a victim to beat up while raping her.

He knew from experience that he did not need to carry burglar tools like pry bars, screwdrivers and other bulky attention-attracting tools for his thievery. The mere possession of such implements could be a felony, especially in the hands of a criminal like LaBelle. He also learned from his arrests as a juvenile burglar that breaking into an apartment by jimmying the door left telltale microscopic tool marks that could be matched to the very implements he was carrying. And it made noise. If he prowled large apartment complexes and tried enough doors the odds were that he would find some unlocked.

⁊

Disappointed that he could not attack Maggie Cross sleeping mere inches from him, LaBelle turned his attention to the dresser where he could make out a watch, wedding ring and other jewelry sitting on top. He tiptoed over to the dresser where he stuffed the watch and wallet into his pockets and picked up the ring. It slipped from his gloved fingers and landed on the dresser top with a resounding metallic clang. That sound immediately roused Bill Cross from his slumber. As he sat up in bed he struggled to clear the fog of sleep that stubbornly clouded his consciousness. Groggily he made out the fuzzy image of a short, stocky black male standing at the foot of the bed.

Startled, he yelled, "Hey, what are you doing here?" as the figure turned and bolted from the room.

LaBelle ran for the front door of the apartment as Cross rolled out of bed, wearing only his underwear. He called out to his wife, "Maggie, call the cops, someone's in here," as he flicked on the bedroom lights and raced down the hallway after LaBelle.

By now LaBelle was in a headlong rush to get away. Once in the hallway he scrambled down the stairs and headed for the front door of the building. Cross was lagging behind. By the time Cross burst through the front door and scanned the darkened parking lot looking for the intruder the fleet-footed LaBelle had disappeared. Concerned about his wife Cross returned to the apartment to await the police.

About this time, Deputy Jerry Birkle was patrolling the Wentworth Apartment Complex in his blacked-out cruiser. The Wentworth complex was just across Q Street from the Citadel complex. It was a midnight cop's dream to be sitting literally seconds away from the scene of a crime. In most cases deputies would be on scene in less than five to ten minutes. This time Birkle was virtually on top of the call. All he had to do was drive across the street.

As Birkle proceeded across Q Street he caught a glimpse of a short black male quickly running south from the Citadel complex. By the time he turned his cruiser around the running figure had disappeared into the vast parking lots of the Wentworth complex. He notified communications that he was searching for a possible suspect when he spotted LaBelle's girlfriend driving slowly through the parking lot. He hung back and watched as she stopped and waited while the same black male emerged from between the buildings and ran to her car. As they drove off, Birkle pulled them over as backup units arrived. He placed them both in custody and impounded their car.

At the office, LaBelle's girlfriend was talkative but stuck to the story that she had merely dropped him off at a poker game. When pressed, she admitted that she didn't know what apartment in the Citadel complex the game was being held and that she had been instructed to drive slowly through both the Wentworth and Citadel complexes until LaBelle reappeared. She denied knowing what LaBelle was up to after he left the car.

LaBelle had ditched his gloves and the items taken from the Cross bedroom before being caught. He wasn't talking but he did agree to give Birkle and the patrol supervisor his fingerprints. As he put it, "You guys have them already," referring to his prior juvenile arrests for burglary. Knowing that numerous hot prowl calls had been reported in the area recently, Birkle had the foresight to ask crime scene technician Bill Kaufhold to take major case prints. Unlike a normal ten-card set of fingerprints that consist of rolling each of a perp's ten fingers, followed by taking all five prints on each hand simultaneously, major case also took the perp's palmprints. It would prove to be a fortuitous decision that ultimately led to taking a serial predator off the streets.

Because neither of the Crosses could positively identify the intruder and none of the items taken from the dresser were found on or near him, LaBelle and his girlfriend had to be released. Birkle completed his usual thorough reports documenting what he had observed and they were forwarded to investigators for follow up. There wasn't much that could be done at that time except to put out a bulletin informing patrol of LaBelle's activities, the physical description of LaBelle and his girlfriend, and their vehicle description. That way if they were spotted again by deputies on other shifts, or by deputies not working the night of their detention, they could be detained and investigated.

Three weeks later, Michael Preston was preparing to leave for work at his job as a garbage truck driver for Waste Management. His wife Michelle was up as usual preparing his lunch and making him breakfast. It was just after 3:15 AM. Unknown to the Prestons, Earl LaBelle and his girlfriend were prowling their apartment in the Fireside Village Apartments on Wilson Drive in Ralston, a southwestern suburb of Omaha. The apartments are less than a mile and a half south of the Citadel and Wentworth apartment complexes where LaBelle had been stopped by Birkle. They are also near LaBelle's parents' home in neighboring La Vista. Young sex offenders often begin their rape careers operating near their homes in areas they are familiar with and feel comfortable prowling. LaBelle was no exception.

Michael Preston was running a little late so he rushed out the door, leaving Michelle showering alone in the apartment. In his hurry he forgot to lock the door. LaBelle and his girlfriend were parked in the lot in front of the building when Preston came out. Earl LaBelle waited until Preston had driven out of the lot before entering the building using the same door Preston had exited. He made his way along the hallway searching for the apartment Preston had just come from. In LaBelle's predatory thinking, with any luck Preston might have forgotten to lock the door, or maybe it hadn't latched. After slipping on his meatpacking gloves he diligently and quietly tried every door as he worked his way down the hallway.

Halfway down he struck gold at the Preston's apartment. Glancing up and down the hallway to be sure he hadn't been seen, LaBelle quietly opened the door and stepped inside. The kitchen light over the table was on along with the lights in the bedroom. He paused to listen and heard the shower running in the bathroom off the bedroom as he locked the door behind him. He pulled a blue bandana from his rear pocket and put it on. It hid his lower face, leaving only his eyes and the top of his head visible.

He moved towards the kitchen where he found Michelle Preston's purse. He poured the contents onto the table and quickly rummaged through them looking for credit cards, cash, and other valuables. He stuffed cash, credit cards and her driver's license into his pockets and turned towards the bedroom as the sound of the shower suddenly stopped.

Michelle Preston had just stepped out of the shower and was beginning to towel herself off when she heard the bedroom door swing open. Thinking it was her husband returning because he had forgotten something, she called out, "Mike…forget something?" There was no response so she leaned out of the bathroom door, still drying herself, "Mike?" she asked.

To her horror Earl LaBelle stood just inside the bedroom door wearing his blue bandana over his face. She started to scream and tried to slam the bathroom door but he had already closed the distance between them. He grabbed her around the neck and pulled the towel from her hands. He spun her around to face away from him and threatened her, "Do what I want and I won't hurt you," as he dragged her from the bathroom backwards toward the bed. She tried to scream but he clamped one hand over her mouth and began to choke her with the other. "Don't scream or try to get away and you won't get hurt." Preston was frozen in fear as her mind raced, trying to figure out a way to escape the horror that enveloped her. "Okay, okay," she pleaded, "I'll do what you want, just don't hurt me, please."

LaBelle pushed her down on the bed and unbuckled his pants. He placed a pillow over her head and ordered her not to look at him. He then flipped her face-down and removed the bandana and raped her vaginally from behind after striking her in the side of her face and head. He punched violently through the pillow as he methodically raped her over and over. Whenever Michelle cried out in pain from the rough handling

LaBelle became more violent. He withdrew from raping her and moved alongside her to savagely pummel her face and head through the pillow while ordering her to shut up. Once she quieted down he resumed raping her as she sobbed quietly into the mattress.

After what seemed like an eternity, LaBelle had spent the anger that fueled his sexual rage. Like most Anger Retaliatory Rapists (ARR) he had difficulty ejaculating. While LaBelle is classified as an ARR, his actions could, and commonly did, overlap other rapist typologies. Depending on the idiosyncratic stressors influencing him to act out, he could gravitate to one end of the violence spectrum or the other; minimally violent in some, extremely in others.

LaBelle withdrew from Preston, reaffixed his bandana, and ordered her not to move as he ransacked the bedroom looking for valuables. As he moved about the room, Preston tried to see what was going on from beneath the pillow over her head. She was still face-down on the bed but could see LaBelle from the waist down. She tried to remember as much about him as possible while she fought back a paralyzing fear that he might rape her again, or worse. She didn't want to do or say anything that might provoke him to resume beating her. After he was finished searching the bedroom, LaBelle stood at the side of the bed before leaving. He warned Preston not to call the police saying, "I know cops downtown. If you call them I will find out and I will come back."

Michelle Preston was terrified after LaBelle departed. She went to a friend's apartment several doors down from hers and woke her up to tell her what had happened. Her friend telephoned the police while Michelle tried to regain her composure. Michelle then telephoned her husband at work and told him what had happened. He got home not long after the police arrived and comforted

Michelle as she talked to responding officers about the attack. Over the next few months her case stalled because Ralston detectives had no suspects. I was working other sex crimes and reviewing patrol reports on prowling in the area, focusing on field interrogation stops of prowlers, but I had no new information and no sexual assaults had been reported in my jurisdiction.

I was aware of the Ralston rape and had contacted Ralston Police Chief Dale Richardson to give him LaBelle's information but I temporarily lost track of the case while investigating sex offenses in other areas of the county. And I didn't want to step on the toes of another department by trying to insert myself into their case. Other than the Ralston rape, things seemed to have quieted down in that district and there were no other reported contacts with LaBelle. All that was about to change.

Around 11:00 PM on Friday, September 13, 1985, sixty-five-year-old Janet Kaminski retired for the night in her third-floor apartment in the Citadel Apartment complex. Her daughter was visiting from out of town and was out for the evening at a party with friends. Lacking a key, she asked Kaminski to leave the door unlocked so she could come in late and not have to wake her up. Kaminski left the hallway light on for her daughter and fell asleep around 11:45 PM after reading in bed. She was a light sleeper, especially when she was expecting her daughter to return. Shortly after 3:00 AM she was awakened by the sound of the front door opening. At first she figured it was her daughter so she called out her name. When there was no response she called out a little louder.

When there was still no reply she sat up in bed. Fear started to rise within her as she heard someone walking slowly, quietly down the hallway towards her bedroom.

Suddenly an ominous shadow started to loom ever larger on the wall outside her bedroom door as the intruder drew closer. She was now frozen in fear trying desperately to figure out what to do. Before she could move, a vision from her darkest nightmares appeared in the doorway. He was backlit by the hallway light but she could see that he was a short, stocky black male with short hair dressed in black with a blue bandana covering his face. He bridged the distance separating them in several quick leaps and pounced on her. He grabbed a pillow and pushed it against her face as he began to punch her through the pillow.

She tried to block the blows using her arms until he grabbed her and forcefully flipped her over face-down on the bed. He ordered her to stop resisting and not to scream. Kaminski later described his voice as unnervingly quiet and calm in spite of the furious pummeling he had just delivered, completely out of character for the rage he displayed as he struck her. She begged him to stop hitting her and promised not to scream or try to escape. That seemed to give him at least temporary pause. She continued to plead while face-down on the bed as he straddled her back. Her voice muffled by the bedding, she said, "I have money, you can have it. Just please don't hurt me anymore."

He again placed the pillow over her head and ordered her not to try to look at him. "Where is the money?" he asked, out of breath from delivering the beating.

Kaminski pointed to the nightstand, "It's in the book. Two twenty dollar bills. And my purse on the kitchen table. It has money, too."

Looking out from beneath the pillow she watched as he fumbled with the paperback book trying to find the money. He was wearing strange gloves that looked like cotton fishnet. She had never seen gloves like that before.

They seemed to frustrate his ability to find the bills in the book so he took them off to thumb through the pages in search of the bills. That one seemingly insignificant act would eventually lead to his downfall. As he placed the paperback on the nightstand to thumb through it he inadvertently touched the heel of his right hand against the surface.

After grabbing the bills he refocused on Kaminski. He pulled down his pants and straddled her on the bed. He was in the process of raping her vaginally from behind when someone turned the knob of the front door. The sound distracted him momentarily as he paused and strained to listen. He climbed off Kaminski and pulled up his pants quickly as Kaminski's daughter started knocking lightly on the apartment door. "Ma, you hear me?" she asked in a hoarse whisper through the front door. Kaminski glanced at the alarm clock. It was 3:20 AM.

Her mind raced, "That's my daughter...and son in law," she said, lying about a man being with her daughter. "They have a key," she added as she noticed the fear in his actions. She wanted to tell him whatever it took to hasten his departure before her daughter got frustrated and left. She also wanted to be sure her daughter didn't stumble into her nightmare and become a victim herself.

LaBelle hurriedly left the bedroom in a panic and headed for the patio door. Kaminski heard the sliding door open and then close. She thought she could hear him climbing down from her patio to the ones below. She waited for a moment while straining to be sure he had gone. Then she climbed out of bed and headed quickly for the front door. Her daughter was just heading down the hallway when Kaminski burst out sobbing.

"I'm not sure if he's gone," she cried out while collapsing to one knee on the hallway floor. Her stunned daughter rushed to her side and asked her what had happened. Kaminski blurted out between sobs, "A man, a black man...he raped me..." she said as her panicked daughter helped her to her feet.

"Is he still in there?" her daughter asked incredulously as she helped her walk to a neighbor's apartment several doors down. They pounded on the door in a panic waking the couple living there who hurriedly ushered them inside.

Patrol deputies were on the scene in minutes. They quickly searched Kaminski's apartment and the surrounding area but LaBelle had vanished. Kaminski was an excellent witness even though she had not seen LaBelle's face. Her vivid description of what she was able to see, especially his clothing, and his actions and comments were invaluable.

While interviewing Kaminski in the hospital a short time later I asked her if her attacker had touched anything while not wearing the gloves. She told me about his handling of the paperback book on the nightstand. Although she was not certain she thought she saw him lay his hand on the nightstand top.

I contacted crime lab technicians still processing Kaminski's apartment and asked them to be sure to dust the top of the nightstand and the paperback book for fingerprints. I found out later that they found what looked like a partial palmprint on the nightstand top. At first they weren't overly excited about the latent lift because it more than likely belonged to the victim rather than the rapist. There were no usable prints on the book.

Later that day I returned to the office to complete reports and check on the status of the lab's processing of evidence from Kaminski's apartment. Because of his hot prowling, combined with the Preston rape, I suspected that LaBelle was the rapist even though he had no priors for sexual violence. The absence of a sexual assault history is a poor indicator of current criminality because every undetected rapist begins their criminal career with no rape priors. Yet they may have committed multiple rapes that either were not reported or were simply not linked to him. Based on the Preston case, I believed that it was probable that there were other victims out there, I just didn't know about them. They, like many other victims of rape, remained in the shadows and suffered in silence.

Bill Kaufhold was processing some of the evidence when I entered the lab. He told me about the partial palmprint and showed me the hinge lifter Sabotka had used to lift it from the top of the nightstand. "Got any suspects for me to compare?" he asked.

"Yeah, I've got several but the guy I like best for this is Earl LaBelle," I replied.

"LaBelle...LaBelle...I think we had him in here a few months back. Birkle nailed him prowling Citadel. I think we got major case prints on him," he responded.

"I'd start with him," I said as I returned to my desk to make phone calls. About an hour later, Kaufhold burst into the detective bay. "It's him! It's LaBelle!" he exclaimed. "It took me a while, but I have more than ten points of identification. Right palm, outside edge, towards the heel," he said breathlessly. It was his first palmprint identification and he was amped, especially since it was a high-grade felony.

To make a positive identification, latent examiners compare the known fingerprints of a suspect with the latent fingerprints, or more technically finger marks left at a crime scene. To be conclusive they must find at least ten points of minutiae, or ten points of similarity between the fingerprints on file and the finger marks lifted from the crime scene. A person's finger- and palmprints are unique and do not change during the course of their life. No two prints have ever been found alike in many billions of comparisons. That's why fingerprints are the gold standard for conclusively identifying a perpetrator. By finding a minimum of ten points of minutiae the examiner establishes that a particular finger mark is individualized, legalese meaning that it is unique to that one individual's fingerprint out of the entire human population on the planet.

Based on the print ID, I obtained an arrest warrant for LaBelle for First Degree Sexual Assault and Robbery and put out a locate on him via a CIB bulletin to patrol deputies and other law enforcement agencies in the area. I spent the next few days searching for him without success at his last known addresses including his parents' home in LaVista, a suburb a few miles from the rape scenes and about 50 miles from Omaha. Several days later, Lincoln police officers stopped LaBelle and his girlfriend while they prowled an apartment complex in that city. When they ran LaBelle he came back wanted on my arrest warrant. They contacted Douglas County Sheriff's (DCS) detectives working the afternoon shift. Sergeant George Whitmore and Detective Randy Brunckhorst drove to Lincoln to transfer LaBelle back to Omaha for booking.

LaBelle's arrest was noticed by local news reporters who contacted me for comments on a piece they were writing about LaBelle's hot prowl and rape crimes. That article was read by Michelle Preston and her husband who called me the next day to ask my help in their case. They specifically noted the similarity in their case with that reported in the paper and wanted to know if I thought the cases were committed by the same man. I told them that I did but cautioned them that I could not barge in on another agency's investigation. After much pleading from them I promised that I would call the Ralston chief and see if he would allow me to assist his investigator resolve that city's case. To my surprise, my call to the Ralston PD the next day was met with relief. The chief had also read the newspaper article and had told his investigator to turn the case over to me since they had no viable leads.

I met with Michelle Preston at her apartment and she walked me through the events of that night. Ralston police had asked our crime lab to process the scene right after the crime was reported but no useful evidence had been recovered. At that time, the only thing that bodily fluids collected after a rape could be used for was to potentially determine the blood type of the offender, if the sample was not degraded or diluted by the victim's fluids. I say potentially determine blood type because about 80 percent of the population secretes a blood protein in their semen and other bodily fluids that identifies their blood type. On the other hand, one out of five do not. Although not as powerful and definitive as DNA evidence, knowing the blood type of the offender could be another link in the evidentiary chain that tied a perp to the crime. Unfortunately, the crime lab was unable to recover adequate fluid samples from the scene to enable forensic testing. They were also unable to find usable fingerprints.

On the slim chance that she might be able to identify LaBelle even though he had concealed his face with the blue bandana, I had the crime lab prepare a six-pack photo array for Preston to view. Photo arrays are quicker, easier and more efficient than physical lineups because they can be assembled from already existing mugshots. Rather than trying to get five stand-ins physically similar to the suspect for the witness or victim to view at the station in person, the crime lab can browse through the voluminous files of mugshots to easily find five fillers to flesh out the photo array.

Some care must be followed in preparing a photo array to avoid having the identification thrown out in court later. The crime lab must choose non-suspect fillers that fit the witness or victim description of the perp. Putting a black male suspect with five white male fillers is a sure way to have the ID tossed. Lesser forms of suggestiveness can also get the ID tossed, such as notable differences in backgrounds or lighting between the suspect and fillers.

The courts also like to see a double blind assembly procedure in which the detective showing the six-pack to a victim or witness is not the one who assembled it. Using a double blind procedure in which the administrator of the showing is unaware of the identity of the suspect in the six-pack lessens the chances of unintentionally influencing the witness's selection.

Horror stories abound in which six-pack IDs were rigged by unscrupulous cops who showed the lineup to the victim while holding it so that a finger pointed directly to the suspect. In other cases the filler mugs were so glaringly different that the suspect stood out like a neon sign. In one case a photo array was constructed using fillers of men with long hippie-type hair when the victim description indicated the perp had a short, close cropped haircut or was bald.

Many courts will accept a six-pack-based ID only if an admonishment is given to the witness. Witnesses are told that the perpetrator may or may not be present and, in the case of a double blind showing that the administrator does not know which person is the suspect. To minimize misidentifications some courts also insist that the administrator assess eyewitness confidence immediately following an identification and to carefully document a witness's response before any response or acknowledgment from law enforcement is given.

Despite Preston being an excellent witness who provided me with a great deal of information, she could not positively identify LaBelle because of the bandana. As much as I wanted to jam up LaBelle for the Preston rape, which I was convinced he had committed, the investigation was stalled for lack of evidence. I tried to interrogate LaBelle after his arrest but he had invoked his Sixth Amendment rights and asked for an attorney. It was a cinch that he wasn't going to confess and the crime scene had failed to yield evidence that linked him to the rape. I also tried to interview his girlfriend but she had disappeared. I found out later that she had left the state shortly after LaBelle's arrest. As I pondered what I could do next to make a case against LaBelle, I remembered a little-used section of state law that allowed the police to obtain identifying physical characteristics from criminal suspects.

Nebraska Revised Statutes, Sections 29-3301 to 29-3307, stemmed from a 1971 legislative bill that allows police to obtain a body warrant to collect identifying physical characteristics, including a voice sample, from a criminal suspect. The Fifth Amendment prevented LaBelle from being forced to incriminate himself through oral communication during an interrogation but the courts have consistently held that right does not extend to non-testimonial procedures. Like other warrants, a body warrant required probable cause to believe the person named in the warrant had committed a criminal offense. It was applied for in the same manner as a search warrant.

I immediately called Preston and asked her if she could remember the exact words spoken to her during the attack. She said she thought she could. I then asked her if she could identify her attacker's voice if he spoke the same words into a tape recorder. Again Preston thought she could do so. Before hanging up I asked her to jot down the exact phrases spoken by her attacker as best she could remember them.

I then started preparing the application for the body warrant based on the facts of my investigation. I included an overwhelming amount of detail to be sure it met the probable cause threshold. I only had one chance and I did not want to come up short if the duty judge refused to issue it because I lacked sufficient probable cause. I began with the history of prowling incidents in apartment complexes in the area, moved on to documenting LaBelle's detention by Birkle for the interrupted hot prowl incident involving the Crosses, the obtaining of a palmprint from LaBelle during that detention, and then on to the rape of Kaminski and the identification of LaBelle's palmprint in that case. I stressed throughout the affidavit the similarity of each crime to the others and that LaBelle had been identified as the perpetrator of a similar crime

I interviewed Preston again at her apartment. Her husband was present and was eager to know how the case was progressing. I told him that our last best hope was the voice ID and asked that he not be present when I talked to Michelle again. She was about to recite the exact words spoken by her attacker and might be unwilling to reveal to her husband exactly what had happened. He agreed and left the apartment for work.

Like my other interview of Michelle Preston, she was an excellent and resolute witness. I was impressed with her courage and determination to help me make a case against her attacker. My job would be nearly impossible without strong, courageous women like her. She gave me five short phrases that she recalled as being the exact words spoken by her rapist. I dictated a report containing the verbatim phrases for the Criminal Investigative Bureau (CIB) receptionist to transcribe into a script. I then found four black males, including two deputies, a city prosecutor and an Omaha officer I knew to read the script into my tape recorder.

I then ran the affidavit by an assistant county attorney friend of mine to be sure I had done an adequate job. After his review I headed for a judge to get it signed. Judge Sam Cooper was the duty judge who was sitting in that afternoon arraignment session in Courtroom 25 on the second floor of the Hall of Justice. Cooper knew me well from my time appearing before him in traffic court while a patrol deputy. He looked up from forms he was completing between arraignments in the packed court and motioned me to approach the bench. "What have you got, Dean?" he asked as he gestured for me to hand him the affidavit and warrant.

"It's a body warrant, judge," I responded. "A rape case. I need a voice exemplar."

He scanned the papers and gestured for me to raise my right hand to swear to their accuracy and truthfulness. "Do you swear?" he asked. "I do," I replied as he quickly signed them and handed them back to me.

I had an excellent reputation with the judges. They barely perused most of my affidavits knowing that I would not burn them by requesting a bad warrant. Some of the other cops in the area had their affidavits studied in detail and scrutinized severely because they had a bad reputation or had burned a judge by seeking a warrant on bad or false information. Many of them had to redo their affidavits because the judge was not satisfied with the truthfulness or sufficiency of the information they proffered, or just didn't trust the officer. Judges are loath to having their decisions reversed on appeal. A warrant from cops with a questionable reputation increases the risk that a judge's decision to grant it could be overturned. In the end, all you have is your reputation and if you lie while testifying in court or falsify an affidavit word spread among the judges that you can't be trusted.

"Good luck," he said as I thanked him and headed for the court clerk's office to get the affidavit and warrant registered on the docket. I then drove to the corrections center where LaBelle was being held. I had him escorted to an interview room off the prisoner booking area and explained what I was there for. He appeared to be slightly nervous but listening carefully to what I said but when I handed him the script and told him to recite it into the tape recorder he refused. He said, "That's some racist bullshit." I explained that the other voices on the tape were also black but he still refused to cooperate. It was obvious that he feared that if he said the exact words on tape that he had said to Preston during the rape she would recognize his voice. The fact that her recollection so accurately matched what was said unnerved him.

Unfortunately, the body warrant statute lacks the teeth to force a defendant to comply with the order. It provides only for the defendant to be held in contempt of court and then only for a maximum of 30 days. That didn't matter much to LaBelle because he couldn't make bond on the Kaminski rape anyway so he was in jail regardless of whether he was held in contempt of the issuing judge.

As a last-ditch attempt to get him to comply I snatched him from corrections and transported him two blocks north to the Hall of Justice to stand before Judge Cooper. He was just finishing arraignments in

Courtroom 25 when I brought LaBelle in. I explained the problem. Cooper took me aside and confessed there wasn't much he could do to force compliance. "The guy's already in jail, Dean…" he said, his voice trailing off at the end. "Not sure what a contempt citation would do for you."

I had one last card to play. LaBelle's defense attorney was a former prosecutor named Don Kleine. I knew Don from prior cases he had prosecuted in which I was the arresting deputy. He had left the County Attorney's office to try his hand at private practice. He would return to the right side of criminal law as Chief Deputy Douglas County Attorney under then County Attorney Jim Jansen. After Jansen left the CA's office to become the Chief Counsel for Creighton University in Omaha, Kleine would eventually run for his old boss's job and be elected county attorney in 2007. I called Kleine and explained what I needed. He assured me that he would get LaBelle to submit to the body warrant after meeting with him the next day. He phoned me afterwards and assured me that LaBelle would now go along with the requirements of the warrant. I returned to the corrections center again and had LaBelle recite the script into the tape recorder.

He stalled before reciting several of the more explicit phrases, apparently fearing that they were especially damaging to his case. After some urging he eventually complied completely and I had my voice exemplar. Next was the most important test. Would Michelle Preston be able to identify LaBelle's voice? If so, I could book him for her rape. If not LaBelle might not ever be prosecuted for that crime.

She arrived at my office the next morning. I escorted her to an interview room where I explained the process and her role in it. I admonished her that her attacker may or may not be on the tape and that she needed to listen to all of the voices and then tell me if she did or did not recognize any of them. She could also ask me to replay the tape if necessary after the entire tape had been played.

She was nervous but appeared to relax as she listened to the first two voices. LaBelle's was the third one followed by two more filler voices. As LaBelle's voice began Preston sat upright in terror. Her eyes widened and her muscles tensed as she gripped the edge of the desk in fear. "That's him, that's him," she blurted out nervously.

"It's okay," I said to calm her. "It's just a voice on the tape. You are safe," I said and cautioned her to continue to listen to the entire tape. I watched as she tried to settle back down. It was difficult to see her suffering the attack all over again by simply hearing his voice. After the last filler she straightened herself in the chair. "That was him, the third one," she said as strength and an air of resolve returned to her demeanor.

"Are you sure?" I asked. "Is there any doubt?"

"None," she replied with confidence. "I am positive that's him. I will never forget that voice."

Based on this ID I arrested LaBelle for the Preston rape. When he came to trial for both rapes about eight months later the prosecutor arranged a plea bargain. LaBelle agreed to plead guilty to the Kaminski rape and robbery in exchange for the Preston rape charges being dropped. Michelle Preston and her husband Mike were outraged. The prosecutor failed to explain his reasoning and they felt cheated that Michelle's rape appeared to be not important enough to warrant a trial. They felt victimized all over again. After all they had endured it was devastating to have rape charges in Michelle's case dismissed almost as an afterthought.

I wasn't aware of the plea bargain until I received a call from Mike Preston the next day. He was angry and hurt that what had happened to his wife appeared to be not important enough to be prosecuted. After speaking to the prosecutor and hearing his reasoning I called the Prestons and explained. The prosecutor could avoid two expensive trials and the necessity of having two victims endure the trauma of testifying by dropping the weaker case and getting a plea bargain for the stronger rape case. The sentencing judge would be aware that LaBelle had committed two rapes in spite of pleading guilty to only one. He would take that fact into consideration at sentencing.

It didn't do much to assuage their outrage but they did understand the legal logic behind the prosecutor's move. Unfortunately, many victims of rape like the Prestons are mishandled by a justice system that works overtime to ensure the rights of the rapist are maintained while expending nary a wisp of consideration for the victims, and then many times only as an afterthought. The prosecutor could have lessened the impact of the plea bargain by exercising some basic decency and empathy for the victim by telling the Prestons in advance of his decision and explaining the legal reasoning behind it. They might not have liked the idea but at least they wouldn't have been blindsided and left with the impression that they were not important enough to merit being told. Leaving them to find out by happenstance added unnecessary insult to injury.

Earl LaBelle received a stiff sentence of 24 to 60 years for First Degree Sexual Assault, Robbery and Burglary. He was released in July 2018.

Chapter Six
Mary Kay Harmer Rape-Murder
A Lamb Lured to a Wolf's Den

> Mary Harmer...was a target for sexual assault...
> because of that she became a target for murder...
> **Prosecutor Sam Cooper**

In 1975, Mary Kay Harmer was a nineteen-year-old living with a roommate in a suburban apartment in southwest Omaha. She was lured to her death at the hands of a Power Assertive Rapist. After being savagely beaten, drugged and raped, she was shot in the head several times and her body callously disposed of. Her anguished family suffered for nearly nine years unable to find her and not knowing for sure what had happened to her. In 1984, an engineering crew discovered Harmer's skeletal remains in an abandoned manhole near Eppley Airport. A caustic substance had been poured over her head in an attempt to dissolve her skull and prevent identification.

At the time her killer, Thomas "Red" Nesbitt, was a member of the Omaha chapter of the Hells Angels Motorcycle Club (HAMC). The HAMC organization is considered an organized crime syndicate by the United States Department of Justice. It is the world's largest and most famous outlaw motorcycle gang (OMG).

There are approximately 400 OMGs in the U.S. (Williams 2010:6). They range from small groups of relatively unsophisticated thugs to well-organized criminal networks. The big dog among OMGs is the Hells Angels Motorcycle Club. As the largest OMG in the world, the HAMC has 200 chapters in 27 countries and an estimated 3000 members worldwide. The FBI estimates that the gang takes in up to one billion dollars a year in illegal drug sales, mostly from the manufacture, sale, and distribution of methamphetamines (Williams 2010:11).

The food chain among OMGs has several levels. At the top sits a handful of hardcore gang members. They operate under a leadership hierarchy consisting of a president, vice president, treasurer, secretary, road captain, and sergeant-at-arms. Large OMGs have franchises in different cities across the country called chapters. The Angel's first chapter outside California was established in Omaha in 1964 (Williams 2010:11).

Gang members are the patch-wearing, motorcycle riding thugs who rake in the lion's share of the drug money and income from other illicit operations like prostitution, stolen property, and extortion. To launder money and fence stolen property, OMGs operate legitimate businesses including security work, tattoo shops, nail salons, massage parlors, pawn shops, antique shops, junkyards, motorcycle shops, strip clubs, limousine services, and hazardous waste disposal. Involvement in the hazardous waste industry serves as cover to transport and obtain regulated precursor chemicals used for methamphetamine manufacturing (Williams 2010:32).

The illicit market in major cities where OMG chapters are located can only support so many members. Their greed dictates that they keep the number of full-fledged, or "patch" members low enough to maximize profits but large enough to give them the muscle to dominate their turf and minimize competition.

Membership in an OMG as a patch member occurs in stages and can take several years to attain. Members are brought into chapters through a lengthy process designed to measure the person's commitment to the gang and to guard against law enforcement infiltration. While the exact steps vary from gang to gang, membership often starts with a wannabe becoming a "friend of the club" or hang-around (Williams 2010:13). A hang-around is invited by a gang member to some club events or to meet members at known gathering places. They perform errands and do small chores for members. The wannabe is continuously evaluated by gang members during the process. If the hang-around is interested, he may be asked to become an associate, a status that usually lasts a year or two. Gang members continue to evaluate the associate as he learns the ropes on how to become a Hells Angel.

While most OMG associates have no interest in becoming full patch members, instead finding other mutually beneficial reasons to be associated with the club, those that do complete the associate stage enter the prospect phase. As a prospect an aspiring gang member can participate in some club activities but does not have voting privileges. During the prospect phase the wannabe is continuously evaluated for suitability as a full member. This can include participation in both legal and illegal activities.

George Christie, former president of the Ventura, CA chapter of the Hells Angels, described life as a prospect. Prospects often guard the gang "members" bikes outside large gatherings and serve them beer and food (Bonner 2015). According to Christie, "Being a prospect in a biker club meant being at the disposal of any member at any time." Prospects also routinely cleaned up the clubhouse. If a gang member broke down on the highway, no matter where or at what time, a prospect would respond.

If the wannabe passes the years-long hang-around associate prospect evaluation process he reaches the point where his membership is voted on by gang members. To make it, the wannabe must receive a unanimous vote from the members. He is then "patched in" by earning the right to wear the full patch consisting of the complete four-piece gang crest worn on the back of the gang "colors." A biker's colors are the sleeveless denim or leather vest also known as a "cut" (Williams 2010:13).

In the case of the Hells Angels, the full cut includes the winged death-head logo beneath top and above bottom semi-circular patches known as "rockers." The top rocker contains the "Hells Angels" gang name. The bottom rocker contains the state or territory of membership. The rectangular "MC" (motorcycle) patch appears below the wing of the death's head. In contrast, prospects are allowed to wear only a bottom rocker with the state or territory name along with the rectangular "MC" or motorcycle patch (Drewery 2003:29).

"Colors" are the official uniform of all outlaw motorcycle gangs. Colors belong to the club and are worn only by male members. They are held sacred by the outlaw gang members. They are festooned with various patches that signify the status and accomplishments of the wearer.

The different colored wings displayed on some colors tell a revealing story of the moral degeneracy and criminality of its members. The acts necessary to earn the wings must be witnessed by other gang members. Blue wings mean that the wearer had oral sex with a cop. Red wings signify that the wearer performed oral sex on a menstruating female. Purple wings mean the wearer performed oral copulation with a female corpse. Green wings indicate that the wearer had oral sex with a woman with a venereal disease. An "eight ball" patch signifies that the wearer committed homosexual sodomy. Similarly, a red cross is earned by committing homosexual fellatio. Gold wings mean the wearer participated in the gang rape of a woman involving 15 or more persons. Gang rape is such an esteemed activity in the twisted morality of outlaw bikerdom that it has its own terminology including "train," "turnout," and "getting off some leg." Examples of the terms in use include "she pulled a train" and "six patch brothers turned her out" (Williams 2010:27).

In the outlaw biker's society, women are bought, sold, traded, or given away within the club. An example of the deplorable treatment of women was provided by an FBI gang expert. He described a 1989 case against south Florida Outlaws club president James "Big Jim" Nolan in which the club kidnapped a Daytona Beach woman, tortured her by burning her breasts with a hot spoon and then gang raped her. By the next day she was dancing and turning tricks at a topless bar owned by the gang (Griffin 1995).

Women are held in such low esteem that many are considered less valuable than a biker's motorcycle. A woman's main value to an outlaw biker, aside from sexual gratification, is daily income. She must give all her money to her "old man"—the biker who controls every aspect of her life. Bikers put their women to work in massage parlors, topless bars, cocktail lounges, and strip clubs. Most of these are covers for prostitution, which is the bikers' most lucrative source of income after drugs (Williams 2010:27).

Biker "bitches" fall into three categories. The first are Old Ladies. They are the wives or steady girlfriends of club members. Old Ladies are considered the exclusive property of the member and can't be used or abused by other club members. In some clubs, they are also authorized to wear "Property of" colors with the name of the biker she belongs to on the bottom rocker instead of the gang's chapter name (Jensen 2015).

The lowest category are the Pass-Arounds. They are women with no long-term relationship with the gang who are shared sexually by multiple members at will, thus being "passed around" (Carlie 2002).

If the Pass-Arounds hang around long enough they are viewed as Sheep or Mamas, the middle category. Aside from sexual services for members and associates, Sheep support the parasitic lifestyle of the sociopaths in the gang by working as prostitutes, dancing in the gang's strip clubs, and hustling drugs. Sheep work and earn for the gang, often working two or more legitimate jobs so that gang members are free to tend to gang business (Mass 2013).

Sheep also help extort money from hapless strip club patrons. In a typical scenario, they size up potential marks who flash large sums of cash, are married and are drinking to excess. After the mark has been liquored up sufficiently and the Sheep has determined he is not an undercover vice cop, she sets the hook by enticing him for sex in a nearby motel or other room owned by the gang. Once in the room and disrobed in preparation for the dirty deed a gang member bursts in with a gun claiming to be the Sheep's angry husband. The mark is then shaken down for his cash, credit cards with their associated PIN numbers, and other valuables with threats of violence or threats to tell his wife and/or employer what he has been up to.

Women are also used to gather intelligence. They take jobs at city, county and state offices where they have access to blank birth certificates, driver's licenses, and other useful documents. Others seek jobs as police records clerks or secretaries, telephone operators, employees in welfare offices, and positions within jails and prisons. They will even sleep with cops to compromise them or gather intelligence.

Women are attracted to this lifestyle for different reasons. Some are emotionally needy or suffer from mental or emotional disorders. They crave the drugs, alcohol, parties, fast bikes and cars, cheap thrills and sex (Carlie 2002). Women with sex addictions seek endless sex every way and any way they can get it. The club becomes their outlet. Many are rebellious teenagers who are trying to strike back at their parents. They numb their minds with drugs and screw themselves silly on the clubhouse floor or on one of its filthy mattresses.

Some females are attracted to the image of bikers as hyper-masculine macho men who lead dangerous, exciting lives. Women without education or futures become somebody when they attach themselves to respected and feared outlaw bikers. Shiftless girls like the freedom from responsibility. As one writer put it, "The unloved and homeless confuse sex with affection and cherish the arms that hold them" (Lavigne 1989).

The outlaw biker world is a testosterone-fueled lifestyle tailor-made for the sociopath. It is male dominated and extremely misogynistic. Occasionally the most dangerous sociopaths that gravitate to Outlaw Motorcycle Gangs export their misogyny and violence beyond the orbit of the gang. When they do, innocent young women often pay a horrendous price. Such victims are called sweeties or cuties. They are women picked up while hitchhiking, kidnapped off a bar stool, or sometimes enticed under false pretenses to a gang party.

Many are taken off the street and brought to the clubhouse or other place for a party. Party is a term used to describe events at which drugs are freely available and used by gang members. Sweeties become the victim of a gang rape and beating. Later, they are released with threats on their life and family if they talk to the police.

Mary Kay Harmer was Red Nesbitt's last known sweetie.

In addition to being a Hells Angel gang member, Nesbitt was a sexual predator, a Power Assertive Rapist (PAR) to be more precise. The psychological profile of PARs hinges on their hyper-masculinity (Groth 1979:56). One expression of that masculinity is through sexual violence. They feel they are not real men unless they take what they want. They rape to prove and display their masculinity.

The PAR is selfish and commits rape because he feels entitled to do so. He sees a victim as nothing more than an object. He takes pride in his masculinity and is often homophobic. He sees his victims as sex objects and believes rape is an act of virility. He will use a moderate level of force if the victim resists and may show a weapon to gain compliance. He will also rape the same victim repeatedly. He couldn't care less about her comfort and well being. It's all about his gratification. If the victim fights, he will double the amount of time he spends with her which further displays his callous nature. One PAR left his victim stranded and naked in an isolated park after throwing her clothes in a duck pond after the rape.

PARs may marry but will almost certainly be unfaithful and prone to domestic violence. Female coworkers often describe such individuals as likely to make sexually inappropriate remarks, engage in unwelcomed touching, and display poor boundaries. He becomes upset and angry if rejected or rebuffed. The typical PAR will use a con approach to disguise his true intentions by getting to know his victim then offering to give her a ride home or walk her to her car.

He may rape the victim vaginally then anally and then force her to perform fellatio afterwards to thoroughly degrade her. He will attack the victim verbally and physically and commit a brutal attack although he doesn't intend to kill. He may slap, hit, curse, and tear clothes as a way to intimidate and control the victim. His motive is to exert power, domination and control over "the weaker sex." During the rape he is very arrogant and doesn't try to hide his identity. Unlike Power Reassurance Rapists there is no apology afterwards.

Everything about a PAR is exaggerated machismo. Many drive muscle cars and work in jobs like construction, as police officers, or as firefighters.

&

Mary Kay Harmer was not Red Nesbitt's first victim. On November 11, 1974, Nesbitt and several other Angels were drinking heavily at the Monkey Mountain Bar on Military Avenue in Omaha when Nesbitt told the others he was going to find a sweetie at the Aquarius Lounge (T. Dempsey, personal communication, February 2007). The Aquarius was located at 72nd and Pacific Street in what was then the west end of the city. It was a popular "Go-Go" bar that catered to a mostly male overflow crowd.

In the mid-1970s go-go dancers were bikini-clad young women employed by the bar to entertain the primarily male patrons. Because city ordinances banned topless dancing the closest thing bar owners could provide to attract men were scantily clad go-go dancers.

They danced on raised stages or tables so that the patrons could see them clearly. They also served as waitresses hustling drinks when not dancing.

Nesbitt arrived at the Aquarius just before midnight. He continued to drink heavily and had to be cautioned by bar bouncers about touching the waitresses and hassling the dancers as he prowled for his next sweetie. He was particularly attracted to dancer Michele McKesson (State of Nebraska v. Nesbitt 2002). When she moved to different tables for her sets Nesbitt followed. He often elbowed his way to the front of the crowd for an unobstructed view.

McKesson was used to attention from male patrons. She was young, shapely and attractive with a beautiful smile. She looked good in her revealing bikini and knew how to dance. She made a lot of money from tips gladly showered on her by enthusiastic patrons. In her recollection, Nesbitt didn't stand out from the throng of other men that clamored to get her attention every night by peppering her with dollar bills. Besides, the bar had strict rules on fraternizing with customers and she didn't want to jeopardize a good paying job (T. Dempsey, personal communication, February 2007)

The bar was fairly busy for a Monday night when the bouncers started urging patrons to finish up as the 1:00 AM closing time approached. McKesson finished her final set just before last call. She and the other dancers congregated as usual in a dressing room at the back of the bar counting their tips and changing out of their bikinis. Many of them were heading out for breakfast at the nearby Village Inn restaurant. McKesson was going straight home so she put on a coat over her bikini and headed for her car in the huge parking lot (State of Nebraska v. Nesbitt 2002).

Her car was parked at the far end of the lot. As she made her way to it, an older model pickup approached slowly. Nesbitt pulled abreast of her as she neared her car. He began his con approach. "Hey, I really loved your dancing tonight," he said after rolling down the window. McKesson continued to walk as the pickup kept pace with her. She glanced at Nesbitt, "Thanks," she said. At first, she wasn't overly concerned because she was accustomed to compliments from inebriated men. Soon Nesbitt being so close to her car in the fast-emptying lot began to worry her but she scoffed at the idea that he posed a threat. Nesbitt's con approach was working. Besides, she was pulling out her car keys and soon would be in her car (T. Dempsey, personal communication, February 2007).

Nesbitt stopped the truck as she started to unlock her car. After putting his truck in park, he continued his con approach, saying, "I'm new to town. Can't quite figure out how to get back to my buddy's house. How do I get to Seward Street from here?" (State of Nebraska v. Nesbitt 2002).

It worked. McKesson paused and stood with her hand on the door handle of her car. "Well," she started, "I think Seward is about a mile and a half north of here. You can get there by going straight up that road," she said as she pointed to 72nd Street.

Continuing the con while working to close in on her before springing the trap, Nesbitt replied, "Great. Hey, I am going to a party there, why don't you come along?"

"Thanks, but I can't tonight. Sorry," she replied

Nesbitt's expression didn't change as he opened the truck door and moved quickly towards her. She was stunned by how fast he was on her. He pulled a gun and grabbed her arm before she could open her car door. He grabbed the keys from her hand.

"Don't fucking scream," he said as he started to push her towards the truck. The truck shielded them from the bar as several waitresses came out. When she started to scream Nesbitt shoved her downwards and put a gun to the side of her head. "Don't fucking do it," he said. "I won't hurt you if you do what I say" (T. Dempsey, personal communication, February 2007).

"Okay, okay," she replied, frightened out of her mind.

After roughly pushing her inside through the driver's side door he ordered her to get on the floor and keep her head down. He threatened her, saying, "If you try anything stupid I will kill you."

McKesson was petrified. Nesbitt placed the gun in his waistband and drove out of the lot. "Where do your parents live? Brothers and sisters? Their address," he demanded. "Don't fuckin' lie to me," he threatened. McKesson meekly recited her parent's address and the address of her sister as she cowered on the passenger side floor. Nesbitt drove to her parents' house first. He pulled up in front and parked. "If you don't do what I tell you, I'll kill you. And then I'm gonna come here and kill them," he threatened while pointing his gun at the house. "If you call the cops or tell anyone I will kill you and them," he added before driving off. He then drove to McKesson's sister's house where he repeated the threat, adding, "I'll kill your sister and her kids" (State of Nebraska v. Nesbitt 2002).

Nesbitt then drove to a house in nearby Carter Lake. He honked the horn twice and got out of the truck to speak to another biker who came out. They spoke in hushed tones as Nesbitt pointed to McKesson who was left sitting in the truck. After a few minutes he returned and drove to a house on North 15th Street (State of Nebraska v. Nesbitt 2002). McKesson tried to memorize the address as Nesbitt grabbed her arm and pulled her roughly across the seat to the driver's door. She repeated the address "2-6-1-9…2-6-1-9," over and over in her mind.

As she sat on the edge of the seat, Nesbitt leaned close to threaten her, "You do what I want and you won't get hurt. If you don't I'll kill you and your mom and dad." He added, "Then I'll kill your sister and her kids. Understand?"

McKesson shook her head meekly. "I'll do what you want. Please don't hurt me," she said as she fought back tears. Nesbitt grabbed her by the wrist and yanked her from the truck.

For the next three hours Nesbitt snorted meth and drank. He tried to force McKesson to do the same. She resisted the dope but drank to keep him from beating her. If she hesitated doing what he demanded he viciously punched her in the face. After ripping her bikini off and slapping her around he forced her down on the bed and raped her twice before passing out. Shortly before sunup McKesson was able to slip out of the house and escape as Nesbitt lay passed out next to her on the bed. She walked for several blocks along the nearly deserted early morning streets until she found a payphone where she called a friend to come and pick her up. Once at her friend's house she was hesitant to call police. Nesbitt's threats against her family reverberated in her thoughts (State of Nebraska v. Nesbitt 2002).

Hours later she finally got up the nerve to report the rape. Two Omaha police officers took her report then drove to Nesbitt's house where they confronted him about McKesson's allegations. To the cops, Nesbitt appeared to be unconcerned. He admitted that McKesson was at the house but claimed the sex was consensual and that she had tried to shake him down for money by threatening to cry rape if he didn't pay up.

The "he said/she said" cast just enough doubt that, when combined with the fact that McKesson had credibility problems stemming from the fact that she danced in a go-go joint for men who tipped her with dollar bills like a stripper, the prosecutors were reluctant to file charges. More significantly, at the time of the rape she was also facing check fraud and forgery charges.

It may never be known for sure but the predatory, cunning, criminally sophisticated nature of sociopaths like Nesbitt committing Power Assertive Rapes suggests that McKesson was targeted as a sweetie since she would be a poor witness with credibility problems precisely because of her occupation. It is also possible that the detour to another Hells Angel's home in Carter Lake before taking McKesson to the house on North 15th Street was so that Nesbitt could get advice about how to handle the cops if his intimidation of McKesson failed to prevent her from reporting the rape.

The other Hells Angel probably suggested that Nesbitt not deny the sex but deflect suspicion back on McKesson by claiming that she had tried to shake him down. As a popular pastime, the Angels have a lot of experience raping sweeties and dealing with the cops afterwards. Having narrowly dodged an arrest, Nesbitt learned from his mistakes with McKesson. The next time he felt the need to satiate the evil desire of his Power Assertive Rapist urges he would guarantee that his next sweetie could not call the police afterwards.

Little more than a year after raping McKesson, Nesbitt's rapist urge reared its sinister head once more. He owed himself another sweetie. Kathy Ray, Nesbitt's old lady, arrived home from her part-time job at a downtown restaurant around 1:00 AM on November 30, 1975. Nesbitt had been doing dope and drinking all night with Wayne Bieber, a fellow Angel who lived next door (Nesbitt v. Hopkins 1996).

Ray had barely set her purse down on the kitchen table when Nesbitt ordered her to call some of her girlfriends over for a party. To disguise his sinister intentions he told Ray to claim it was a housewarming party with a group of their classmates and to target her girlfriends from high school. Because of the late hour, Ray was not having any luck until she telephoned Gayla Jorgensen, Mary Kay Harmer's roommate, in an apartment at the Timbercreek Apartment complex near 138th and Harrison Street in southwest Omaha. Jorgensen said she was willing to attend the party to reconnect with classmates she was assured would be there.

Ray and Brigitte Kohlert, Bieber's old lady, left around 2:00 AM for the crosstown drive to pick up Jorgensen and Harmer. After Ray and Kohlert arrived at the girl's apartment, Jorgensen changed her mind and decided not to go. Ray, Kohlert and Nesbitt later alleged in court testimony that Harmer decided to go without her roommate because she was assured there would be drugs at the party. Harmer then left with Ray and Kohlert who drove her to the North 15th Street address.

The trio arrived around 3:00 AM. After they were inside, Nesbitt told Kohlert and Ray to leave and they both went next door to Bieber's house. On the way they met Wayne Bieber coming to join Nesbitt. That left Harmer alone with Nesbitt and Bieber. Ray claimed that she returned to the house on three occasions, twice at Kohlert's insistence, because she feared Wayne Bieber was having sex with Harmer (Nesbitt v. Hopkins 1996). This was a valid concern because it is doubtful that Bieber was playing solitaire while his patch brother Nesbitt was beating, drugging, and raping Harmer.

The first time Ray returned, Nesbitt refused to let her inside. He told her to tell Kohlert that no one was having sex with Harmer. That failed to satisfy Kohlert who was beside herself worrying what her old man was doing in the house with Nesbitt and Harmer. She pestered Ray to go back a second time. An hour later, Ray returned to the house and found that Nesbitt was "upset, very upset." He again refused to let her inside. He asked her, "If Mary got raped; what would she do?" Ray told him that Harmer would go the police.

It was mid-morning the third time Ray returned. She pushed her way inside because she had to get ready to go to work at her part-time job as a waitress. Nesbitt was visibly upset and nervous. Ray claimed that when she opened the bathroom door she saw Harmer's "coat in a pile right when I opened the door." An irate Nesbitt yelled at her to get away from the bathroom, screaming, "Did you see her? Did you see her?" Harmer's lifeless body was in the bathtub with the shower curtain drawn, hidden from Ray's view. By murdering her in the bathtub the bikers could contain the mess and wash any evidence down the drain afterwards (Nesbitt v. Hopkins 1996).

Ray left for work sometime later. Nesbitt and Bieber stripped Harmer of all of her clothing to prevent identification and washed off the blood and evidence of the rapes before wrapping her in a roll of carpet from Bieber's garage. They placed her in Bieber's garage while they tried to figure out where they could dump the body (T. Dempsey, personal communication, February 2007).

Ray later claimed that when she returned home from work in the early morning hours of Monday, December 1, 1975 changes had been made to the house. She said in a later deposition for court that "The rugs were gone. The throw rugs in the kitchen, right when I walked in…were gone…." She said that Nesbitt told her he had burned the throw rugs from the bathroom and kitchen in a trash barrel behind Bieber's house. She also smelled the strong odor of bleach throughout the house, and saw Nesbitt was washing the bedding from the front bedroom in the washing machine.

Nesbitt ordered Ray to help him clean by mopping the floors in the kitchen and bathroom. He ordered her to "scrub down the bathroom from ceiling to floor; everything." Nesbitt also told her to clean up any blood she saw. Ray testified later at trial she saw blood "in front of the refrigerator," and in the bathroom on the shower curtain. Nesbitt told her the blood was from Harmer because he had "bloodied her nose to keep her in line." Nesbitt also asked her if she could "handle it" if the "Feds" were involved in investigating Harmer's death. Ray was told to say that Harmer had been at their house the night before but was gone when they awoke in the morning. In explaining what happened to Harmer, Nesbitt told Ray, "Let's just say she died of an overdose" (Nesbitt v. Hopkins 1996).

Later at trial, Nesbitt admitted that there had been drugs at the house. Among them was amyl nitrate. Known on the street as poppers, amyl nitrate also has the potential to facilitate rape by relaxing the smooth muscles throughout the body including the vagina and the sphincter muscles of the anus. When inhaled it can also incapacitate by causing temporary dizziness and confusion.

Adhering to the outlaw biker code, "He's my brother, he's not always right but he's always my brother," Bieber later gave conflicting statements about what he knew about Harmer's murder. At one point Bieber stated that Nesbitt told him he might have "fucked up," indicating that he had raped Harmer. The two of them discussed whether Harmer should be let go or killed to keep her from notifying the police. Bieber vehemently denied any involvement in Harmer's rape or murder. He testified later in court that he and Nesbitt spoke about getting shovels, digging implements, and lye. And he admitted that he burned Harmer's clothing for Nesbitt.

By now Harmer has been missing for more than 24 hours. Her roommate, Gayla Jorgensen, was worried when she didn't return after leaving with Ray and Kohlert. Unable to reach Ray, she telephoned Harmer's parents who called the police. Because the apartment complex where Jorgensen and Harmer lived was outside the city limits in suburban Omaha, the Douglas County Sheriff's Department was notified (T. Dempsey, personal communication, February 2007).

On Monday evening, December 1, 1975, detectives from the sheriff's department were waiting for Ray when she left her full-time job at the World-Herald Newspaper in downtown Omaha. Ray nervously called Nesbitt who picked her up and invited the deputies to the house to discuss Harmer's disappearance. Both Nesbitt and Ray stuck to their story and told detectives that Harmer was at the house for a party. They had gone to bed and Harmer was gone when they woke up in the morning. They had no idea where she had gone (Nesbitt v. Hopkins 1996).

Nesbitt, knowing that the place had been scrubbed of evidence and that Harmer's body was hidden next door in Bieber's garage, even offered to let the detectives "look around." They left after searching the house and finding no sign of Harmer. That night, Bieber and Nesbitt dumped Harmer's body in an abandoned manhole less than a half mile from the house. They poured lye on her in an attempt to dissolve her skull to hinder identification (T. Dempsey, personal communication, February, 2007).

Nesbitt was rattled after the detectives came calling. He and Ray left for Chicago "not very long" afterward. They left in a hurry and took very little with them. In Illinois, Ray assumed the name "Colette Royce," and Nesbitt began using the name "James Clark." Nesbitt worked sparsely and lived off the income of Ray's two jobs (State v. Nesbitt 1987). It wasn't long before Ray tired of the stress of life on the run and trying to live under an assumed identity. And she missed her friends and family back in Omaha. This was aggravated by Nesbitt who was showing signs of increased stress by drinking more than ever and using huge quantities of dope as he ramped up his violence against her. She finally had enough and fled back to Omaha.

In July 1977, Ray contacted Omaha attorney Art O'Leary and arranged to meet with detectives to tell them what she knew about Harmer's murder. Because she hadn't actually seen the body, and had no idea where it had been dumped, detectives were still stymied. She did give them the alias being used by Nesbitt and the address where he lived outside Chicago.

In the meantime, detectives from both the Douglas County Sheriff's Department (DCS) and the Omaha Police Department (OPD) continued to work the Harmer case. OPD got involved because detectives believed that Harmer was killed at Nesbitt's N. 15th Street address inside city limits. Mary Harmer's body still had not been located in spite of extensive publicity about her disappearance in the local media.

With their daughter still missing, in desperation the Harmer family hired an Omaha private detective named

Denny Whelan to do what they believed the police were unable to do. Whelan was a hard-drinking, chain-smoking private eye with a reputation for skirting the law for his clients. There were only four people who had firsthand knowledge of what had happened to Mary Harmer: Nesbitt, Bieber, and their old ladies. Nesbitt and Bieber were hardcore Hells Angels and weren't talking. Whelan devised a plan to go after what he perceived as the weak links in the case, the old ladies (T. Dempsey, personal communication, February 2007). Police detectives had focused on Ray since her breakup with Nesbitt. It was hoped that as a disgruntled former old lady she could help make the case against Nesbitt. That left Bridgett Kohlert who had recently married Wayne Bieber. It is likely due to the intense heat of the police investigation that had tangled up Bieber that Wayne married Kohlert to prevent her from being forced to testify against him.

The exact nature of what transpired next still isn't known for certain but Whelan was accused in court filings by Nesbitt of allegedly snatching Bridgett Kohlert-Bieber and holding her captive to force her to reveal everything she knew. He was intent on finding Harmer's body using methods unavailable to the police. Unfortunately for Whelan, Beiber and Nesbitt did not confide in either of their old ladies when they dumped Harmer in the abandoned manhole. And neither old lady had been an eyewitness to the rape or murder. Nor had they had actually seen Harmer dead. Other than suspicions of what happened, combined with incriminating statements made by Nesbitt to Ray, without a body neither Whelan nor the police could make a case against Nesbitt for murder.

In an attempt to reinvigorate their stalled case, DCS detectives flew to Chicago in March 1978. Based on information revealed by Ray they arranged for Cook County (Illinois) sheriff's detectives to go to Nesbitt's address in Homewood to pick him up for questioning. They wanted another crack at him to see if they could get him to confess. True to form, Nesbitt refused to talk and asked for an attorney. He was subsequently released (State v. Nesbitt 1987).

Apparently, the incident so rattled Nesbitt that he used his Hells Angel sources to obtain a new identity under the name Michael Stein (U.S. v. Nesbitt 1988). He obtained a fake passport under this name and fled the country for Brazil in late 1978 where a gang of bikers had formed a nascent OMG four years earlier in Rio de Janeiro. They were eager to forge alliances with the notorious HAMC in America and aided Nesbitt by providing him with work and a place to stay.

Nesbitt, along with other Angels, are reputed to have instructed them in how to manufacture meth and taught them the criminal techniques of the HAMC. The infusion of the criminal expertise of Nesbitt and other Angels into the primordial stew of Rio's outlaw biker subculture came to fruition five years later when the Rio franchise of the Hells Angels Motorcycle Club became the first Angels chapter in South America (T. Dempsey, personal communication, February 2007).

Detectives knew that Harmer had been raped and murdered by Nesbitt but they didn't have a body and the case went cold until late summer 1984 when an engineering crew opened a long-abandoned manhole near the airport. They were stunned to find skeletal remains and reported it to police. An autopsy revealed that the remains were of Mary Kay Harmer. Etchings on the teeth and skull suggested a caustic substance was poured on her head while tissue was still present. The sludge samples taken from the manhole revealed high calcium and pH levels associated with caustic alkaline substances such as lye. The skull had two holes consistent with bullet wounds. Due to the length of time that had passed it was impossible to determine the exact cause of death. But now that they had Harmer's remains, sheriff's detectives could obtain a murder warrant for Nesbitt. It was entered into the National Crime Information Center so that if he was contacted by cops anywhere in the United States he could be arrested.

To escape the heat of the investigation, Bieber and his new bride had left Omaha in March 1976, about four months after the murder. They moved first to Monticello, Utah then on to Imperial Beach, California, a suburb of San Diego (State v. Nesbitt 2009). After they were informed in late summer 1984 by other Hells Angels that Harmer's body had been found, Wayne Bieber contacted San Diego attorney Tom Humpherys, who contacted Douglas County authorities and arranged for immunity agreements with state and federal officials for Wayne and Bridget Bieber in exchange for their testimony against Nesbitt.

Prosecutors were not happy granting immunity to Wayne Bieber, believing that he was more deeply involved in the rape and murder of Harmer than he admitted. They swallowed a bitter pill and accepted the reality that they had no other choice. The statute of limitations had expired on any crimes he might have committed raping Harmer, helping Nesbitt hide the body or aiding and abetting the murder by destroying evidence. And prosecuting Bieber for Felony Murder—a legal ruling that allows a defendant to be charged with first-degree murder for a killing that occurs during a dangerous felony he participated in, like rape, even if the defendant is not the actual killer—was virtually impossible based on the scant evidence. More importantly, they needed Bieber's testimony about statements made by Nesbitt about the rape. No one else could establish an unequivocal link between Nesbitt and Harmer's death.

Meanwhile, Nesbitt had tired of South America and had returned to the Chicago area in 1984 after the Rio HAMC chapter he helped midwife had been formed. He brought with him his latest old lady, a Brazilian woman named Ana DaSilva. The next and final break in the case occurred when Nesbitt was caught in a clever sting by federal authorities.

In early 1983, the United States Drug Enforcement Administration (DEA) started an undercover business in Elk Grove Village, Illinois, a suburb of Chicago (U.S. v. Nesbitt 1988). It was known as North Central Industrial Chemicals, Inc. The initials of the business, NCIC, are the same as the National Crime Information Center that held an entry for the murder warrant for Nesbitt. No one can claim that DEA agents lack a sense of humor, in this case a richly ironic one.

NCIC offered a variety of chemicals and lab equipment for sale. Its customers were discretely profiled to determine whether or not the chemicals or equipment purchased were being used for illegal purposes, especially the manufacture of controlled substances (U.S. v. Nesbitt 1988). As part of the profiling process, a DEA chemist reviewed a copy of the customer's receipts in an attempt to identify the potential use of the chemicals purchased. If the chemist determined that the type or amount indicated that they were intended to produce illegal drugs, the DEA would launch a more thorough investigation. The company's prices were considerably higher than those charged for comparable chemicals from other companies in the Chicago area. Purchasers' willingness to pay indicated that they were more concerned with maintaining their anonymity than seeking competitively priced supplies like a legitimate business would do to maximize profits.

In October 1984, James Nesbitt, Thomas Nesbitt's brother, visited NCIC along with Ana DaSilva, and placed an order for equipment and chemicals. Among the items ordered was phenylacetic acid, a chemical used to synthesize P2P. P2P is a necessary precursor in the preparation of methamphetamine. Based upon the meth production potential of phenylacetic acid and the type and amount of chemicals purchased by Nesbitt and DaSilva, the DEA concluded that they could be used to manufacture methamphetamine. The DEA placed them under surveillance when they returned to NCIC to pick up their order (U.S. v. Nesbitt 1988).

In the ensuing days, James Nesbitt placed several telephone calls to NCIC to order more chemicals and lab equipment. When he picked them up he was tailed by agents to his home in Crete, Illinois. During the late evening hours of October 24 and into the early morning hours of October 25, DEA agents obtained a search warrant and conducted a search of Nesbitt's house. He voluntarily gave up the location of the lab where the chemicals were to be used. He took DEA agents to a secluded rural residence in New Carlisle, Indiana owned by Douglas Massey. The agents maintained surveillance of the house while they tracked down Massey to find out the details of who rented the property. Nesbitt claimed the meth cook was a biker named Michael Stein (U.S. v. Nesbitt 1988).

Massey told them that he had been renting the house to a man named Michael Stein since in August 1984.

The agents obtained a second warrant to search the New Carlisle house on October 26. A man who identified himself as Stein was present during the search, as was Ana DaSilva. As suspected, the house was a clandestine meth lab, a huge one. Agents found a photocopy of a chemical formula for preparing methamphetamine along with a quantity of meth in the bedroom of the house. It also contained several documents bearing the name Michael Stein including one bearing Thomas Nesbitt's picture. They found a Brazilian work permit as well as payroll stubs from a Brazilian company listing the employee as Michael Stein. The DEA estimated that the clandestine lab had the potential to produce 115,000 individual doses of methamphetamine. At the conclusion of the search, the DEA arrested Michael Stein and Ana DaSilva.

In court three days later, Stein came clean and identified himself as Thomas Nesbitt. That led to the discovery that he was wanted in Nebraska on the murder warrant. From November 1984 through mid-January, 1985 Nesbitt fought extradition to Nebraska. Eventually he was returned to Omaha to stand trial for Harmer's murder. He was convicted on April 17, 1986 and sentenced to life imprisonment without the possibility of parole (U.S. v. Nesbitt 1988).

Following his conviction for murder, Nesbitt was returned to Indiana to stand trial for the DEA charges. On November 17, 1986 he was convicted of conspiracy to manufacture methamphetamine and the manufacture of P2P. He was sentenced to concurrent terms of five years imprisonment on each charge to run consecutive to his Nebraska murder sentence.

Over the years, Nesbitt has appealed his murder conviction at least five times, alleging police and prosecutorial misconduct, violations of his constitutional rights, and incompetent legal counsel, among other claims. Having apparently abandoned his "my rights have been violated" ploy in May 2018, Nesbitt filed an appeal to the Nebraska Supreme Court in which he claimed that his circadian rhythms were being disturbed due to prison overcrowding (Nesbitt v. Frakes 2018).

As of this writing, Nesbitt, now in his early 70s, has claimed that he suffered from a debilitating spinal condition that caused him sciatic nerve pain and restless leg syndrome and that he is required to sleep from 2 AM to 10 AM every day in order to prevent paralysis. He alleged that his sleep patterns were being disrupted because the Nebraska State Penitentiary was overcrowded and because his solitary confinement cell, designed for one inmate, was being double-bunked.

Nesbitt has lost every appeal. That may provide a small measure of comfort to the family and friends of Mary Kay Harmer, knowing that her killer will take his last breath behind the cold gray walls of the state penitentiary in Lincoln. Society breathes a little easier knowing that a vicious serial rapist and murderer will never again prowl the innocent in search of his next unsuspecting sweetie.

Chapter Seven
David Burdette Series
The Ten Most Eligible Women Rapist

You're a wanton, animalistic and depraved person,
...society has to be protected from you...
District Judge Jerry Gitnick

In March 1982 a series of rapes occurred in the Omaha metropolitan area. The rapist in each case was described as a white male who surprised his victims at home in their beds or as they got ready to retire for the evening. He restrained them by binding their hands behind their backs with duct tape and gagged them by taping their mouths shut. He also used duct tape to blindfold them before forcing them face-down on the bed and raping them anally and vaginally. He demanded to know where their money was, then stole from their purses. Before fleeing, the intruder told the victims to wait ten to twenty minutes before getting up.

Behavioral analysis indicated that the rapist was a classic Anger Retaliatory Rapist (ARR). To review, the primary motivations for this type of rapist are power and aggression. The ARR rapes out of retaliation for perceived wrongs by women (Groth 1979:42). Because of this the attacks are intended to degrade and humiliate the victim. Instead of attacking the object of his rage directly he directs his anger at a surrogate. Not all ARRs physically beat their victims. Sometimes the anger and violence and the desire to dominate and humiliate is satiated by the violence inherent in the rape itself, especially if it involves anal intercourse, which is considered especially degrading and may also be painful.

As previously mentioned in Chapter Five, rage-based rapists are difficult to profile and apprehend because their attacks are stress-based. They are triggered by a relationship ending or job loss that leads to a spontaneous eruption of violence.

Consistent with the ARR classification, psychological assessments following the arrest of this rapist showed that he possessed a seething, long-simmering, chronic anger against women and all of society. Unlike the explosive rage of some ARRs, his anger was expressed in a more controlled, methodical manner that bled off his pent-up aggression.

The first reported rape occurred around 3:00 AM on Wednesday, March 31, 1982. Carol Melner was living alone in her residence on North 78th Street in Omaha (Burdette v. Britten 2009). The suspect had gained entry through a back window by pulling off the screen. As she was going to bed, the suspect grabbed her from behind and tossed her onto the bed. He bound her arms behind her back with duct tape and gagged her by putting tape over her mouth. He also blindfolded her. He then sexually assaulted her both anally and vaginally. When he was done he asked her where her billfold was and took her money. He warned her to wait ten to twenty minutes before getting up. In spite of being tightly bound with duct tape, Melner was able to hop outside to a neighbor's home and call police.

The second assault took place nineteen days later at about 2:30 AM on Saturday, April 19th. Peggy Griffon, recently divorced, was with her four-year-old son in the house she had just rented on N 53rd Street in Omaha

(State v. Burdette 1999).The rapist broke in and waited for her to get off the phone and retire for the night before he attacked. While she fell asleep the intruder skulked around the darkened house searching for valuables. She was awakened when he clamped a hand over her mouth and roughly flipped her face-down on the bed before binding her wrists behind her back and gagging her with duct tape. He rolled up a pillowcase as a blindfold that he duct-taped over her eyes. He told her to be quiet or he would kill her and her son. Like the previous attack, he raped her anally and vaginally.

Peggy's son was sleeping on a couch in the living room and did not wake up during the assault. As in the prior rape he asked where her money was and left after taking a gold cigarette lighter worth $500 that her brother had bought for her in Germany. Similar to the previous crime, Griffon was able to free herself and call police. There were no signs of forced entry but a side window in the kitchen had been left unlocked.

The third incident occurred eight days later in the early morning hours of Sunday, April 25, 1982. Jeanne Leno was living in a home on Chris Lake in unincorporated Sarpy County just south of Bellevue, Nebraska (State v. Burdette 1999). Bellevue is a suburban city south of Omaha. Leno was asleep in bed when she was awakened by an intruder who climbed on top of her. As in the prior rapes, the suspect used duct tape to bind her hands behind her and to blindfold and gag her. He then sexually assaulted her anally. After the rape, he rummaged through her belongings looking for money before leaving. As with the previous crimes, Leno was able to free herself and get to a neighbor's home to call police. This time, the intruder had gained entry through the sliding glass door which may have been left unlocked.

At one point during Jeanne's attack the suspect taunted her, asking, "What makes you so eligible?" before mentioning that he had seen her picture in a magazine article featuring Omaha's ten most eligible women. Leno never got a clear look at her attacker but told Sarpy County Sheriff's detectives that she thought that he was white but his voice "sounded black." The comment about Leno appearing in a magazine article didn't seem significant to investigators at the time because they were unaware of the other attacks.

As word spread among investigators in the metro area that a serial rapist was at large, a meeting was arranged in early May at Omaha Police headquarters at 15th and Howard Street to compare notes and discuss investigative strategies. Detectives were initially baffled because there did not appear to be any pattern that could be used to predict where the suspect might strike next. The wide geographical dispersion and the varied age and employment of the victims did not indicate a pattern that could be used to identify how and why victims were targeted.

At the meeting, detectives from various agencies in the area discussed the details of their cases. It is always helpful to have fresh eyes look at a case to spot things that might have been missed or have become camouflaged to the detectives working the case amid the minutiae of the details. Nothing seemed to stand out until Omaha Police Detective Mary Lou Lawson heard the comments made to Jeanne Leno in the Sarpy County case. On a hunch Lawson got a copy of the March 1982 issue of Omaha Magazine. It contained an article by Nancy Jacobs titled "Omaha's Ten Most Eligible Women," which profiled successful single women in the Omaha area. Lawson was stunned to see that the first reported victim, Carol Melner, was listed in the article. She was puzzled about

the second reported rape involving Peggy Griffon. She
was not mentioned. And the article did not include the
addresses of any of the women featured. To complicate
matters the two victims named in the article were not
listed in the phone book. Lawson was at a loss to figure
out how the rapist found their address until someone
pointed out that Polk Directories were available in the
Public Library.

In the days before the Internet and online sources
that have virtually eliminated personal privacy, Polk
Directories were an invaluable source used by detectives
to track down witnesses and suspects. They had the
potential for darker uses as well. Polk routinely sent
out representatives who canvassed every neighborhood
obtaining the names of the residents, where they worked,
their job title, how much money they earned, the names
of everyone living at the address, whether they were dual
income or not, the age of the head of household, if there
were multiple adults in the household, whether or not
they were retirees, and similar demographic information.
The information compiled by Polk was intended to be
used legitimately by marketers and researchers. Unlike
the scant information in phone books, Polk Directories
included a wealth of information that could also be used
by rapists.

A detective grabbed the department's copy of the
latest Polk Directory and found that the address of nearly
every woman mentioned in the article was listed. He also
found that one of the Ten Most Eligible women had once
lived at the address where Peggy Griffon had been raped.
It was Griffon's misfortune to move into a house where
the intended victim of a serial rapist formerly lived.

During the course of the investigation it was learned
that the rapist used the Polk Directories in the South

Omaha Library at 28th and Q Street to find some of his victims. The remaining women named in the article were hurriedly contacted and warned about the ongoing investigation. Several mentioned that they had received threatening and obscene telephone calls from an anonymous caller. They also mentioned that there were signs that someone had tried to break into their homes.

Once the targets of the rapist had been identified, a task force was quickly organized to establish stakeouts in the homes of the remaining women named in the article. There was an added sense of urgency because some of them were already being stalked. OPD set up surveillance on five locations, Sarpy County had one in their jurisdiction and detectives from the Douglas County Sheriff's Department set up on Lakehurst Drive in Riverside Lakes, a subdivision just south of the small town of Waterloo in the western part of the county.

I was assigned as backup during the stakeout. We knew the approximate time of the attacks, the suspect description, and his method of operation, but his identity eluded us. The stakeouts were scheduled to run for two weeks after which the strategy would be reevaluated if no contact had been made. On the last day of the stakeouts, as expectations waned for lack of activity, the Ten Most Eligible rapist struck again.

In the early morning hours of Monday, May 10, 1982, fifteen days after the last rape, he came calling. My partner, Dave Vencalek, and I were backing up Detective Lynn "Pat" Mason who was the inside man at the home of Pamela Maynard in Riverside Lakes. She and her child had gone to bed around 11:00 PM and the darkened house had been deathly still for hours. At around 2:05 AM Mason heard footsteps on the deck. Through the closed window blinds he saw the shadow of someone moving along the deck towards the rear of the house. He then heard the shadowy form try the locked screen door followed by the sounds of the screen being cut.

It was less than an hour before the stakeouts were scheduled to end. Mason notified Vencalek and me by radio and hurriedly roused Maynard and her child from their beds. He ushered them to a downstairs bathroom where they locked themselves in. The suspect saw Mason and fled.

Vencalek and I arrived within a minute or so after leaving the stakeout location temporarily to assist another agency with a help an officer call nearby. When the help call was cancelled we quickly returned to the stakeout site. We found the faint traces of footprints on the deck from dew on the grass. We also saw the cut screen. Mason stayed in the house with Maynard and her child while Vencalek and I began to search for the rapist. It was a nightmare of a place to search with numerous overturned or covered boats, boat docks, shrubbery, raised wooden decks around the back side of the walkout houses that backed up to the lake, and a million shadows where a suspect could hide.

Two houses down from the stakeout location, Vencalek found an unlocked sliding patio door on the lower level. The house was dark inside with the only light visible from a basement bathroom. We slid the door open slowly and paused to listen. It was utterly still so we pushed the door open and slipped inside. The patio door led to a family room in the walkout basement. As our eyes adjusted to the darkness we could see a woman asleep on the couch. She was laying partially on the couch with one leg resting on the floor. She was breathing fairly heavily and was naked except for a robe partially covering her. It was open at the front exposing the front of her body. An empty bottle of Tanqueray gin lay on the floor next to the couch with an empty glass on its side next to it, the shriveled remnants of a lime still visible.

The women appeared to be in her mid-30s. She was obviously passed out from the gin. Vencalek was transfixed by her nudity. "Should we cover her up?" he asked.

"No! You'll wake her up and scare the crap out of her." I replied. "Leave her be and let's check the rest of the house."

"Why bother?" Vencalek responded. "He wouldn't have passed this up."

He was right. We quietly slipped out the way we came in. Sleeping beauty was none the wiser for us having been there.

The upscale neighborhood consisted of nearly 200 homes. Searching it thoroughly was a daunting task. We began with the houses on either side of the stakeout location. They were both locked up tight. The entire neighborhood was eerily still in the darkness of the early morning hours. Nothing was moving and with the coolness of the night we would have heard if a car was started anywhere near us or the sounds of a suspect running through the brush. One advantage we had was that the subdivision was secluded with only one way in or out via 228th Street. It was situated about a quarter mile south of West Dodge Road—a four lane state highway also called Highway 6.

In spite of it being a normally slow shift spanning the late Sunday into early Monday morning hours, patrol deputies were busy running from call to call. And no K-9 unit was available to track the suspect. Because the subdivision was secluded I was sure the rapist was still in the area because no car had left since Mason notified us that he had a nibble. Being that far outside the city it was easy to assume our suspect had not walked there. We decided against calling in reinforcements to help with the search.

I left Vencalek to patrol the area on foot while I headed to find a spot to watch the road in and out of the subdivision. I remembered a place just east of the intersection of 228th and West Dodge Road from my patrol days. It was the entrance to a farm field on the south side of the road surrounded by trees and adjacent to the Elkhorn River. I backed in, cut my lights and switched off my brake lights. From there I could see any car leaving the neighborhood but could not be seen. With Vencalek watching close in and me watching the only way in or out I was certain that the suspect was bottled up and could not leave without being seen.

Over the next several hours only two cars left the neighborhood. I ran the plates on both and they came back to residents. Even though I was being eaten alive by mosquitoes I remained parked in the brush watching… waiting. About 5:45 AM I was in desperate need of a transfusion from the mosquito bloodletting. They were so thick they were flying up my nose. I decided to make a pass through the neighborhood. Dawn was fast approaching and the rapist would have to make his move soon to get away unobserved before sunrise when the subdivision would begin to come alive. As I turned off 228th Street onto the Wilson Avenue entrance to the subdivision I inched along with my windows down and my headlights and brake lights still off, pausing often to look and listen. Vencalek was still on foot on South Shore Drive on the other side of the subdivision. I hoped that his movements throughout the night had kept the suspect off balance and confined to the northern end of the subdivision where I now prowled. Both Vencalek and Mason advised me by radio that nothing was moving near them. I was starting to worry that the rapist had found a way outside our perimeter.

I continued to creep along Wilson Avenue. As I approached the intersection with Shorewood Lane I paused to scan the area and listen yet again. I was focused on a row of cars parked in a common area across the street from the houses when I caught movement out of the corner of my eye. It came from the shadows between two houses about a half a block ahead of me. I remained motionless in my idling car and watched as a white male emerged from the shadows. I picked up my binoculars and peered at him through the windshield. Because I was blacked out and stationary he didn't see me right away.

By the way he moved and the condition of his clothing it was obvious he was not a resident coming out to get into his car to leave for work. Instead of paying little or no attention to his surroundings, as most innocent people do, his body language said he was keyed up and he was looking right and left and behind him as if he was trying to see if he had been spotted. And he walked in a slinking manner; smoothly, quietly with gliding steps in a stealthy way, not upright and with purpose as an innocent person usually moves.

I radioed Vencalek and Mason that I had a suspect on Wilson Avenue at Shorewood Lane and continued to watch him with my binoculars. As he stepped slowly from the shadows I could see that his pants appeared to be wet from dew from the knees down and there appeared to be grass and weeds on his pant legs as if he had been hiding in tall grass. I was surprised that he still hadn't seen me because even though I was motionless with my lights off the area was illuminated by streetlights.

As he stepped from the shadows he stiffened on seeing me and froze in place near the street as I raced up and slammed my unmarked unit into park before jumping out to confront him. He tried to act nonchalant as I rounded the front of the car with my gun drawn. He stood there with his hands in his pockets. I was in plain clothes so I announced in a loud clear voice, "Sheriff's Department! Show me your hands!"

I scanned his face. He looked oddly familiar. He said nothing as he slowly removed his hands and opened them for me. "All right, man," he replied. "I'm just looking for a place ta fish," he said as he gave a target glance towards the tree line across the street.

Target glances occur when a suspect telegraphs his intention by, for example, looking at an escape route or at your weapon if he is considering a gun grab. It is a pre-escape or pre-attack indicator based on body language. The best counter to it is to point it out immediately to let him know you are on to him. "Don't even consider running for those trees. I'll drop you before you can cross the street," I said to dissuade him from bolting.

He responded with mock surprise, "What? Man, like I said, I was looking for a place ta fish."

As soon as he opened his mouth I recognized him as David Burdette. He had been locked up awaiting trial on rape charges when I began my career as a deputy assigned to the courthouse jail in 1978. He had served 15 months in a Missouri prison for felonious assault (Hunziker 1982). In 1977, five months after his release from prison he was arrested again for a Sarpy County burglary for which he was sentenced to three years in the Nebraska Penitentiary in Lincoln. A year later he left jail on a weekend furlough but didn't return. He was arrested by Omaha Police after a 50-year-old woman reported that a man entered her home, put duct tape over her eyes and bound her with bed sheets. During the attack Burdette told her he just wanted her purse but then spread her legs apart and told her, "Don't make me hurt you." He was frightened off when the woman's screams woke her son (Hunziker 1982). At the time I encountered him in the jail, he was awaiting trial on that rape charge. Burdette was sentenced to one year in prison for second-degree sexual assault in that attempted rape and another year for escape. He was released December 17, 1980.

I ordered Burdette to place both hands behind his back as I moved in and speed-cuffed him. Once he was restrained I spun him around. "What are you doing out here, Dave?" I asked. "You still live at 20th and Y in south 'O'?" He looked at the ground, "Yeah, still there," he replied with a barely perceptible sigh. He glanced at me and continued, acknowledging that he remembered me from the jail, "Like I said, O'son, I was jus' lookin' ta fish." As he spoke, I remembered Jeanne Leno's description of her rapist as a white male who "sounded black." I thought to myself that Burdette could sound like a black person to a bewildered, frightened rape victim.

I looked him in the eye, "In the dark, with no gear, at a private lake? You're a long way from home, Dave." He looked at the ground and said nothing in response. "Are you on paper?" I asked, referring to parole for his 1978 rape charge. He didn't look up, "Nope, jammed it." Jamming means he served the full sentence instead of seeking parole. Hardcore incorrigibles jam their time rather than seek early release on parole because they don't want to live under the strict rules of parole.

Parole is the provisional release of an inmate from state prison. The parolee agrees to certain conditions prior to the completion of the maximum sentence, such as obeying the law, refraining from drug and alcohol use, avoiding contact with victims, obtaining employment, and maintaining regular contacts with a parole officer (PO). Many hardcore cons feel that these conditions are so onerous that they are willing to do extra time to avoid it. Living within the constraints of law-abiding parole hampers a con's ability to live the lowlife criminal lifestyle.

Most parole agreements also mandate surprise home visits during which POs look for signs of drug or alcohol use, guns or weapons and other illegal activities. The three or more years of parole also includes alcohol and drug monitoring as well as monthly office visits. Recidivism rates for parolees average sixty-eight percent (Alper 2018).

"Where's your ride?" I asked. He twisted his back to motion with his cuffed hands towards an older model Dodge Dart parked on the grass in the overflow parking area across the street. "It's the yellow one...over there," he replied, motioning with his head towards the car. The location was over three blocks away and around the corner from the stakeout location on Lakehurst Drive.

Like all experienced rapists, Burdette possessed a high degree of criminal versatility and expertise. He knew that he was less likely to be noticed if he parked farther away in a common area rather than making a rookie's mistake and parking too close to the target. Being farther away meant he stood a better chance of sneaking back to his car undetected if things went south. He would be outside the immediate focus of any law enforcement response. The only thing that prevented him from escaping this time was Vencalek on foot in the area, which kept him off balance. He was unable to get to his car after the aborted break in. That, plus me doing the unexpected by patrolling while blacked-out and waiting until near sun-up when he would be pressured to get out of the area surprised him as he made his way to his car for the getaway.

Burdette didn't know about the stakeout. At that moment he mostly likely assumed that at worst he might take a hit for attempted burglary. Lt. Bob Tramp wanted him booked for attempted burglary so we had time to prepare search warrants on his car and home in cooperation with the other agencies involved to link him to the completed rapes. Later, when his car was searched with a warrant, we found duct tape matching that used to bind prior victims, rubber gloves, a knife and other bindings in his car. Detectives searching his parents' home at 20th and Y Street, where Burdette lived at the time, also found a copy of the Ten Most Eligible Women issue of Omaha Magazine, the distinctive cigarette lighter stolen during the Griffon assault, and other evidence linking him to the rapes.

The arrest generated extensive news coverage. It also received national coverage during the Tuesday, May 18, 1982 NBC Evening News with anchor Tom Brokaw. There was something deeply sinister in the Ten Most Eligible Women rapist case that roused primal fears. Burdette ultimately pleaded guilty to the first-degree sexual assault charges in the rapes of Carol Melner and Peggy Griffon. Charges for the rape of Jeanne Leno filed against him in Sarpy County were dismissed. He pleaded not guilty to the attempted sexual assault in the Pamela Maynard case but was found guilty after a trial. He was sentenced on December 1, 1982. During sentencing, District Court Judge Jerry Gitnick told Burdette, "You're a wanton, animalistic and depraved person, and society has to be protected from you," before sentencing him to 22 to 30 years (UPI Archive 1982).

Psychiatric reports in Burdette's pre-sentence investigation indicated that he gave several reasons for the rapes including saying that he hated women. The reports describe a man who showed no remorse or guilt and who confided to doctors that he "couldn't stop" the string of rapes and attempted rapes he committed. One of the psychiatrists who examined Burdette noted, "You don't cure people like this...you...try to isolate them from opportunities to have this happen" (Hunziker 1982). Burdette told psychiatrists the women in the magazine reminded him of his two sisters. He said he was blamed all his life for the wrongs of his sisters and that his parents favored them over him. He also said that he hoped one of the women in the magazine might want to marry him if he "made love to her."

Characterizing the violent rape of a woman as "making love" after terrorizing her, violating her in the most intensely personal and devastating way, threatening to kill her and her child, binding her with duct tape, gagging her and placing a pillowcase over her head is typical of the callousness, lack of empathy and extreme self-centeredness of a sociopath. Further evidence of Burdette's lack of empathy includes claims to the psychiatrists examining him that he didn't "hurt" his victims (Kentsmith 1982). In Burdette's twisted narcissistic logic he did not harm anyone, "maybe emotionally only," and he certainly did not "hurt them physically."

Like all criminals Burdette was highly skilled and well-practiced at concocting lies and justifications for his crimes including claiming he was "hurting and depressed" over the loss of a job and so "I just hurt them the way I've been hurt." His extensive criminal history depicts a cunning, evil predator who was a diagnosed sociopath. In spite of the fact he was doing life on the installment plan with his frequent trips to prison, he skated in and out of the revolving door of criminal justice each time, robbing, raping, and beating a growing list of often female victims and leaving in his evil wake incredible fear, trauma, and suffering.

Burdette is a glaring example of the dangers sociopaths pose to society. His troubled past began in his preteen years. Burdette's criminal history dates to 1969 and includes arrests for burglary, sex assault, escape from prison and robbery (Brunkow 1998). At age 11 he was sent to the Omaha Home for Boys for acting out as a juvenile and breaking into houses. The Home was established in 1920 for at risk kids and has a remarkable history of diverting kids from the path of life-long criminality. They weren't successful with Burdette. Like all sociopaths he wasn't amenable to treatment. From the age of 13, Burdette moved in and out of mental hospitals and state correctional institutions, accused or convicted of at least nine sexual assaults or attempts. He was sentenced to three years for burglary in Nebraska's reform school at the Youth Development Complex in Kearney at age 15.

One of his first attempted rapes occurred when he was 15. An attractive young woman in the neighborhood soon fell under his rapacious gaze. She lived with her boyfriend several houses away on the same block. Burdette began to surveil her by window, peeping at night (Kemling 1983). Over a couple of weeks he watched as she undressed, showered and made love with her boyfriend. One day he noticed that she was preparing to wash her car in the driveway. He also noticed that her boyfriend was nowhere in sight. He snuck through the adjoining backyards and surreptitiously approached the back of the garage as she used a hose to wash the car. He savored her female form in her tight-fitting shorts and her braless halter top.

The driveway was flanked on one side by a short flagstone retaining wall. Burdette looked around and saw that no one was in sight. He crept up and grabbed a stone from the wall and snuck up behind the woman as she crouched down to wash the front wheel. He clobbered her over the head with the stone, rendering her semi-conscious. He then dragged his stunned, groggy, and utterly helpless victim behind the garage where he hurriedly pulled down her shorts and pulled her top up around her neck to expose her breasts.

As Burdette was pulling down his shorts to rape his incapacitated victim her boyfriend unexpectedly came out of the house. Not seeing his girlfriend and with the water running down the driveway he began to frantically call out her name while looking for her. Burdette panicked and slipped back through the backyards to his parents' home. He watched as the police arrived followed by an ambulance that took the woman to the hospital for her head wound. Later, as the police officer stood on the front sidewalk talking with the boyfriend and jotting notes on a clipboard, Burdette nonchalantly walked up and asked what was going on. The officer brusquely ordered him to move along (Kentsmith 1982).

Burdette began having attendance problems in the sixth grade and two years later was placed in an alternative school (Kemling 1983). By ninth grade he had dropped out of school. In March 1971, he failed to return to the youth center after being let out for a hernia operation. Within a month he had been arrested in connection with the rape of a 23-year-old woman and the attempted rape of a 21-year-old woman who fought him off with a fork.

Burdette spent one year in the maximum security unit at the Douglas County Hospital and then, at age 16, was committed to the Lincoln Regional Center, a state psychiatric hospital, by the Douglas County Board of Mental Health. In 1972, he escaped from the regional center for an hour when he was taken to the dentist. He spent four-and-a-half years at the state psychiatric hospital center before escaping again (Hunziker 1982).

As he matured, Burdette's criminal expertise increased along with his dangerousness. He moved to Kansas City in August 1975 where he was sentenced to two years for aggravated assault and was confined to a mental hospital in Fulton, Missouri. He was released in November 1976. In June 1977, he was sentenced to the Nebraska Penal and Correctional Complex for burglary (Kemling 1983). While incarcerated there he was charged for administrative offenses that included the homosexual rape of two other inmates and an escape attempt. Inmates committing crimes inside prison walls are often disciplined in administrative hearings rather than being charged with crimes because it is a simpler and more effective way to maintain control. None of the administrative charges resulted in criminal charges and he was released back into society in December 1997.

In court-ordered psychological exams following his Ten Most Eligible Women rapes, he confessed to raping his first victim as a "young kid while on drugs." He admitted raping a "couple of times" during that period but was evasive about the details.

As part of a pre-sentence investigation following his conviction in the Most Eligible Women rapes, the court ordered a psychological examination at Douglas County Hospital, 42nd and Woolworth Street in Omaha. Psychologist Dr. John Hunziker interviewed Burdette in November 1982 (Hunziker 1982). A second court-ordered exam was conducted for sentencing purposes the same month by psychiatrist Dr. David Kentsmith at the University of Nebraska College of Medicine, 42nd St & Emile Street (Kentsmith 1982). A third assessment was a Nebraska Penal and Correctional Complex Intake Classification Assessment by Mark Kemling and David Kanive in Lincoln in January 1983 as Burdette began to serve his prison sentence for the rapes (Kemling 1983).

What the various exams revealed is a chilling portrait of a cold-blooded serial predator. It is the image of an untreatable, incorrigible sociopath with an already lengthy criminal history of violence including serial rapes. Equally ominous, the psychological assessments revealed Burdette's deep-seated hatred of women and society and his eagerness to act violently on that hatred. One of the psychiatrists evaluating Burdette noticed a tattoo on his left forearm of a devil, its tongue extended, and a naked woman lying across that tongue (Kemling 1983).

Burdette refused to participate in sex offender rehabilitation programs in prison and declined to apply for parole. He did not want to be encumbered by those restrictions upon release because they would have limited his ability to indulge his evil desire any time he felt its sinister urges. He was released after serving half of his sentence under Nebraska's good time law. The law, enacted in 1969, provided a day-for-day credit for time served. Burdette served a day and got a day lopped off his sentence, gratis, regardless of whether or not he participated in rehabilitation therapies.

Burdette served his time at the maximum security state penitentiary in Lincoln and, as he neared release, at the medium security Omaha Correctional Center. Due to his notoriety as the Ten Most Eligible rapist, a

TV news reporter was waiting for him as he departed the Correctional Center in East Omaha when he was released on April 30, 1998. Burdette was clearly agitated about being hounded by the reporter as he wheeled his meager belongings through the parking lot in a broken-down grocery cart. The persistent reporter asked him if women had anything to worry about with his release. Burdette's response was priceless, "A woman has a better chance of being struck by lightning than being raped by me."

Due to quirks in Nebraska law that had accrued over the years, there was no way to incapacitate a dangerous sexual predator like Burdette via indefinite civil commitment in a psychiatric institution as there had been prior to 1992. Civil commitment proceedings are used to remove habitual sex offenders from society for extended, sometimes indefinite, periods of time. Civil commitment for sex offenders can happen after they've already served the prison sentence for their crime and without having violated any other laws. Instead of punishment for past crimes, this form of involuntary confinement is based on the risk that an individual may commit offenses in the future. The U.S. Supreme Court upheld civil commitments in Kansas v. Hendricks, but when Burdette jammed his sentence in 1998, there was no law in place to commit him civilly as a sex offender to protect society. The only restriction on Burdette was the requirement that he register as a sex offender with the Douglas County Sheriff's Department when he moved back to Omaha after release.

Burdette had targeted the Ten Most Eligible Women because he despised what they stood for: strong, successful and socially adept women. He also knew that since they were not married there was a good chance no man would be in the house to prevent him from indulging his evil desire. This particular aspect of his modus operandi would reappear in another form in his future predations. Only this time they would exhibit an uncommonly cruel and callous disregard for the suffering of others at the time of not only their shattered physical security but their emotional security as well. It would make Burdette the poster boy for indefinite incarceration for being one of the most dangerous sexual offenders among us.

Nebraska was the second-to-last state in the nation to enact a community notification statute stemming from the federal Megan's Law (Megan's Story n.d.). Megan's law was created in response to the murder of Megan Kanka in July 1994. Megan Kanka was seven years old when Jesse Timmendequas lured her into his house, raped her, and then killed her by strangling her with a belt. He then dumped her body in a nearby county park. The next day he confessed to investigators and led them to the site.

Megan Kanka's murder was a preventable tragedy. Her killer had two previous convictions for sexually assaulting young girls. In 1979, he pled guilty to the attempted aggravated sexual assault of a five-year-old girl. Astonishingly he was given a suspended sentence. After failing to go to counseling he was sentenced to nine months in prison, a remarkably light sentence considering the gravity of the crime (Megan's Story n.d.). In 1981, Timmendequas pleaded guilty in the assault of a seven-year-old girl and again was sentenced to an unbelievably light prison sentence of six years at a diagnostic and treatment center—essentially a mental hospital—for sex offenders. Timmendequas reportedly participated little in the treatment program while incarcerated. He was described by one therapist who treated him at the facility as a "whiner" who spent most of his time sleeping. Another therapist stated that she believed that

Timmendequas would eventually commit another sex crime targeting young girls.

The murder generated national outrage that led to the introduction of Megan's Law. The law requires sex offenders to register with law enforcement and disclose their location under the federal Jacob Wetterling Act. The full name of the law is the Jacob Wetterling Crimes Against Children and Sexually Violent Offender Registration Act. Jacob Wetterling was an eleven-year-old who was abducted by a stranger in Minnesota in 1989. He was missing for almost 27 years until his remains were found on September 1, 2016. His killer, Danny James Heinrich, was a convicted child sex offender who agreed to disclose the location of Wetterling's remains in exchange for not being prosecuted for the murder (Peralta 2016). The law requires states to implement a sex offender and crimes against children registry.

Together the two laws helped strip away the cloak of anonymity that sexual predators hid behind when they preyed upon the innocent. The new law provided two major vectors to inform the public: a sex offender registry for law enforcement that can be queried by concerned citizens, and community notification when a dangerous sex offender moves into a neighborhood. A law similar to Megan's Law, had it been in place at the time, would have informed Megan Kanka's parents that they had a dangerous child rapist for a neighbor.

With only the gossamer protection of the Sex Offender Registry requirements standing between Burdette and society it was only a matter of time before other women would endure their worst nightmares at his hands. It didn't take long. Approximately six months after his release from the penitentiary, Burdette was raping again. On October 14, 1998 Annette Blackman was living on a farm with her two daughters, ages seven and nine, on State Street outside Omaha (State v. Burdette 1999). Her husband Terry had died two weeks earlier in a motorcycle accident on September 30th. His death was listed in the obituary column of the Omaha World Herald newspaper.

Blackman had retired for the evening around 10:30 PM on October 13. Her two daughters were in bed with her. That night was the first night she and her daughters had stayed by themselves overnight in their home since Terry's death. Sometime after falling asleep Blackman was startled awake by an intruder who placed a hand over her mouth. She could feel that the hand had a latex glove on it. He asked her where her purse was before getting her and her two daughters out of bed and leading them to the hallway. He ordered them not to look at him as he herded the terrified trio ahead of him out of the bedroom. After a few minutes he put the children back into bed with their mom and tied one child to each of the Blackman's arms with plastic zip ties that he had brought with him as part of his rape kit. In a stunning case of sadism he forced the terrified children to witness their mother's rape while ordering them to lie face-down and not to look at him (State v. Burdette 1999).

Blackman could hear the intruder going through her drawers in the room as well as her daughters' room. He found her husband's magazine to an antique World War II pistol and asked her where the gun was. Blackman told him it was in one of the dresser drawers. After retrieving the pistol he returned to the bed and blindfolded and then gagged Blackman with one of her late husband's ties. He then ripped some sheets into strips and tied Blackman's legs apart after forcing her face-down on the bed. Blackman could hear her attacker taking off his pants before he penetrated her anally and vaginally with his penis as her terrified daughters sobbed hysterically. Blackman, frightened out of her mind, tried to comfort and reassure them by pleading with her attacker not to harm them.

As he was raping Blackman, the rapist told her daughters he was not hurting their mother and that "mommy liked this" (State v. Burdette 1999). After 5 to 10 minutes Blackman heard the intruder say he was not "going to waste the bucket" before withdrawing his penis and putting his pants back on. That comment apparently referred to his inability to achieve orgasm—a typical sexual dysfunction among rapists, especially Anger Retaliatory Rapists. The intruder then went downstairs and found Blackman's purse and came back upstairs. In another callous act of sadism before leaving he hit Blackman and her daughters on the buttocks as they lay face-down on the bed and warned them not to call the police or he would return and kill them.

Blackman waited to be sure her attacker had left the house before struggling with her daughters to get free of their bindings. She promptly called 911 and patrol deputies responded. Sheriff's detectives determined that the point of entry was a window in the living room where a screen had been ripped off the frame. Blackman could not identify her attacker because she never got a look at him. And he was an experienced rapist; he wore latex gloves to avoid leaving fingerprints, blindfolded Blackman and prevented her and her daughters from looking at him to identify him later, and wore a condom to eliminate leaving DNA behind. Detectives were initially stymied because they didn't have much to go on to identify him.

Then a huge break in the case occurred. Blackman's neighbor, Jane Frost, was working a few miles from the

Blackman residence. At around 12:30 AM she was driving home with her husband. As they proceeded westbound on State Street, Frost noticed a black Ford Bronco with a red stripe down the side parked on the side of the road by the driveway leading to the Blackman residence (State v. Burdette 1999). Because it stood out to her, she slowed down and got a partial license plate number of "1-HB." She also believed the plate had a "7" in it. The next day when she heard about the Blackman rape she contacted the Sheriff's Department and told them what she had observed.

Detectives put out a bulletin with details of the rape and the suspect and vehicle description including the partial license plate number provided by Frost. They then began a computer search for all Ford Broncos registered with the partial license plate and all of its possible permutations. Before they received the vehicle list from data processing they got another huge break based on heads-up police work.

Several days after the rape on October 17, Sergeant Pat Thomas, a relative of Blackman, was on patrol when he observed a Ford Bronco with a red stripe bearing Nebraska license "1-HH87" westbound on Maple Street in West Omaha approximately five miles from the Blackman residence. As Thomas followed the Bronco, he observed it fail to signal several lane changes and pulled it over because it matched the description of the vehicle observed by Frost.

The driver of the vehicle was David Burdette. As if suffering from a guilty conscience, which psychopaths don't possess, or more accurately because he feared detection and wanted to appear to come clean to deflect suspicion, Burdette immediately informed Thomas that he was a registered sex offender. Thomas filled out a Field

Interview (FI) card and passed the information on to detectives.

A FI card is used by deputies to document informal police contacts during the course of patrol. They have required fields to be completed by deputies documenting the name, date of birth, address, telephone number, and physical descriptors of the person involved including where the contact occurred, vehicle descriptors and space for a short narrative explaining why the person was contacted and under what circumstances. The FI card is commonly used to document a contact which does not rise to the level of an arrest or citation. Thomas also followed up the FI card by personally stopping by Criminal Investigative Bureau (CIB) at the end of shift to talk directly to detectives working the Blackman case.

CIB supervisor Sergeant Bill Jackson and lead Detective John Pankonin were alarmed after checking Burdette's criminal history and sex offender registration details. They realized that they were dealing with one of the most notorious serial rapists in Omaha history, classified as a high-risk sex offender. Due to the lack of evidence in the case they also realized they would have to surveil Burdette continuously to prevent him from raping again while gathering enough evidence to arrest him. They immediately informed the CIB commander and senior department officials of the details of the Burdette case. They asked for a task force to be organized with the Omaha Police Department based on Burdette's level of dangerousness, his past history, and the fact he appeared to be raping again.

On October 21, 1998, detectives from both departments began a 24-hour surveillance of Burdette. Task force leaders realized that manning the round-the-clock surveillance would quickly overtax their staff. To solve that problem they sought assistance from other divisions in both departments as well as devising a plan to perform the observation with less manpower. Jackson and Pankonin prepared an affidavit for a court order requesting authority to install a GPS transmitter on Burdette's truck. They also devised a clever ruse to get access to his vehicle to surreptitiously install the tracker. By employing GPS tracking they could follow Burdette using a looser tail than they could accomplish by eyes-on surveillance alone. That would minimize the chance that he would spot them while simultaneously enhancing their ability to know where he was at all times. The risk was too high for anything less.

Following a criminal suspect is not like it appears on TV and in movies. They always show the surveillance vehicle close to, and easily observable by, the target. In real life that would quickly lead to getting burned and the target would know he was being watched. In reality, the type of route the target takes affects his ability to spot surveillance as well as the ability of detectives to remain within range. When following someone on an interstate highway, for example, detectives might be able to follow the target undetected for hours since it's only natural that they would going in the same direction. That plus the ability to mask the surveillance vehicle by sliding in behind another vehicle, or hanging back much farther than you can on city streets without losing the target, make it fairly easy to maintain watch, even from a pronounced distance.

Conversely, if the target is driving through a congested urban area and making a number of turns and stops along the way, following him without getting burned is more difficult. The human brain filters out randomness and seizes upon patterns. While it's expected that a random car might make the same two or three turns in a row any movements that continue to mirror the target's actions dramatically increase the chance he will notice the same car in his rearview mirror. That is why surveillance teams use multiple and different makes and types of vehicles combined with frequently handing off the eyeball, or eyes-on surveillance, of the target to different detectives during the course of the watch.

The best surveillance vehicles are those that do not stand out. A beige, five-year-old sedan or compact SUV fits the bill. And they can't have noticeable peculiarities such as dents, rust, spoilers, window, bumper stickers or police radio antennas for obvious reasons. And it shouldn't be either too clean or too dirty.

Effective surveillance takes practice. Inexperienced detectives tend to begin following too soon or they hesitate and lose the target in heavy traffic or at a missed traffic light. Following too quickly or closely at the outset will make the target notice you. With practice you learn to allow the target a short amount of time to drive off. Later on when you're miles down the road he'll wonder why the same vehicle from his neighborhood is still behind him. Experienced detectives let the target get down the block a ways before they ease into traffic. It's all about avoiding becoming one of the four "sames" used by professionals to detect surveillance: same person, doing the same thing, at the same time, at the same location. In the case of following a target in a car it involves seeing the same vehicle, especially at different locations.

Losing a target is normally not a huge deal. And it is sometimes preferable to lose them rather than risk getting burned and tipping him off that he is under surveillance. You might miss the criminal acts he commits or the people he associates with after he loses you, but you can pick him up later when he returns home. Given Burdette's level of dangerousness it was imperative that he be under constant surveillance to prevent him from raping another woman while detectives gathered evidence to make a case against him. Losing him was not an option. Using a GPS transmitter to augment physical surveillance helped ensure that he would not slip away while minimizing the chances he might spot detectives following him and ruin the chance to making a case against him in the shortest time possible. Anything less presented an unacceptable risk to the public.

The ruse involved Burdette's status as a high risk registered sex offender. From Deputy Thomas's FI card they noticed that Burdette was driving a different vehicle from the one he had registered on his release from the penitentiary. They issued a "locate" for Burdette under the pretense that he needed to update his sex offender information. Locates are similar to the "all points bulletins" or APBs commonly mentioned on TV shows or in old movies. They are usually supplemented by a CIB bulletin notifying patrol deputies to stop and detain the person named and the reason for the locate. They include descriptive information such as vehicles the person is known to drive, his last known address, other locations he may frequent, people he is associated with, and a physical description, among other information. Locates are entered into the local law enforcement database so that any officer stopping the person named in the locate is instructed to contact the issuing authority, in this case sheriff's detectives.

Because of the manpower-intensive demands of the 24/7 surveillance, CIB requested assistance from other divisions within the sheriff's department. I was the Training Division commander at the time and volunteered myself and two of my trainers who were experienced detectives to assist. We would work the overnight to free up detectives to handle day shift duties when the bulk of investigative efforts necessary to make a case against Burdette would occur.

My shift began at 9:00 PM on October 26. The overnight team included Detective Ed Vanatterin another sheriff's vehicle, me in my unmarked Training Division car, and two Omaha Police detectives in another unmarked. The three-car team we relieved advised us that Burdette had arrived at his apartment around 7:30 PM. They watched as the lights came on in his apartment on the third floor of the Rorick Apartments after he parked his Bronco in the lot south of the building.

Located on South 22nd Street, the Rorick had been a part of the downtown Omaha landscape since 1953. Originally it was constructed as an eleven-story structure with 235 apartments and parking for 100 in a lot on the south side of the building. For 22 years it was also home to a series of FM radio stations with studios in the building and a transmitter tower on the roof. In 1980, a severe storm toppled the tower and the FM stations moved to different digs. Around that time, the Rorick succumbed to the urban blight that surrounded it. It became a cockroach-ridden low-income apartment building plagued by prostitution, drug dealing, and occasionally lethal violence.

The Omaha Police Department (OPD) detectives set up to watch the south lot where Burdette's Bronco was parked. From their perch they could also see the door he used to enter and exit on the south side of the building. I set up on 22nd Street just north of St. Marys Avenue. St. Marys is a one-way street heading west at that location. To go east Burdette would have to go south on 22nd Street to Leavenworth Avenue, a one-way that heads east at that location. He would have to pass the OPD detectives to do so. Vanatter set up on St. Marys to watch the main entrance. From my vantage point I could see the only other exit to the building, the entrance on the east side of the building.

We knew that the court order had been signed late that day and the plan was to stop Burdette the next morning on his way to work using the pretext of the locate to update his sex offender registration. Burdette usually left for work at his job as a laborer for a parking lot maintenance company around 6:30 AM. He normally drove west on St. Marys before catching the freeway at 28th Street. We would follow Burdette and direct patrol deputies to traffic stop him once he headed for his morning cup of coffee at a 7-Eleven in West Omaha near his job. After the stop, the ruse would play out. They would inform Burdette that he was being detained based on the locate for failure to update his sex offender monitoring information. In the meantime Jackson and Pankonin would proceed to the location of the stop and transport Burdette to sheriff's headquarters purportedly to update his sex offender information. His truck would be impounded and transported to the impound lot where the GPS device would be implanted.

Burdette's apartment was dark all night and his truck remained parked in the lot. All was still in and around the Rorick. Shortly after 2:30 AM I started my car to chase off the chill of the cool fall night. As it idled I saw a hump approaching me walking north on 22nd from St. Marys. Vanatter also saw him and called me on the radio, "Heads up, Deano. You got a low-knuckler approaching you at twelve o'clock. He was trying car doors on St. Marys."

"Yeah, I see him," I responded.

I was hunkered down in my car with the doors locked and the mirrors adjusted to be sure no one could sneak up on me from behind. I had a Remington 11-87 shotgun on the floor and was wearing my .40 caliber Smith and Wesson Model 99 in a paddle holster on my hip. As I remained motionless the hump continued to approach me by walking slowly in the middle of the street. He was obviously looking for an easy take, perhaps hoping to find an unlocked car or one he could break into to steal a laptop, cell phone, or other valuables a careless motorist had left in the car.

At first he wasn't sure which car was idling so he crept towards me slowly, trying to determine where the motor noise was coming from. Once he pinpointed it he walked up slowly to the front of my car and tapped on the hood while trying to peer inside the darkened interior. He appeared to be trying to determine the condition of the person inside. The area is a known drug market populated by hookers and lowlife urban cretins. This predator likely thought he had a drug abuser, perhaps passed out or overdosed, that he could sweep in and rob or even carjack with little or no resistance. He tapped on the hood again saying, "Hey brother. You okay? You okay, man?"

I remained motionless and hunkered down in the seat as I tried to suppress a smile at the surprise I was going to unleash on the hapless hump. I reached slowly to my side, unsnapped my holster, and drew my .40. I held it next to my leg as the hump started to approach the driver's side window. He must have thought better of that tactic and slowly walked around the front of my car to the passenger side. He tapped on the hood again, repeating, "Hey brother, you okay?" Emboldened by my lack of movement and failure to respond to his comments he walked up to the passenger door and tried to open it. I quickly slid over the seat and lowered the electric window as the astonished hump was trying the door again. I thrust my gun into his face and yelled, "What the fuck you doing, shit lips?"

The hump's eyes widened and he gasped as a look of terror shone on his face. He shot backwards, tripping over his feet, and landed unceremoniously on his ass on the sidewalk. He jumped up and raised both hands saying, "Okay, man, don' shoot, don' shoot!"

I yelled through the open window, "Get the fuck out of here, asshole!" as the hapless guy scrambled up the hill to get away.

Vanatter was laughing as he radioed me, "I think you scared ten years off that hump's life. He was all ass-over-elbows trying to get up the street and away from you."

"If we weren't tied up he would be in cuffs now," I responded. "Probably clear a bunch of thefts and maybe a robbery or two…the friggin' hump."

Around 6:30 AM on Tuesday, October 27th, Burdette left his apartment and walked to his Bronco in the parking lot. We didn't want to tip our hand and let Burdette know he was being surveilled so we hung back and watched from a distance as he took his normal route towards his job in West Omaha. I radioed the designated patrol deputy waiting to make the stop that we were on our way to his location. He responded that he was in position and waiting. Once Burdette got close, the patrol deputy pulled him over and initiated the ruse to implant the GPS device. He informed Burdette that he was in violation of the sex offender registration requirements because he had failed to notify the sheriff's department that he had changed vehicles. Burdette was detained until Jackson and Pankonin arrived.

Jackson asked Burdette to come to headquarters because he was in violation of the sex offender registration requirements. Burdette agreed to accompany him and his vehicle was towed to the impound lot. There deputies hard-wired a GPS transmitter by connecting it to the battery and secreting it in the engine compartment. The hockey-puck-sized device was nearly discovered about a week later when Burdette took his vehicle to a car repair shop for a new battery. Either the technician failed to spot the device, or figured it was none of his business, and Burdette was none the wiser.

As the tracking device was being installed, Burdette was updating his sex offender registration at sheriff's headquarters. Pankonin began the process with a blank form and took his time as he went over the questions with him. Pankonin needed to buy time for deputies to get the transmitter installed. Burdette answered the questions and volunteered additional information. He told Pankonin that he had committed sexual assaults in 1982, stating that at that time he and his girlfriend saw an issue of a local magazine featuring a list of the most eligible women in Omaha. Burdette told his girlfriend the women on the list were probably better lovers than she was and she replied that he would never know. Burdette claimed that he took that as a challenge and that he proceeded to rape "two or three" of the women on the list to find out.

Burdette, like all sociopaths, was an expert and well-practiced liar with a thoroughly developed but entirely fraudulent litany of excuses and justifications for past crimes. Blaming his girlfriend for the rapes because she supposedly challenged him to stalk, rape, and rob women is as flimsy an excuse as it is bogus. One of the hallmarks of a sociopath is the ability to spin an absurd lie without embarrassment. While people with normally functioning consciences would be ashamed to try to pull off such a lame dodge, Burdette was oblivious to such social strictures.

Continuing his sociopath hustle, no doubt thoroughly enjoying his verbal chess match with police, he went on to tell Pankonin that he was now 43 years old and too old and not in good enough shape to do something like that again. He added that during the 1982 assaults he did not use a weapon because he believed he could physically overpower his victims with his hands and did not need one. He also told Pankonin that during those assaults he was not wearing a condom but now he would wear a condom because of sexually transmitted diseases and because police would need only a small sperm sample to make a DNA identification (J. Pankonin, personal communication, 2005).

Burdette must have gotten a sociopathic rush as he savored getting over on the detectives as he played them by feigning innocence and contrition while asserting that he was not able to rape anymore due to his supposed advanced age and poor physical condition. Unknown to him, Pankonin and Jackson already had his number. They knew he had raped Blackman and they were professionally and expertly laying the groundwork to end his predations once and for all. While Jackson watched Pankonin's interview via a monitor in CIB he had no way of knowing just how pivotal his personal role in arresting Burdette would ultimately prove to be. It would be a Hollywood ending to a violent predator's criminal career.

After the tracking device was installed, investigators used it to track Burdette's movements while also following him using as many as four vehicles. The additional member of the surveillance team was a detective manning the computer that tracked the GPS transmitter. The computer was located at the off-site, or "hole" as it was called, where all of the undercover federal, state and local cops were officed. Then, the hole was located in a nondescript strip mall on the north side of town. From that location the monitoring detective called out Burdette's direction of travel provided by the GPS tracker to the detectives following Burdette.

A slight technical hiccup with the transmitter soon appeared. When Burdette passed under a bridge or the signal was otherwise attenuated between the transmitter and the satellite, like when the Bronco was inside the auto repair shop when Burdette had his battery replaced, detectives monitoring it from the offsite computers lost the signal. Normally when the transmitter was clear of the obstruction that blocked its signal it would begin transmitting again within a minute or so. However, when the signal dropped off the detective manning the computer had to reboot the entire GPS program in order to reacquire the signal. That took up to three minutes, and Burdette was essentially free of GPS tracking during that time. You can get lost in less than five seconds during an eyes-on surveillance amid the congestion of an urban environment. Three minutes is a veritable lifetime in surveillance terms and meant that Burdette could be in the wind unencumbered by our tail to commit another rape. The danger to his potential victims was substantial. It complicated efforts and forced those following Burdette to maintain a closer tail to avoid losing him when the GPS transmitter went down.

In spite of the technical problems, over the next six weeks detectives from the Sheriff's department along with detectives from the Omaha Police Department followed Burdette around the clock. They witnessed him stopping and going through numerous neighborhoods. While heading to work or back home, he would pull into out-of-the-way neighborhoods where he would slow to five miles per hour in front of certain houses then drive around the block. It was the attention Burdette gave to one house in southwest Omaha that led Detective Joe Mainelli to spot a pattern that ultimately led to the next break in the case.

One afternoon on his way home from work, Burdette drove out of his way to S. 140th Avenue. As he had in eight other neighborhoods he slowed to five miles per hour as he passed the house then proceeded to drive around the block and pass by the house again. It was the home of Susan Hartman, a woman in her 30s. Mainelli recalled seeing an obituary for Hartman's husband in the newspaper. He had identified Burdette's targeting MO. All of the homes, including the Bennington one where Blackman was raped, were ones where tragedy had struck. Each home was occupied by a widow who had put an obituary in the paper.

On November 25th, task force detectives followed Burdette to the Hartman home again. He was obviously homing in on her as his next victim. This time he appeared to be looking for a place to park his Bronco so he could approach the house unnoticed. He drove through the Woodridge apartment complex parking lot on S 141st Plaza. Hartman's home backed up to the north end of the complex. From there he sat in his truck and stared at the rear of the house. Three days later, around 10:00 PM on November 28, detectives followed Burdette to the same area. This time they observed him park in the apartment complex lot and get out of his vehicle. As they watched he made his way from the parking lot to the back fence of Hartman's home. He was learning his prey's habits like when she went to bed, and if she watched TV in bed or went to sleep immediately. He was also searching for security vulnerabilities to exploit to gain entry like window screens that could be cut or pried off or doors left open or unlocked.

At one point, Burdette climbed a large evergreen tree on the edge of the apartment complex property and proceeded to surveil Hartman's house. As detectives watched Burdette with night vision binoculars they saw him masturbate while sitting in the tree staring at the Hartman home. After he was finished he climbed down out of the tree and left the area in his Bronco. They realized he would attack soon, if not that very night. They needed to approach Hartman immediately and tell her that she was in the crosshairs of one of the most notorious serial rapists in Omaha history.

Other detectives maintained surveillance of Burdette as he headed to a bar on Grover Street. Like many other rapists Burdette used alcohol before his rapes. Sergeant Jackson approached the Hartman residence to warn her. He explained the situation and assured her that Burdette was being watched and that she was safe. He told her that detectives might have to place a female officer in her house as a decoy. Jackson left around 11:30 PM but soon got word that Burdette was heading back towards the widow's home. He immediately turned around and raced back to Hartman's house. He asked the terrified widow for permission to hide in her kitchen at the rear of the house. He then asked her to lock herself in the bathroom.

Meanwhile detectives followed Burdette to the Woodridge apartment complex parking lot. They again used night vision optics to watch him as he parked his Bronco in the lot and stuffed latex gloves, bindings and a screwdriver into his pockets. They contacted Jackson by radio and warned him. The tension was palpable as other detectives moved to positions where they could assist Jackson in making the arrest. They stationed themselves out of sight on the street in front of Hartman's house and in the darkened yard of an adjacent house as Burdette crept slowly through the parking lot heading towards a rear gate in the chain link fence surrounding Hartman's backyard.

In the house, Jackson readied himself. He had an earpiece for his radio and listened to detectives as they tracked Burdette approaching the house. A few minutes later one of the detectives warned Jackson that Burdette was at the fence line. Jackson removed the earpiece and prepared himself for the encounter.

Jackson is a big, powerfully built detective. He stands over six feet tall and well over 280 pounds. As he stood in the shadows of the kitchen he heard the gate to Hartman's backyard opening. Seconds later, Burdette stepped up onto the patio and slipped on a pair of latex gloves. He opened the sliding glass door that Jackson had unlocked, parted the blinds and entered the kitchen. Once inside he paused to let his eyes adjust to the darkness. Before he could move, Jackson yelled "Sheriff's Department! Don't move!" as Burdette turned to flee back out the door. Jackson caught him in mid-stride before he could make it outside. He tackled Burdette and slammed him roughly to the floor as the rest of team rushed to the house to assist.

Burdette was stunned, both literally and figuratively. As he cuffed him, Jackson told Burdette, "You're under arrest." Burdette sighed as Jackson stood him on his feet with his hands cuffed behind his back. He looked at the floor and said, "You've got me. I'm going back to the penitentiary." In addition to the latex gloves he was wearing, and a screwdriver and two 36 inch lengths of nylon rope in his pocket, he also had two condoms in his wallet.

In May 1999, Burdette was found not guilty of the rape of a 31-year-old Bellevue woman that had occurred in July 1998. The judge in that case said police were overzealous and the woman's identification of Burdette as her attacker was tainted. Sarpy County prosecutors had said Burdette found her through an ad for a moving sale that included her address in a local shopper newspaper. Douglas County prosecutors were more successful. On August 20, 1999, Burdette was convicted after a jury trial of one count of First Degree Sexual Assault Second Offense, two counts of Burglary, one count of Robbery, and one count of Attempted First Degree Sexual Assault (Brunkow 1999). Burdette was sentenced to 35-60 years imprisonment on the First Degree Sexual Assault Second Offense conviction, and 20-40 years imprisonment on each of the remaining counts. Each sentence was to be served separately and consecutive to the others for a total sentence of 115 to 220 years.

Burdette's 1982 Ten Most Eligible rapes were perpetrated against women that he was reasonably sure would be alone because they were single and without male companionship that could interrupt the fulfillment of his evil desire. His 1998 rapes were perpetrated against women he knew would be alone because they were listed in newspaper obituaries on the deaths of their husbands. Targeting widows so soon after the deaths of their husbands was part of his sadism and callous hatred of victims already suffering what was likely some of the most significant grief imaginable. As mentioned above, it served both MO and signature needs. He knew they were much more likely to be alone in the wake of their husband's death, making them attractive targets. By attacking them in the aftermath of such monumental grief he intensified the satisfaction of his sadistic pleasure by inflicting further pain on already tremendously suffering victims.

The news of the guilty verdicts made Peggy Griffon, one of Burdette's 1982 rape victims, whose young son was asleep in an adjacent room while she was being raped, shiver with emotions of elation and relief. She told a news reporter, "I was so happy, knowing that he's going to be put away for a long time and that he's not going to hurt another woman again" (Heinzl 1999). Like many other rape victims, Griffon said she had feared for her safety when she learned that Burdette was back on the street after serving more than 15 years in prison for the 1982 rapes. The PTSD that time had helped to ease resurfaced. Long-dormant fears began to haunt her anew. She had trouble sleeping. Every night she double-checked the locks on her doors and windows. "I was afraid he could track us down. You lose your sense of trust and your sense of security."

Burdette weaponized sex to serve his evil desire to punish, hurt and degrade women that he blamed for all of the perceived injustices he had suffered in his life. I have arrested many violent sociopaths in my career but few were as cunning and dangerous as David Burdette. I was proud to have arrested him for his first series of rapes in 1982 and to have assisted the team that arrested him in 1998 in what I hope and pray are his last rapes.

Chapter Eight
Christina O'Day Rape-Murder
The Babysitter Killers

> I've been on the bench for...years
> and heard many murder trials,
> this...is by far the most brutal I've ever heard.
> **Judge Robert Burkhard**

One of the most pernicious myths of rape is that it is an alternative expression of passion, perhaps just an overly aggressive expression of sexuality. The reality is that rape is a life-threatening crime. During the attack victims may straddle a precariously shifting line between life and death. Depending on the motivation of the rapist, murder is an ever-present possibility during any sexual assault.

Some rapists intend to destroy their victim from the outset. In the case of many Anger Excitation Rapists (AERs), the sexual torture of the victim is so severe that survival is unlikely. The intricate fantasies that drive AERs to abduct and torture their victims center on escalating torture that culminates in the destruction of the victim. Her death after a prolonged period of torture and suffering is the ultimate turn on.

In other cases the victim may be murdered by an Anger Retaliatory Rapist (ARR) when things get out of hand, perhaps because she fights back or resists. The rapist increases his violence to ensure both control over her and to vent his pent-up aggression against her. By objectifying her as the target of his rage, the ARR is one giant step closer to disregarding her humanity to satisfy his evil desire to sexually express his rage while simultaneously beating her to take his anger out on a symbolic scapegoat. The ARR uses extreme physical force to dominate his victim up to and including bruises, cuts, and broken bones. He acts out of anger and in retaliation against her. His overriding goal is to physically beat her up. If she resists he may escalate the violence potentially to lethal levels.

A third circumstance involves murder of the victim during what the FBI classifies as Secondary Felony Rape. The primary intent of the offender is rape with a second felony also planned, usually robbery or burglary (Douglas 2006:302). Killing the victim is not the primary focus of the crime. The rape and burglary are compounded by the additional crime of murder to silence the victim. In many cases the murder is an unplanned event committed almost as an afterthought. This is evident in the O'Day rape-murder case described below since the offenders were not armed and were forced to find a weapon at the scene to commit the murder. Like other cases of secondary felony rape the non-sexual assault crime is planned and committed knowing the victim would be present and is carried out after the rape. The offender typically targets the specific victim and the crime scene and has been in the area before. Although the murder is not planned there is nothing random about the rape and burglary.

In the early morning hours of March 21, 1990, unspeakable evil, inspired by a power enthroned in the bowels of hell, enveloped a middle-class tri-level home near 110th and Z Street in the Brookhaven subdivision in southwest Omaha. When the horror of what had happened became known, the normally tranquil suburban neighborhood was shaken to its core, as was the rest of Omaha. In the wake of the evil that night, Christina O'Day, a beautiful, immensely popular, red-haired, 17-year-old Millard South High School senior, was left to suffocate and bleed to death in a slow, agonizing way. Two teens, 16-year-old Christopher Garza and 18-year-old Wayne Brewer, sodomized, beat and tortured her before strangling her and slashing her wrists repeatedly with a fourteen-inch butcher knife. As the horrors of that night unfolded, an eight-year-old girl lay in bed in an adjacent bedroom paralyzed by fear at the sounds of what was happening to her babysitter.

The road to the horrors of that night began innocently enough a year earlier. Martha Bushon was a recent widow who started working the night shift at U.S. West Direct in downtown Omaha. She needed to find someone who could babysit by spending the night at her house to take care of her eight-year-old daughter.

O'Day would drive to the Bushon house every weeknight between 10:45 PM and 11:10 PM and park her car in the garage. Bushon would then leave for work. On Mondays, Bushon usually attended a university class from 7 PM to 9:45 PM and would go to work directly from class.

Christopher Garza had met Wayne Brewer about a month before the murder when both worked at the Kentucky Fried Chicken (KFC) restaurant at 108th and Q Street. Garza had dropped out of Millard South High School at the beginning of the school year. Garza and Brewer were rudderless, subsisting on the margins of society while working part time for minimum wage. That left them a lot of time to plot to indulge their evil desires. On Monday, March 19, 1990, Garza and

Brewer purportedly went to visit Garza's mother who lived several blocks away from the Bushon home. Garza later claimed that since it appeared that his mother was asleep he drove out of the area but missed a turn and ended up by happenstance on the street where O'Day was babysitting. He claimed he saw O'Day pulling into Bushon's driveway and decided to stop and visit with her (State of Nebraska v. Garza 1992).

Like all sociopaths, Garza was a well-honed and habitual liar. Brewer testified later that instead of a chance encounter, Garza had intentionally driven by the house before turning around and stopping. Garza knew O'Day from school and claimed to have been a former boyfriend. He also knew O'Day babysat overnight during the week. That marked her for the monstrous horrors that lay ahead because she was the perfect prey; unsuspecting, accessible, and isolated.

At 11:10 PM, Garza and Brewer rang the doorbell of the Bushon home and O'Day answered. She asked Garza what he was doing there and told him to leave. Brewer and Garza then left. Martha Bushon, who happened to be home that particular Monday night, heard the doorbell ring and thought it was odd that someone would come to the house that late. She stood at the top of the steps leading to the hallway and bedrooms beyond in order to see who was at the door. Garza and Brewer's plans were temporarily derailed by the unexpected presence of Martha Bushon that night.

The following night, March 20th, Garza and Brewer were driving around the area waiting for Bushon to leave for work. They had agreed to break in and steal from the house because, according to Garza, he needed money for car insurance. Both Garza and Brewer knew full well that O'Day and eight-year-old Beth Ann Bushon would be in the house. They returned to the Bushon house at approximately 2:30 AM on the morning of the 21st. Garza, already an accomplished thief and burglar, headed directly for the phone line at the back of the house and cut it. He wanted to be sure that he could indulge his evil desire that night without having to worry about someone calling the police. Garza then broke in through a basement window at the back of the house and let Brewer in through the front door. Brewer immediately began looking for things to steal in the living and dining rooms and moved a TV and VCR near the front door. Garza headed up the stairway and down the hallway to the master bedroom where O'Day was sleeping (State of Nebraska v. Garza 1992).

Brewer told investigators later that after Garza had been upstairs for a while he "heard the door open... looked down the hall and saw Garza and O'Day" go into Beth Ann's bedroom and "told her to go back to sleep." He described watching Garza enter Beth Ann's room, hearing Garza tell the child everything was okay. He said Garza was holding a crying Christina by the arm.

Beth Ann had been awakened by the loud cries of her babysitter in the adjacent bedroom. She had nodded when Garza poked his head in to say everything was okay and could he just shut her door. The eight-year-old spent the next three hours in abject fear listening to sounds that would haunt her for the rest of her life. The running down the hallway, the tromping up and down the stairs, the creaking of the birdcage downstairs and the squawking of Sunshine, her pet cockatiel. And the horrible crying, crying, crying of her beloved "Chris," as she called Christina O'Day (Grace 2016).It is obvious that O'Day selflessly sought to protect eight-year-old Beth Ann by reassuring the young girl to make sure she stayed in her room and away from the evil that had befallen them. After reassuring the child, Garza dragged O'Day back into the master bedroom and closed the door. He then beat her savagely, stripped off her night clothes and so brutally raped her vaginally and anally that it resulted in bruising and tears of her anus and vagina.

Meanwhile Brewer continued to look for things to steal on the entry level of the house. Sometime later Garza came downstairs and told Brewer, "Go have some fun." Brewer claims that he originally refused to go upstairs but after Garza mocked him he went to the master bedroom. He found O'Day on the bed sobbing with her hands over her head tied to the headboard. She was gagged with a scarf and wearing only a t-shirt but had no obvious injuries. In a transparent attempt to minimize his culpability, Brewer claimed he was in the room for only 5 to 10 minutes when he raped O'Day. Brewer then went back downstairs and sat on the couch. Garza returned to the bedroom to check on O'Day and came back down. He went into the kitchen to get a 14-inch knife and returned to the bedroom. As Garza went back upstairs Brewer asked him what he was doing but received no response (State of Nebraska v. Garza 1992).

Brewer followed Garza back upstairs a short time later and stood in the bedroom doorway where he saw Garza pulling away from O'Day and "blood spurting in the air." Garza and Brewer then went back downstairs and hurriedly carried the stolen items out to O'Day's car in the garage. Brewer then followed Garza, driving O'Day's car to a secluded spot where they transferred the stolen items into Garza's car. He then drove her car to another secluded spot along the banks of the Missouri River opposite Honey Creek, Iowa just north of Omaha where they pushed the car into the river. The stolen items were later discarded. As mentioned before, the offender almost always specifically targets the victim at the crime scene and has been in the area before. The O'Day murder bears this out. The thefts from the house occurred only after O'Day was raped and left for dead and the stolen items were thrown away shortly after leaving the scene of the murder. So much for the pretense of burgling the house for money to pay an insurance bill.

The department's involvement began, as most cases do, after a call came into 911. Shortly after 6:30 AM, a resident living a few doors down from the Bushons reported that a distraught neighbor child rang their doorbell saying that she thought her babysitter was dead. Patrol deputies responded immediately and talked to the girl. She was visibly shaken and upset and said she was eight-year-old Beth Ann Bushon. She told them where she lived and that bad people had hurt her babysitter Chris last night. She added that she thought her babysitter was dead.

Deputies checked the Bushon residence and found the babysitter, 17-year-old Christina O'Day, partially out of the bed in a face-down position on the floor in the upstairs master bedroom. Blood soaked the mattress and pooled on the floor next to her body. She was naked with a blue electrical cord wrapped tightly around her neck. A blue scarf had been shoved down her throat and a white hat had been tied over her mouth and nose. Pantyhose and a narrow red belt were used to bind her feet together. She had a huge gash on her right wrist. The scene was extremely bloody with huge swaths of blood spatter on the bed, nightstand, and floor. The presence of lividity made it obvious that she was dead.

Patrol deputies immediately called for detectives and the crime lab. After an initial briefing by patrol deputies on what they had seen, investigators and crime lab personnel conducted a hands-in-pocket walk through of the scene. They gloved up with rubber gloves and booted up with disposable evidence booties to prevent leaving fingerprints or introducing contaminants into the crime scene that might be on their feet.

The hands-in-pocket approach minimizes the urge to pick things up and examine them before the crime lab has had a chance to photograph everything and process the scene for latent evidence like fingerprints, DNA and blood evidence, hair and fibers, tool marks and other trace evidence that might be lost if disturbed before it can be processed. A Royal Canadian Mounted Police axiom describes why this limited incursion is so vital during the initial stages of a homicide investigation, "A victim can be killed only once, your crime scene can be killed a thousand times" (Olson 1999:2).

The hands-in-pockets incursion is predicated on the exchange principle first discovered by Dr. Edmond Locard of France (Forensics Laboratory n.d.). Locard, who was known as the "Sherlock Holmes of France," discovered that every time an individual comes in contact with a place or another individual, something of that individual is left behind at the place and something of that place is taken away with them. He reduced his fundamental principle to the phrase, "Every contact leaves a trace." The next time you cringe in anticipation of your grandmother's obligatory hug and sloppy but lovingly delivered kiss remember that after she walks away and you straighten up and begin to breathe again fibers from her clothes will be on your clothes and fibers from your clothes will be on hers. Not to mention her saliva on your cheek. Or when a person talks on the telephone cells from his or her mouth are exchanged with the receiver. Theoretically it is possible to gather this material and perform DNA analysis to identify the telephone user.

Each of us is a veritable trace evidence magnet collecting small, often microscopic traces of the places, things, and people we have been in contact with. Likewise, we are also spreaders, depositing many of those same items at the places we visit and upon the people we meet throughout the day. The infamous Wayne Williams child murder case in Atlanta in the early 1980s hinged on the exchange of carpet fibers from Williams' car and home to his victims. He was convicted because fibers found on the body of one of his victims matched fibers from the carpet in his house.

Locard's exchange principle works every time and in all places under all circumstances. When evidence is not found after a criminal has been at a scene it may be because the traces of it were too small to be detected or collected, or they may have been disturbed or obliterated by people or conditions that rendered them undetectable. If a careless cop wanders needlessly through a crime scene he or she may step on and destroy footprints left in soft earth near a basement window used to break in, for example. Similarly, rain or wind blowing through an outdoor scene can wash or blow away delicate trace evidence. There is a reason that wise criminals will dump a homicide victim in a river. By doing so they virtually guarantee that most of the trace evidence of their crime is washed away.

Practically, the technology to collect DNA material in this manner is still beyond the capabilities of most forensic labs. Its closest application today, and not available at the time of O'Day's murder, is touch DNA. It is so sensitive that it only requires seven or eight cells from the outermost layer of a suspect's skin. That miniscule amount is not visible to the naked eye and is transferred literally by as little contact as touching an item—hence the name "touch DNA."

In other cases, exchanged material may be obliterated or removed either intentionally or by happenstance. A body exposed to the elements will often yield little trace evidence. Careless scene preservation and processing, or no processing at all, is the number one cause of botched crime scenes in which trace evidence is destroyed, improperly processed, or missed entirely.

Although there are common items which are frequently collected as evidence such as fingerprints, shoeprints, and bloodstains, literally any object can be physical evidence. Less common examples include the palmprint that tied Earl Labelle to the rape of Janet Kaminski described in Chapter Five. I've also heard of a murder case that was cleared when a barefoot suspect left prints from the soles of his feet in his victim's blood. Anything that can be used to connect a victim to a suspect or a suspect to a victim or crime scene is relevant physical evidence. In many cases apparently unimportant objects at the scene later prove to be critical to linking it to a suspect.

A fracture match is one such innocuous object that can be an important link between a suspect and a crime scene. If you tear a piece of paper in half and hold the two halves together you have a fracture match. No two tears are exactly alike. One half of a tear can always be matched to its other half. Likewise, if a half or part of something is found at a crime scene it can be matched to the other half of something found on a suspect. Fracture match would play a role in tying one of the perps to the O'Day homicide.

During the hands-in-pocket walk-through a detective noticed a sheet of paper on the kitchen counter with a corner torn off. He later remembered it when examining Christopher Garza's car and found what appeared to be the missing corner. By making the connection between what could have been an easily overlooked item the detective tied the suspect to the crime scene before other trace evidence had even been processed.

After discovery of the body by patrol deputies, crime lab personnel, including technicians Bill Kaufhold and Dave Sobotka, along with supervisors Deputy Ray Paulison and Sergeant Dave Krecklow, began the painstaking and laborious task of processing the house for evidence. It took the better part of the day. It wasn't long before they found the 14-inch butcher knife taken from the kitchen used to kill O'Day and a hydraulic door closer removed from the front storm door that was used in a futile attempt to bludgeon her to death.

While crime lab personnel processed the house, detectives contacted Martha Bushon at work and informed her of what had happened. Other detectives arrived and began a canvass of the neighborhood. Because of the early morning hours no one had seen or heard anything useful. Martha Bushon mentioned a suspicious incident that had occurred the night before. She told detectives that she didn't have class that night and happened to be home when the doorbell rang around 11:30 PM. Thinking it was strange that someone would come to the house that late she stood at the top of the stairs to see who was at the door. She told detectives that O'Day knew one of the boys and said his name was "Chris." Bushon said she could identify him if she saw him again.

Detectives next notified Sheila O'Day of her daughter's murder. From her they learned that "Chris" was probably Christopher Garza. He had been a former classmate who also used to live in the neighborhood. She didn't know the identity of the second person with Garza at the Bushon home the prior evening. Based on that information, detectives fanned out and began to track down Garza, eventually speaking to his grandmother and other relatives. From these contacts word quickly spread about the murder and that Chris Garza was wanted for questioning.

Beth Ann told detectives that she woke up at 2:30 AM because she heard crying coming from the bedroom where O'Day slept. She said that when her door was opened she only saw one man, and apparently did not see Christina O'Day standing with Garza in the hallway outside. She told detectives that for the next three hours she heard her beloved Chris crying, some whispering and muffled talking, the door to her birdcage on the main level of the house slam and her pet cockatiel Sunshine squeaking. She also told detectives that she heard footsteps, the front door slam (apparently when Garza and Brewer left), and the sound of the overhead garage door opening and then closing. She fell back asleep after that and did not awaken again until she heard O'Day's alarm clock going off at 6:30 AM. Beth Ann slipped on some pants, crept cautiously outside her bedroom and peered inside her mother's room. She was horrified to see blood on the pillowcases and sheets. In the darkness she was unable to clearly see O'Day's body covered with a comforter and lying partially out of the bed in a face-down position against the floor.

Frightened beyond belief, brave little Beth Ann crept downstairs where she was horrified to see her beloved Sunshine's feathers all about and the bird lying dead on the floor. The home had been ransacked. Frantically she reached for the phone to dial 911 but the line was dead. She opened the front door and ran to a neighbor's house. She told detectives, "I rang the doorbell five times, but nobody answered." She added, "I went to the next house and rang the bell three times, but nobody came. I went to the third house and rang it once, and they were home. When [the neighbor] answered the door, I told him, 'I think my babysitter's dead.'"

The shock and horror of that night reverberated throughout the Omaha area and beyond. There hadn't been a high profile brutal murder involving such vulnerable victims in a while and there was incredible pressure to find and arrest the "babysitter killers." The city was on edge with rumors running rampant that no woman was safe and children were in jeopardy. As long as the perpetrators remained at large the metropolitan area was gripped by a fear it hadn't known in quite some time.

For the next 16 days, six detectives, including me, doggedly worked to develop leads that ultimately led to the arrest of the perpetrators. I was working Vice-Intelligence when O'Day was murdered. My partner was Deputy Mike Buglewicz. We were both ordered to drop what we were doing and assist homicide detectives in the O'Day murder. The need to make a maximum effort right after a homicide occurs is based on the "Golden 48" theory; if detectives don't have a lead, a suspect or an arrest within 48 hours their chances of solving the case are cut in half (Olson 1999:3).

Due to the high profile nature of the case we were working non-stop to find Garza and identify his companion. We knew he had been to the Bushon home the night before the murder but we were not sure who he had been with. When his manager at KFC told us that he was friends with coworker Wayne Brewer we began to look for him as well.

Late in the morning of March 21st, Garza received a telephone call from his brother's girlfriend (State v. Garza 1992). She told him that sheriff's detectives were looking for him in connection with the murder. Garza immediately called his mother at work. She came home to take him to the police station. By mistake, Garza and his mother went to the OPD, assuming it was the city police who were handling the investigation. They arrived at OPD headquarters at 15th and Howard Street shortly after noon.

At the police station, Garza was escorted to an interview room by an Omaha Police detective to wait until sheriff's detectives arrived. Garza told the OPD detective that he and Brewer had been with each other on the night of the 20th and into the early morning hours of the 21st. Garza also said that he knew the victim, claimed to have dated her a "couple times" and had seen her on the 19th. He added an alibi saying that he and Brewer had visited several friends in Omaha and Council Bluffs Tuesday evening and early Wednesday and then returned to Brewer's residence where they stayed the rest of the night.

Sheriff's Detectives picked up Garza and transported him to sheriff's headquarters at 115th and Burke Street for further questioning. Continuing the OPD detective's line of questioning they asked Garza if he knew O'Day. Garza admitted seeing her on March 19th as Martha Bushon had reported. Garza told them that on the morning of the murder he was at Brewer's house and denied any involvement. Both the sheriff's detectives and the OPD detective saw scratches on Garza's arms.

None of the evidence from the crime scene had been processed yet and an autopsy had not yet been performed. Without a confession, and lacking the full details of O'Day's injuries and an official cause of death, the detectives let Garza go after he agreed to give saliva, fingernail scrapings, hair samples and photographs taken of the suspicious injuries to his arms.

That evening, Brewer contacted the sheriff's department and agreed to come in for questioning. Brewer arrived at DCS headquarters with his mother at approximately 11 PM. The lead detectives working the homicide conducted the interview as I watched through a one-way mirror. At first Brewer refused to confess to any involvement in the murder and tried to stick to the alibi used by Garza that the two of them had been asleep at Brewer's mother's house at the time the murder occurred.

A key goal of an initial interview is to lock a potential suspect into a story that can be attacked or disproved later after the investigation has yielded evidence and the facts of the case are sufficient enough to know what happened and who was involved. As the interview of Brewer wore on we noticed that his chin and shoulders had slumped forward, the volume of his voice had lowered and he looked fatigued. He appeared to be holding something back. His body language telegraphed that he was losing the will to continue his evasion.

After an hour asserting that he had been asleep at his mother's house at the time of the murder, Brewer sighed, looked resigned, and asked to speak with his mother in private. Detectives left the interview room for about 10 minutes as Brewer's mother counseled him to "do the right thing and get it off your chest." After his mother indicated that Brewer was now ready to talk, the detectives reentered the room to resume the interview.

His mother was standing in the hallway just outside when they asked Brewer whether he was ready to talk. Brewer hesitated but his mother interjected through the open door, "You know, Wayne, you know why we came out here. Tell the man what happened." Brewer then proceeded to give an extensive confession to detectives in his mother's presence.

When Brewer was finished, the lead detective left the room and asked to consult with Detective Randy Brunckhorst and me. He wanted to know if we thought he should get a taped confession. Both Brunckhorst and I pushed for the taped confession because of the weight it carried in court, especially to jurors. There was something compelling in hearing the actual voice of the perp confessing to the murder and laying out the details of the crime. And it deflated false assertions that the defendant was coerced or somehow otherwise tricked into confessing.

Brunckhorst assisted the lead detective in taping Brewer's confession, which concluded at 2:35 AM on Thursday, March 22, 1990. Brewer then led deputies Mike Buglewicz and Neil Paulison to where the victim's automobile had been dumped into the Missouri River. Brewer was then booked for criminal homicide and lodged in the Douglas County Corrections Center. Over the next few days, he contacted the lead detective several times to reveal where evidence could be found. He then led him to the locations.

I was assigned to attend O'Day's autopsy the next day along with crime lab personnel. Autopsies were and continue to be conducted in the morgue in the basement of the Douglas County Hospital at 42nd and Woolworth in Omaha. Dr. Blaine Roffman was the forensic pathologist on duty that day. He had also been to the scene of the murder the previous day. I have attended many autopsies in my career but O'Day's was different. The waste of a young life squandered to satiate evil desire affected me more than I realized at the time.

It's one thing to watch the autopsy of some deserving creep who died at the hands of another lowlife. Such zero sum violence barely causes a ripple in the fabric of society.

But to see a beautiful young woman on the threshold of the immense potential so needlessly, senselessly, and selfishly murdered was profoundly heart-rending. It is the type of evil that shreds the fabric of society. My stoicism was severely tested that day.

O'Day's autopsy revealed numerous injuries: a deep traumatic laceration on the left side of her forehead, a large area of swelling over the right forehead, a deep blunt injury between the eyebrows and upper portion of the nose from being bludgeoned by the storm door closer, petechial hemorrhaging of the eyes and around the neck caused by strangulation by the electrical cord twisted tightly around her neck, a laceration on the inside surface of the left upper lip, a blackened left eye, bruising and tearing caused by vaginal and anal penetration, two dark linear-pattern bruises on the right back side, a bruise on the left shoulder, and another one over the right hip.

Lead pathologist, Dr. Blaine "Bud" Roffman documented a large, gaping laceration on the right wrist which extended to the bone. It had severed all of the superficial tendons as well as producing a 90-percent laceration of the radial artery and a nick in the ulnar artery. He also found seven superficial lacerations on the wrists similar to hesitation marks seen in suicides. They occur when someone is not sure they want to complete the act before making the fatal cut. In the case of O'Day, the hesitation marks indicated that her killer was inexperienced and was unaware how much force was necessary to cause a fatal wound.

Roffman said that the large wrist laceration was inflicted while the victim was alive and continued to bleed profusely until she died. In his opinion she died as a result of three injuries, any one of which alone could have killed her: bleeding to death from the laceration of her wrist, strangulation as a result of the electrical cord tightly wrapped around her neck, or asphyxiation caused by the scarf shoved down her throat and the hat covering her mouth and nose, aggravated by the position of her body lying halfway out of the bed with her face turned against the carpet.

According to Roffman, all of the injuries were inflicted while O'Day was alive as evidenced by the bruising and hemorrhaging. They were silent witnesses to the savage brutality of the beating, rape and murder. And they were evidence of the horrendous, prolonged suffering she endured before her death.

Roffman pointed out that after any of these three fatal injuries O'Day would have been conscious at least 3 to 5 minutes before dying. Roffman also stated that she could have been saved by simply untying the cord around her neck, changing the position of her body, removing the blockage to her mouth and nose, or placing a tourniquet on her arm, depending on which injury had been inflicted at the time. His autopsy left no doubt about the savagery and wanton cruelty of the crime.

Garza disappeared after that first interview. Deputies spread out and scoured every place where he might be hiding but he was in the wind. Several of us participated in the surveillance of his girlfriend's house for several days without success. Garza's girlfriend, Donna Coffin, told us that on Monday, March 19th, Garza had shown her a picture of the victim and told her that he was mad at her, a transparent attempt to justify the unjustifiable via a lame attempt to legitimize her murder. Coffin also stated that a day before the murder Garza had asked her to provide an alibi in the event the police were looking for him. She told us that she wasn't sure at the time whether Garza was serious regarding the alibi but in retrospect she had no doubt of his intentions and that he had killed O'Day.

Other detectives were watching his mother's house and anyone connected with him. When we learned that he had left the area we obtained a warrant for a wiretap on his mother's phone. It wouldn't be necessary. There weren't too many places a 16-year-old murder suspect could hide for very long.

Garza went to his girlfriend's house the day before his arrest. We had pulled our surveillance by then to follow up other leads on his whereabouts and we missed him by mere hours. Garza told his girlfriend that he had seen the victim the night of the murder and that he and Brewer had broken into the house through the basement window in order to steal. Garza also told her that it was not until after they left the Bushon home that Brewer told him he had killed O'Day. Coffin's sister Chris told detectives that Garza had told her he had broken into the house where O'Day had been murdered through a basement window and "robbed" it but denied killing her.

The pressure of the dragnet finally wore Garza down and he turned himself in on April 6th. After processing he was taken to an interview room where he asked Detectives Craig Madsen and Jim Westcott if Brewer had "spilled his guts." They told Garza that Brewer had told his side of the story and had implicated him. They ramped up the pressure by adding that tests were being conducted on blood and semen at the scene that would soon reveal who had been involved. The detectives asked Garza whether he would like to tell his side of the story and Garza agreed.

Garza admitted that he had been with Brewer at the scene but that he had not killed O'Day. He said that he and Brewer had gone to the house to rob it, that he had cut the screen to a basement window at the rear of the house and crawled in, looked around, tied up O'Day and then gone downstairs, gathered a videocassette recorder and other items ready to steal while Brewer remained upstairs. Garza admitted having sexual intercourse with O'Day after which he went back downstairs, collected the items and put them in his car. He claimed that O'Day was alive when he left.

According to Garza, Brewer told him after they left the house that he had killed O'Day. In response to Westcott's question, Garza said that yes, he was "there when it happened." When asked whether he would be willing to give a tape-recorded statement he repeated several times that it was "First Degree Murder and it don't make no difference," but he would not give a recorded statement.

A sustained media frenzy erupted in the aftermath of the murder. Martha Bushon and her extended family worked hard to shield Beth Ann from the horror of that night and the incessant news reporting that dominated local coverage. This was a feat given the intensity of the publicity. The story was so widely covered that a Douglas County District Court judge decided to draw a jury for the Garza trial from two western counties several hundred miles away from the Omaha metropolitan area.

At trial, Garza maintained his innocence, saying he was home asleep when the murder happened. His family complained that the all-white jury was biased against him because he was half-Latino. His attorney raised questions about Brewer's testimony implicating Garza, noting that Brewer faced the death penalty and had reason to blame Garza. As a juvenile, Garza could not be sentenced to death under Nebraska law, while Brewer, who was an adult, could be.

For Garza, crime ran in the family. Christopher Garza's older brother, Michael, and his cousin, Steven, were convicted of an attempted rape a year and a half before the O'Day murder (State v. Steven Garza 1990). They targeted an intoxicated female at a party at an apartment complex, jumped her in the dark as she left the building, and hit her in the face, knocking her to the ground. They dragged her to the side of the building before threatening to "fuck (her) in the ass." Michael Garza pinned her to the ground while Steven Garza pulled down her pants and then pulled out her tampon and threw it in her face before unbuttoning his pants to rape her.

The victim was able to fight enough to get free as a neighbor heard her screams and saw two men struggling with a woman wearing no pants. The neighbor called the police who arrived within minutes. The victim suffered two black eyes and lost the feeling in her face for about three months. She also had scrapes and bruises on her arms and legs. She identified her attackers from a six-pack photo array and the cousins were convicted and sentenced to prison.

Several years earlier, the Garza family lived in the Brookhaven neighborhood not far from the Bushon home. I was working several rapes of female joggers in the area. Michael Garza was named as one of several suspects in those rapes. I was not able to make a case against him because, among other reasons, the victims were unable to identify their attacker because he had blitzed them from behind and forced them not to look at him during the assaults.

I set up a decoy operation using undercover female deputies to jog in the area on the days of the week and at the times of the previous rapes. They were wired with a body wire and under continuous surveillance by undercover deputies in the hope that the rapist would strike again. Unfortunately, one of the victims was the girlfriend of the head of a federal law enforcement agency in Omaha. Unbeknownst to me or any of the deputies working the decoy operation at the time, the boyfriend ordered his agents to surveil the Brookhaven Park at 115th and Monroe Street near where one of the rapes had occurred. They spent days in and around the area and likely scared off the perpetrator as numerous residents reported being contacted by them and seeing them watching the area in their unmarked cars.

They lacked the jurisdiction to do any of the things they were doing because the rapes were not federal offenses. And they failed to inform me that they were working the case, probably because they knew it would unleash a shitstorm of protest that would immediately shut them down. More importantly, their amateurish antics interfered with and probably derailed an expensive, manpower-intensive undercover police operation that stood a fair chance of netting the rapist. By making the area too hot for him to operate in, they may have squandered the best opportunity to catch a serial predator. Michael Garza was not charged with those crimes and the cases went unsolved. They were closed and filed when the statute of limitations expired after three years.

Federal arrogance in believing that they could better investigate a case they had absolutely no training or experience working, coupled with unprofessional antics by the head of a federal law enforcement agency, may have let a violent sexual predator evade arrest. Instead of heeding the axiom that he was too close to the case to remain objective the agent forged ahead with deleterious effect. When a cop abandons the objectivity that makes him effective he is prone to doing amateurish, even clownish things, like the fed did in this case.

I learned later from several disgruntled agents who were taken off cases they were working to essentially perform this off-the-books personal investigation for the agency head that an inspector general (IG) had been tipped off about the unauthorized investigation and other abuses. IGs are the oversight/watchdog authorities that investigate allegations of wrongdoing within a federal agency. The IG's investigation reportedly skewered the agency head. He finished his career at a backwater posting as a result.

⁂

The senseless rape and murder of high school senior Christina O'Day shocked the city in its cold-blooded savagery. The thought that an eight-year-old girl lay frozen in fear listening to the horrors unfold in an adjacent bedroom sent shudders through parents everywhere. The shock was palpably amplified after it was discovered that the killers were two teenagers themselves. District Judge Robert Burkhard, the judge who presided over the trial of Christopher Garza, cited the brutality of the murder when declaring that Garza should never be freed. "I've been on the bench for a number of years and heard many murder trials," Burkhard said during Garza's sentencing. "This one is by far the most brutal I've ever heard" (Grace 2016).

The O'Day murder hit all of the emotional nerves: teenage victim; savage, brutal rape and murder; the place and time it occurred; all heightened by the presence of a small vulnerable child listening helplessly through a wall in an adjacent bedroom and powerless to intervene. The babysitter murder triggered a primal fear revealing the vulnerability of and need to protect our children. The fragile sense of safety people had known in what many viewed as crime-free suburban neighborhoods was shattered. If it happened there, what prevented it from happening anywhere?

The high profile arrests of Brewer and Garza allowed the community to breathe a sigh of relief that the babysitter killers had been taken off the streets. A sense of normalcy slowly returned to the area as attention turned to the equally high profile criminal trials. While Brewer's mother was instrumental in having her son do the right thing and confess to his involvement in O'Day's rape and murder, that sense of righteousness turned defensive as her motherly instincts kicked in at trial as she sought to defend her son from a potential death penalty. Her original urging that Wayne Brewer do the right thing and come clean had evolved as both mother and son now claimed that detectives had violated Brewer's rights by coercing a confession and failing to inform him of his Constitutional rights to an attorney and against self-incrimination. The courts were unmoved by the assertions at trial and again later when Brewer appealed his conviction.

After separate trials in 1991, both Brewer and Garza were convicted of first degree murder and use of a weapon in commission of a felony. Each was sentenced to life in prison without the possibility of parole. The heinous nature of the murder, aggravated by the media frenzy surrounding the investigation, and the arrests and subsequent trials, all combined to deprive O'Day's family and friends of the ability to properly grieve. Incessant media attention forced the O'Day and Bushon families into the public eye, denying them the privacy and space to move on. It prolonged the grieving process by forcing them to relive their pain and sorrow with each news story.

In the years after the murder, Martha Bushon wrestled with the emotional impact on her eight-year-old daughter who lost her babysitter—more a big sister—in the most horrific manner possible (Grace 2016). She struggled mightily to shield her from the reality of that night and restore a sense of normalcy to her life. Unfortunately no one can un-ring that bell, at least not completely. Beth Ann's memory of the events immediately following the murder was hazy. She knew that both young men were eventually charged with robbery, rape, and first-degree murder. She remembered talking to police officers and testifying at Brewer's trial, but she didn't know the details of how truly horrific Christina O'Day's murder had been until years later.

As time passed, Martha Bushon knew that she had to escape the intrusive media coverage and the horribly suffocating memories. She pulled up stakes in Omaha where she had family and moved herself and Beth Ann to the southeast. She was able to transfer her job to BellSouth, later AT&T. They lived in various states including North Carolina, South Carolina, and Georgia. She sold the house where the murder occurred for far less money than it otherwise would have brought because the high profile news coverage of the murder made it a stigmatized property. Estimates vary but experts believe that the loss in property value due to stigmatization ranges from ten and thirty percent. Not only do the murder victim's survivors suffer horrendous emotional and psychological injury, they often sustain significant financial injury as well (Grace 2016).

In high school, Beth Ann learned more details about the murder using the newly emerging Internet. She plunged into deep depression and suffered fear and terrible guilt. She returned to Omaha to see her

childhood counselor and even briefly attended Millard
West High School, the same school Christina O'Day had
attended, before returning to the southeast. She finished
high school, attended college, got married and got a job
working as a fundraiser for a child advocacy group. She
has tried to move on and has been successful in building
a life for herself that isn't defined by the horror of that
night (Grace 2016).

Then the inconceivable happened. In 2012, the U.S.
Supreme Court upended the peace and security the
family and friends of Christina O'Day had known since
Christopher Garza's conviction for her murder in 1991.
The court ruled that, based on research showing adolescent
brains are not fully developed and juveniles under age 18,
like Garza at the time of the O'Day murder, he could not
be held to the same level of accountability as adults. In
Miller v. Alabama, a stunning case of judicial activism,
U.S. Supreme Court Justice Elena Kagan, speaking for
the court majority, wrote that a sentence of life without
parole on a juvenile "...prevents taking into account the
family and home environment that surrounds him—
and from which he cannot usually extricate himself—no
matter how brutal or dysfunctional" (Miller v. Alabama
567 U.S. 460 (2012)).

As Justice Alito noted in the Miller dissent,
"Determining the appropriate sentence for a teenager
convicted of murder presents grave and challenging
questions of morality and social policy. Our role, however,
is to apply the law, not to answer such questions. Nothing
in the Constitution supports this arrogation of legislative
authority."

The Miller decision forced the state to resentence
Garza in 2016. That decision opened old wounds and
re-inflamed the pain and sorrow of Christina O'Day's

murder. While the tremendous void in Sheila O'Day's life never healed, time had at least eased the most acute pain. It had been the same for Beth Ann Bushon.

Now that sense of peace was shredded. News reached Beth Ann that in early 2016 a judge would hold hearings to resentence Christopher Garza for the O'Day murder. That sent Beth Ann into a spiral of worry. Her long-dormant Post Traumatic Stress Disorder came back with a vengeance. The memories, the fear and the crushing guilt that she didn't do more tormented her. She had trouble sleeping. She started waking up at 2:30 AM, the exact time she remembers first hearing Christina O'Day's cries. She told a reporter later, "I relive it all, over and over" (Grace 2016).

Beth Ann wasn't the only one experiencing the tearing open of old emotional wounds. Sheila O'Day described to a reporter the emotional roller coaster surrounding Garza's resentencing, "It's been hard to come to terms over the years—the anger frustration, sorrow...I wish I knew her. It's like your child left 26 years ago and you never saw them again. I believe she's at peace, but I still don't know her. I wish I could, I wish I could" (Chiodo 2016).

Even twenty-six years after the murder, Sheila O'Day said that something as simple as a glimpse of red hair made her remember that her life has never been the same. "Her red hair; her hair was beautiful," she said. "After she was gone I would catch a glimpse of a woman with red hair and I'd have to stop and look and just think, 'oh yeah—never mind.'"

O'Day told a TV news reporter that "The Supreme Court decision was a shock when it happened.... The act that [Garza] committed was thought out—it wasn't random." She said that she can't stand to think her daughter's killer could get a chance at life because "Christina was cheated out of hers. I miss the fact she wasn't able to grow up, have an adult life—maybe get married, have kids. I miss that. I resent that. I resent that."

She said the resentment is as tough to subdue now as it was on the day of the crime. "It could have stopped. They could have left. They terrorized an eight-year-old little girl…that is way wrong." She added that she misses everything about her daughter, "Ya know it's been 26 years; I've had my other two kids around. I know them, I see them. I don't know Chris. I don't know what she's like now. I wish I did. That's what I miss. I miss not having her in my life" (Chiodo 2016).

Beth Ann was determined to do something. She knew she couldn't bring Chris back but she could protest the potential early release of her killer. She returned to Omaha to attend the resentencing. For Beth Ann, the prospect of Garza leaving prison before he died was "my worst nightmare come true." Beth Ann Bushon, now Beth Ann Tuerff and 34 years old, returned from Georgia where she lived to attend the sentencing. She said "it was a second chance at justice for Christina O'Day" (Grace 2016).

Tuerff told a TV reporter, "I mean I wake up in the middle of the night and I can relive it all. It's on my mind way more frequent than I would like to admit." In advance of the hearing Tuerff said, "I kind of feel like this is a gift from Chris. This will happen, be done again and I will move on with my life." Tuerff wanted to give voice to Chris's suffering and to her own. She wanted to move on. "I couldn't save her then," she said. "But testifying at the hearing is all I can do [to] make sure he spends the rest of his life in jail" (Chiodo 2016).

The hearing took place on Tuerff's 34th birthday. Though she was not able to testify she was allowed to read a statement to the court. At the hearing the emotions were as raw as they were back then. Tuerff, fighting back tears, read her statement with Sheila O'Day standing by her side. Tuerff said that 26 years later the crime still haunts her like it was yesterday. She said that Christina O'Day's family still suffers pain and anguish, as she does. She told the court that the resentencing had brought back her nightmares, fear, depression, and guilt. She urged the judge not to let Garza ever go free. "I couldn't save Christina that night," Tuerff said. "But I can do everything in my power to keep Mr. Garza where he belongs today." Garza, sitting mere feet away, turned red and hung his head as she spoke (Grace 2016).

The statement Beth Ann read in court included the following: "I am the eight-year-old little girl that was in the next bedroom while Christopher Garza tortured, raped, and murdered Christina O'Day. Twenty-five years later…[that night] still haunts me like it was yesterday. The fear, anger, sadness, depression, and guilt I have had to live with has consumed many years of my life. The nightmares, fear of being alone, fear that Garza would come after me, and guilt. Immense guilt: the guilt that I couldn't save her, guilt that I graduated high school and Christina never got to do so, guilt that I had a chance in life when she didn't because I didn't get up earlier and save her in time, the pain and guilt that I have felt for her family. These thoughts and feelings have led to years of major depression, post-traumatic stress disorder…many years of counseling and reliving this terrible tragedy…I am that terrified, innocent eight year old little girl who Christopher Garza shut in her bedroom after Christina began screaming. I couldn't save Christina that horrible night 25 years ago…." (Chiodo 2016).

Garza was resentenced to 96 to 110 years in prison in spite of Douglas County Attorney Don Kleine's request that the judge impose the maximum of life in prison without parole (Hammel 2018). By factoring in Nebraska's "Good Time Law" that effectively cut most sentences in half, and given credit for time already served, Garza would be eligible for parole in about 23 years. Garza, 42-years-old when resentenced, could be out of prison by age 65. His partner in crime, Wayne Brewer, was 18 when he participated in O'Day's rape-murder and is ineligible for resentencing. He continues to serve a life sentence without the possibility of parole. He will die in prison.

Following Garza's resentencing, Sheila O'Day faced the news media once again, "It's been hard to come to terms over the years—the anger, frustration, sorrow—but it's time to move on. I feel justice has been served." She added that the person who suffered the most was Beth Ann. "Of all of us she suffered the most I think. She had to relive this from eight years old—just a child—how do you process that?" (Grace 2016).

Chapter Nine
Henry Kamphaus Series
The Canyon Road Rapist

Being with a prostitute is like having a cup of coffee,
when you're done you throw it out.
Anonymous John

I was slightly more than a year away from retirement when a case more ominous than your run-of-the-mill rape case, if you can call it that, cropped up. Shortly after 3:30 AM on Wednesday, November 29, 2006, Thomas Matthews was awakened by a naked women screaming for help and beating on his front door. The house on Canyon Road sits back from the road in the heavily wooded Ponca Hills area just north of Omaha. When he got to the door, Matthews found 21-year-old Holly Black on his porch. She was mostly incoherent and had been badly beaten and raped.

Patrol deputies arrived quickly, followed shortly afterward by a rescue squad and paramedics from the Ponca Hills Volunteer Fire Department. Deputies tried to sort out what had happened as medics treated Black before transporting her to Methodist Hospital on Dodge Street. As she was treated for the sexual assault in the emergency room, Black regained her composure and told deputies what had happened.

She had been plying her trade as a prostitute working the stroll on Leavenworth Street at Park Avenue in downtown Omaha. Around 2:00 AM, a "John," later identified in the course of this investigation as Henry Kamphaus, pulled up in a white minivan. Thinking he might be an undercover cop, Black was initially hesitant to transact a deal. The closer she looked at him the more she was convinced he was not a cop. He appeared to be in his thirties, heavyset with strange eyes. She walked up to the passenger side of his van and leaned in, "You lookin' for a date?" she asked.

Kamphaus responded, "How much for 'half and half'?" The term "half and half" is street lingo meaning he wants to pay for vaginal intercourse and oral sex.

Black replied, "$100 for more than you can handle, hon."

The driver fumbled for his wallet. "I got $25, how 'bout it?"

Black sized up the driver. He was pudgy in his thirties with closely cropped hair and a short goatee. He was smoking Marlboro cigarettes. Up close, it was even more apparent that there was something weird with his eyes. She looked closer in the dimly lit interior of the van and finally figured out what was wrong—he was cross-eyed. She also noticed that he had a nickel-sized mole near his right ear. He said his name was "DJ."

"Not enough," she replied. "Gotta do better than that for a good time."

"C'mon," Kamphaus replied. "Maybe I can come up with $50."

"That'll buy you a straight," Black replied, lighting a cigarette and casually blowing the smoke into the van as she continued to lean into the window. "Straight" is street lingo for a straight lay referring to basic sexual intercourse. She glanced up and down the street to be sure the cops weren't nearby.

"I got $75. That's all I have. Now how 'bout it?" Kamphaus asked as he pulled out some twenty dollar bills and waved them at her.

"Okay," Black replied as she hopped into the passenger seat. "Pull over there," she said, pointing to the deserted parking lot of a nearby grocery store.

"I got a fantasy place...wanna do it outdoors," he replied as he headed north on Park Avenue until he got to Douglas Street where he turned east to 28th Street. Once there he turned north and entered the North Freeway at the interchange with the 480 freeway just south of Creighton University campus. He continued northbound until the freeway merged with North 30th Street just south of Fort Street.

By now Black was getting nervous. "Where you takin' me?" she asked. Kamphaus looked at her calmly, "I got a perfect place in mind. Not far from here." As they continued to drive northbound her fear increased. She thought about jumping out of the van as they drove past Miller Park but reconsidered because he hadn't done anything overtly threatening yet. And it had been a slow night and she needed the money.

Pimps are vicious, unrelenting parasites who demand that their hookers meet a dollar quota each night or face a beating. If they fail one night the deficit is added to the next night's quota. As they continued northbound and got farther and farther out of the city Black started to panic. Her survival instincts were beginning to kick in as her fear of being murdered began to override her fear of her pimp.

When they stopped for a traffic light at McKinley Street she tried to open the door but fumbled in the dark with the unfamiliar locking mechanism. Kamphaus reached over suddenly and grabbed her by the hair, yanking her violently towards him. He grabbed a large bladed knife from between the seats and pressed the blade to her neck, "If you do as I say you won't get hurt. If you don't…I'll kill you."

"Okay, Okay, I won't do nothin'," she responded as he released her hair. She sat upright in the seat and began to weigh her options. There weren't many, at least not many good ones. They continued northbound, passing under Interstate 680 where 30th Street ended and North 31st Street began. They were now in the secluded, rolling, heavily wooded Ponca Hills. Black was completely lost having never been in the area before. She noticed that the houses were now farther and farther apart as they left the congestion of the city behind.

The pavement and the street lights ended as they passed Rainwood Road as 31st Street changed to Canyon Road. Ominously, the trees lining the unpaved road blocked out even the scant moonlight of the overcast night. The area was dark and desolate in the early morning stillness. By now Black was in a full panic. She was sobbing and near hyperventilating as she feared what he would do to her isolated in the dismal emptiness of the unfamiliar and menacing area.

As they continued northbound they passed a driveway. Black noticed that there appeared to be a house set back off the road. She could make out lights barely visible through the thick growth of trees and underbrush. They continued for another block or so, then Kamphaus pulled off the road just around a bend. He grabbed Black by the hair and brandished the knife again. "Get out. This way," he ordered as he yanked her hair roughly, dragging her over the console between the seats and out of the driver's door. She lost her footing and fell to the ground as he violently pulled her from the van. She started to scream as he pulled her to her feet by her hair and then began to punch her in the face and breasts.

He grabbed her by the throat, "Shut up or I'll cut your throat," he said as he began to push her off the roadway and into the brush. There he ordered her to disrobe and kneel. Once completely naked and on her knees he pulled down his pants and ordered her to "suck my cock," as he held the knife to her throat. Black begged for her life, "Please. Please, I'll do it all, just don't kill me."

"Shut up and suck it," Kamphaus ordered as he put the knife in his back pocket and pulled out a pair of pliers. "I'm going to pull your tits off," he said in a strangely calm voice as he reached down and cupped one of her breasts in his hand. Black screamed and started to stand up, forcing him to drop the pliers and use both hands to subdue her. He threw her on the ground face-down and began to punch and kick her. He then raped her vaginally for a while as she lay writhing face-down in the dirt. To keep him from beating her she tried to comply with what he was doing while her mind raced, desperately thinking about how to escape.

Black sensed a chance to get away when he withdrew himself from her vagina and leaned over, apparently looking in the dark for the dropped pliers. While he was momentarily preoccupied she bolted for the road. In the darkness, she stumbled on the uneven terrain and nearly fell, screaming for help as she ran. Afraid to look back, she headed for the driveway about a block away that she had noticed earlier, screaming hysterically as she scrambled naked and bruised along the dark roadway.

Climbing over a low hedge adjacent to the gated drive, she raced up the driveway to the front door of the house where she screamed for help while frantically beating with both fists on the door. It was the home of

Tom and Deborah Matthews on Canyon Road. In his call to 911 Tom Matthews told dispatchers that there was a naked and "badly beaten and very incoherent" woman at his front door claiming she had been raped (WOWT 2007a).

Meanwhile her attacker panicked after she bolted. He tried to run after her but quickly realized that he didn't want to risk chasing a naked screaming woman down the road fearing that a passerby might happen upon them or a resident might hear the commotion and call the police. Kamphaus quickly gathered up her clothing and got in the van, driving northbound on Canyon Road. By the time Black had reached the front door of the Matthews' home the perp had already vanished.

Violence and prostitution go hand in hand. In many ways, prostitutes are the perfect victims for serial rapists. The covert nature of the sex-for-money transaction requires that prostitutes go with the John to a secluded place away from the initial encounter. It is a convenient means of ensuring that the rapist has a compliant victim under his control before departing the area where witnesses may be present and then transporting the victim to another location with no witnesses where he can rape her—or worse—without interruption.

Prostitutes also make easy targets and rapists targeting prostitutes often strike again because the attacks usually go unreported. Most prostitutes are reluctant to report a rape because it reveals that they were breaking the law prostituting themselves. When rapes do get reported, usually because the victim has been beaten so severely she requires hospitalization and hospitals are required by law to report such violence to police, responding officers are often reluctant to handle the case the same way they handle rape reports from "innocent" rape victims.

The pernicious attitude of some police officers towards prostitute victims holds that they somehow deserve it or can't be raped because they sell their bodies for money. This attitude has been stubbornly resistant to change. As recently as 1991, police in a southern California community closed all rape reports made by prostitutes by placing them in a file stamped "NHI," an abbreviation for "No Human Involved" (Farley 2012:1). In 2009, prosecutors in Detroit, MI began to wade through a backlog of more than 11,300 unprocessed rape kits that were found in a police storage warehouse (Shamus 2017). Eight years later they found that nearly 1,000 serial rapists had assaulted multiple victims, some a dozen or more, and were never charged. They estimated that it would take at least another three years to process the remaining rape kits. Michigan State law requires a 90-day turnaround time on rape kits. Obviously that was not happening in Detroit.

The problem is not restricted to Detroit, however. There are an estimated 400,000 untested rape kits in the country. As one prosecutor involved in the Michigan backlog noted, only a small minority of rape victims file a report: "I think nationally the number is about 20 percent of rapes…that means there is much more sexual assault going on, that it's much more pervasive than people think" (Shamus 2017).

The prosecutor also said the mindset of police investigators is also something that must change. Specifically, the callous disregard of victimization must cease: "We reviewed many, many police reports where the officers dismissed (victims) because they didn't act the way they thought they should act.… They just closed cases, even cases where I think they believed the victim.… They closed cases because the women had worked as prostitutes or had mental illness issues or had substance abuse. Didn't believe them, didn't care, and this was one issue that led to the backlog of these kits."

Another prosecutor believes racism may have played a role in the Detroit debacle. "I can use Detroit as an example, 86 percent of our victims in these untested kits are people of color. You're not going to find too many blonde-haired, blue eyed white women…because their kits are treated differently, their cases are solved.… If you're a person of color, if you're a different economic class, then your case across the board…not just sexual assault—they're treated differently" (Shamus 2017).

The Detroit scandal also revealed that the impact of ignoring rapes is not confined to that jurisdiction alone. Once prosecutors got the rape kits into FBI's CODIS, the national Combined DNA Index System database, they found that serial rapists had committed crimes ranging from burglary to homicide in at least 39 other states. The frustrated prosecutor noted, "No one would be saying this, and you wouldn't even have to ask that question, if we were talking about homicides.… Because it's sexual assault, for whatever reason, it's very easy for some folks to sweep this under the rug" (Shamus 2017).

And it isn't just the police. In March 2017, a Canadian judge was forced to resign after he blamed a rape victim for not avoiding the assault during a 2014 rape trial. Justice Robin Camp asked the alleged victim why she didn't keep her "knees together" during the sexual attack that occurred to the then 19-year-old woman on a bathroom sink in 2011. "Why didn't you just sink your bottom down into the basin so he couldn't penetrate you?" Camp asked the woman during the trial. "And when your ankles were held together by your jeans, your skinny jeans, why couldn't you just keep your knees together?" Camp also incorrectly called the woman the "accused" more than once during the trial and he even told her that "pain and sex sometimes go together." The man accused of rape was ultimately found not guilty (Guardian 2017).

In another rape by Kamphaus that occurred around the time of the Black case, Omaha Police officers refused to take a report from the victim because she was a prostitute (Devin 2007). As in the Black case the victim had been badly beaten. She had been driven to the hospital by a passerby who found her stumbling dazed and incoherent along the street after she had jumped out of Kamphaus' van. Following state law, the hospital notified the police that they were treating a potential rape victim who had been badly beaten up. Responding officers justified their refusal to take a report claiming that the victim was intoxicated and gave conflicting details about what happened (Detective T. Walter, personal communication, 2007).

Researchers have discovered what most cops know from street observation: violence is endemic in prostitution. Rape, battering, and torture are points on a continuum of violence that occur regularly in prostitution. A study of 200 prostitutes in San Francisco found that 70 percent had been raped (Farley 1998:39). Researchers found that prostitutes are raped on average eight to ten times per year. As one researcher described it, "They are the most raped class of women in the history of our planet" (Hunter 1990).

The violence endemic to hooking does not always stop at rape. A sex buyer explained that in prostitution, "she gives up the right to say no." Another "John," or customer, told researchers that he clarifies the nature of his relationship to the women he buys: "I paid for this. You have no rights. You're with me now" (Ending Exploitation n.d.). A Canadian report on prostitution and pornography concluded that girls and women in prostitution have a death rate forty times higher than the death rate for all women in Canada (Farley 2017).

Ignoring rapes of prostitutes is shortsighted on three levels. First, no woman is beneath the protection of the law. Unlike the glamorous Hollywood portrayals of prostitution, most famously in movies such as "Pretty Woman," most prostitutes of the street walker variety do not sell their bodies for large sums of cash to handsome, high-class clients on satin sheets in five-star hotels. Most of them are addicted to drugs and many are forced into prostitution against their will by violent pimps. Studies show that sexual abuse during childhood is another common denominator (PCAR 2013:2). The reality of the sordid, seedy, and violent nature of street-walker life destroys the myth of prostitution that underpins the view that it is a victimless crime. To disregard the rape of a prostitute is to demean the sexual abuse of all women.

In addition, rapists targeting prostitutes often attack women who are not prostitutes. Many rapists are opportunists who target victims based on access and vulnerability. Some are highly attuned predators are capable of spotting signs of weakness and vulnerability from often subtle behavior and demeanor cues such as posture, walking style, even facial expressions and lack of awareness of surroundings.

In a classic 1981 study, known as the Grayson/ Stein Study, researchers Betty Grayson and Morris Stein asked convicted criminals to view a video of pedestrians walking down a busy New York City sidewalk unaware they were being taped. The convicts had been to prison for violent offenses such as armed robbery, rape, and murder. Within a few seconds they nearly unanimously identified which pedestrians they would have targeted (Grayson 1981:69). Their choices were not based on gender, race, or age. Some petite, physically slight women were not selected as potential victims while some large men were. What the researchers found was that the criminals were assessing the ease with which they could overpower the targets based on nonverbal signals such as posture, body language, pace of walking, length of stride, and environmental awareness.

The researchers analyzed the body language of the people on the tape and identified several aspects of demeanor that marked potential victims as easy marks. One of the main precipitators is a walking style that lacks "interactional synchrony" and "wholeness." Perpetrators notice a person whose walk lacks organized movement and flowing motion. Criminals view such people as less self-confident perhaps because their walk suggests they are less athletic and fit. As a consequence criminals are much more likely to exploit them. Like predators in the wild, violent criminals often attack the slowest in the herd. People who drag their feet, shuffle along, or exhibit other unusual gaits are targeted more often than people who walk quickly and fluidly.

It is important to remember that rape is motivated less by sex and more by the desire for control and power. Sexual predators look for people they can easily overpower. As one researcher described it, "The rapist is going to go after somebody who's not paying attention, who looks like they're not going to put up a fight, who is in a location that's going to make this more convenient" (Hustmyre 2009).

Drinking and drug use also mark a person as a potential victim. Most cops know that it is a robber's dream to "roll a drunk" and take what they want because a drunk is incapable of effectively protecting himself. Drug and alcohol intoxication dulls awareness of one's surroundings and blunts survival instincts and the ability to spot approaching trouble. It also leads people to place themselves in dangerous situations by decreasing their ability to evaluate the consequences of their actions and distorting their ability to predict how others perceive them. It's like wearing a giant flashing "Rob Me" sign.

The Detroit rape kit processing scandal described above highlights the dangers of ignoring the rapes of prostitutes and other victims. The Detroit cases were ignored largely because police officers felt the women didn't act the way they thought stereotypical rape victims should act.

Another reason ignoring rapes of prostitutes is shortsighted is that some rapists targeting prostitutes are the rarest but most dangerous rapist type. The rapist's actions in the Holly Black case were more ominous than less violent serial rapists because they suggested that the perp was an Anger Excitation Rapist (AER). As previously described, the AER is by far the most dangerous type. He is often referred to as a sadistic rapist. As the rarest type of offender AERs commit less than five percent of all rapes. However their violence towards their victims eclipses the impact of their low numbers.

The typical AER wants to inflict emotional and physical pain and is sexually aroused by the pain and suffering of his victims. Legendary FBI Agent Roy Hazelwood describes the AER: "He's the predator of all predators when it comes to rapists.... He's the most meticulous" (Dietz 1990:163). In spite of their rarity, rapes committed by AERs often generate sensational headlines because of the bizarre and extremely savage nature of the attacks. The AER uses ritualism, bondage, or other acts of sexual sadism. His targets are vulnerable women whom he can control. The AER is aroused by their suffering, particularly if they struggle to escape. A noted researcher described this type of offender, "He's a sexual sadist. He's punishing women because he believes them to be evil and powerful, so he's trying to take away that power. He has deep and complex fantasies" (Dietz 1990:163). The physical injury inflicted during the torture is often so prolonged and severe that the victim dies.

The typical AER puts a great deal of planning and forethought into his attacks. He stalks his victims by car, prowling well outside his normal areas of operation like his home or work. He often carries a "rape kit" with all his needed tools, such as duct tape, scissors, bindings, ice packs, dildos, a ski mask, pantyhose, etc. His intent is to degrade, torture, and kill. It's the only way he can get sexual satisfaction.

His psycho-social background often includes being raised in a single parent household and suffering from physical and sexual abuse. He's most likely intelligent, often educated, and usually has no arrest record. Because of the elaborate planning, AERs avoid the haphazard nature of less well-planned rapes that often trip up more spontaneous rapists (Pinnizotto 1998).

The more experienced AER takes his victims to an area prepared in advance where he can have complete control and seclusion to take his time while torturing and raping them. Typical of such preplanning were the actions of serial killer duo Charles Ng and Leonard Lake. In the mid-1980s, they transformed a remote cabin near Wilseyville, California east of San Francisco into a rape, torture, murder and corpse disposal factory for as many as 25 victims (Welborn 2011). The master bedroom in the cabin held a four-poster bed that had electrical cords tied to each of its posts. Bolted through the floor at each corner were heavy eyebolts and above it a 250-watt floodlight had been fastened to the wall. Its mattresses were heavily stained with dried blood from multiple victims.

The property also contained an incinerator with thick fireproof walls capable of withstanding extreme temperatures like those necessary to turn human bones into ash. They built a torture chamber they called the "dungeon" next to the cabin. It was filled with hand and power tools, many encrusted with dried blood, used to torture, murder and dismember their victims (Greig 2005:132). The dungeon was a well-prepared soundproof torture chamber containing several hidden rooms and disguised movable walls, with two-way mirrors to observe their captives.

One hidden room, described by detectives as a "hostage cell," was absolutely dark with even the air ventilation holes modified so that no light entered it. It was reminiscent of the terrifying scenes of rookie FBI agent Clarice Starling, played by Jodie Foster, being stalked by serial killer Buffalo Bill wearing night vision goggles in his blacked out basement in the movie "The Silence of the Lambs." The utter darkness of the room hints at the sadistic impulses of Lake and Ng who used a night vision rifle scope to view their captives through a two-way mirror. Few things elevate fear more than helplessness in utter darkness. That is why so many AERs blindfold their victims, to intensify their fear and suffering, which then feeds the AER's sadistic impulses.

Some AERs are so adept at their crimes they have kept victims bound for days or weeks, torturing and raping them at will. Todd Kohlhepp, a 45-year-old registered sex offender, bought a 95-acre property near Woodruff, South Carolina and paid $80,000 to have a six foot high chain-link fence installed around it. He also bought several shipping containers and had them delivered to the property. In October, 2004, detectives were brought to the property when tracing the last known cell phone signal of a couple reported missing since August. There they found 32-year-old Kala Brown chained inside one of the shipping containers (48 Hours 2016).

One detective described her as "chained up like a dog." The body of her boyfriend, Charlie Carver, was found in a shallow grave nearby. The couple had disappeared when the woman went to do some cleaning on Kohlhepp's property. Her boyfriend accompanied her. She told investigators that Kohlhepp shot and killed her boyfriend in front of her. "He didn't want to kill me, he wanted to keep me," Brown said. Kohlhepp confessed to killing at least seven people. Brown told detectives that Kohlhepp bound her by her ankles, wrists and neck and sexually assaulted her over several weeks (48 Hours 2016).

The AER often tells his victims exactly what he plans to do to them in order to increase their fear. It's not the injury that excites him; the fear the victim experiences is what satiates his evil desire. Many AERs are very ritualistic, planning every detail of the abduction, torture, rape, murder, and disposal of the body—if he has become a killer at this point.

While not all AERs will progress to lust murder, some must engage in ever-increasing levels of sadistic torture to feed their evil desire. Lust murder is the term coined by FBI Agents Roy Hazelwood and John Douglas in an April 1980 article in the FBI Law Enforcement Bulletin

(Hazelwood 1980:9). It refers to fantasy-driven sadistic torture and mutilation murders committed by serial murderers like Ted Bundy, Jeffrey Dahmer, and John Wayne Gacy. The natural outcome of that escalation is murder, the ultimate form of domination and control over a human being. Everything has to go according to script down to the last detail, including having the victim say specific things in order for the rapist to obtain sexual satisfaction. Typically the AER's victim will be lucky to get away with her life.

Serial killer Rodney James Alcala, known the "Dating Game Killer" because of his 1978 appearance on the television show "The Dating Game" in the midst of his murder spree, is estimated to have raped, tortured and murdered as many as 130 women from California to New York (Gardner 2010). Investigators say that Alcala sadistically toyed with his victims by strangling them until they lost consciousness, then waiting until they revived, repeating the process several times before finally killing them. In that way he prolonged his sexual arousal stemming from the fear and suffering and the ultimate form of domination and control over the life and death of another human being.

The AER may have a wife or girlfriend with low self-esteem who actively participates in abducting victims. They will even go so far as raping and torturing them to please him. An infamous example is Gerald Gallego, one of Sacramento's most notorious killers. Gallego was a classic sexual sadist (Christensen n.d.). He used his wife as a lure to help him kidnap and murder nine women in his quest for the perfect "sex slave," often mentally torturing his victims by having them watch their friends be raped and murdered as they awaited the same fate.

❧

At approximately 3:45 AM on April 19th, 2007, the Matthews home on Canyon Road was again the scene of a naked prostitute banging on the front door screaming for help. The victim this time was 23-year-old Rose Riva. Like Holly Black the preceding November, Riva had been working the stroll when she was picked up by a John and driven to Canyon Road. He had the same physical description as Black's attacker. Following the same script he used with Black, Riva's rapist threatened her with a knife, dragged her from the van by her hair and slapped her around before forcing her to undress. He then raped her both vaginally and orally.

This time the rapist produced a vibrating dildo while raping Riva and used it to torture her as she lay naked and writhing in the dirt. He used the dildo to roughly violate her vaginally. Like with Black, he also said to Riva that he was going to "pull your tits off." When he dropped the knife and struggled to find it in the dark, Riva bolted and fled running naked to the Matthews home.

Counting the rape of the prostitute that Omaha Police officers refused to investigate, the Canyon Road rapist was now up to at least three victims. In addition to his increasing toll, the introduction of the dildo marked an ominous escalation in the level of violence and underscored the sadistic urges that typify an AER. The use of a vibrator was clearly not for the sexual pleasure of the victim. It was used to demean, degrade, and inflict sexualized pain and suffering..

As Criminal Investigation Bureau Commander I seldom had the time to review every report coming in for investigative follow up. I relied on my sergeants and lieutenant to give me a heads up on unique or most serious or high profile crimes so that I could inform the sheriff and chief deputy. The news media often went over reports looking for stories and to interview victims and witnesses for the human angle to crimes. The last thing I wanted was for a reporter to call the sheriff to interview him about a crime he was unaware of. Getting blindsided by the media is never a pleasant experience.

When both the day Sergeant Matt Martin and the bureau Lieutenant Steve Glandt asked to speak to me one morning I knew something was up. They proceeded to give me an overview of the Holly Black rape and were concerned that we were dealing with the type of rapist violence they had not seen before. As they laid out the details of the rape I began to share their concern. Black's rapist appeared to be an Anger Excitation Rapist (AER). His threatening to pull off Black's breasts exhibited his sexual sadism—the hallmark of this type of rapist.

The AER may be the rarest type of rapist statistically but they are serial predators who are notorious for their cruelty to their victims, which can easily rise to homicidal levels as the rapist needs ever increasing levels of sadistic torture to satisfy their evil desire. The fact that the victim was a prostitute also raised my concern because they are society's disposable victims. Many AERs target hookers because the cash-for-sex transaction is tailor-made for their needs. The strongly fantasy-based nature of prostitution plays directly into the psycho-emotional needs and desires of an Anger Excitation Rapist.

Serial killer Gary Ridgway is a notorious example of an AER who preyed on prostitutes. He is known as the Green River Killer after the river where many of his "victims" bodies were dumped. He murdered woman and girls, many of them prostitutes, in and around Washington State during the 1980s and 1990s, often dumping their bodies in the Green River near Seattle and rural King County. He was convicted of 48 murders but confessed to twice that number after his arrest. Ridgway intentionally targeted women he knew the police wouldn't get too worked up about. He said, "I picked prostitutes because I thought I could kill as many of them as I wanted without getting caught" (Lee 2018:48).

Going over the crime reports after the Riva rape, I was alarmed. Not only did we have a serial rapist but he appeared to be an "increaser"—a rapist who continually ups the ante on each successive rape. It is estimated that increasers comprise less than 25 percent of all rapists (Pinnizotto 1998). However, they commit substantially more rapes with a shorter time period between them than non-increasers. The FBI found that non-increaser rapists they studied averaged 22 rapes before capture and raped on an average of every 55 days. Increasers averaged 40 victims and raped every 19 days (Pinnizotto 1998). More ominous, increasers also escalate the level of violence in each attack.

The FBI identified five crime scene behaviors common to increaser rapists: (1) no negotiation with the victim; (2) lack of victim reassurance; (3) use of bindings; (4) transportation of the victim from the encounter site; (5) macho offender image (Pinnizotto 1998). The Canyon Road rapist exhibited three of the behaviors. He didn't negotiate with his victims like a Power Reassurance Rapist might do. He simply produced a knife and used force or threats to gain compliance with his demands. Unlike some rapist types, especially the Power Reassurance Rapist, he didn't try to reassure his victims about their comfort or safety during the attack. And unlike many rapes that occur near or at the spot where the victim is first encountered, like a woman accosted while asleep in her home or a woman grabbed off a jogging trail and raped in the brush nearby, the Canyon Road rapist transported all of his victims from the location where he first encountered them miles away to the seclusion of Canyon Road where the attacks took place.

We were dealing not only with the rarest of the four types of rapists, we were also dealing with a rarity among AERs. The increaser factor, added to the Anger Excitation Rapist type, foreshadowed the potential of life-threatening levels of sexual torture in subsequent rapes. There was a sense of urgency when I spoke with my command staff and discussed setting up surveillance on the prostitute strolls downtown and in the Canyon Road area. The manpower demands would be extensive and draining so I called my undercover narcotics sergeant to have him clear his calendar for a couple of weeks to assist in the operation. It would take detectives from both narcotics and the criminal side to get the job done because we would have to watch two and possibly three locations. The most probable spot was Canyon Road. It was the common denominator in each rape. But in case the rapist changed his preferred location we also had to cover other stroll locations in and around downtown.

It was assumed that since the Omaha Police were adamant that no crime had occurred in the case of the prostitute victim they had blatantly refused to investigate they would be unwilling to participate in the surveillance even though it was in the heart of their jurisdiction. That fact was bolstered by my detective working Sex Offender Monitoring. He had spoken with other Omaha detectives about the growing number of victims picked up on the stroll and taken to Canyon Road (Detective T. Walter, personal communication, 2007). They voiced the opinion of their superiors that any prostitute crying rape wasn't worthy of their time. We were on our own.

The pushback was immediate. My sergeant in investigations was worried about pending cases that our overworked detectives would have to shelve during the operation or pile onto a small number of already stretched-thin investigators who would be holding the fort while other detectives conducted this investigation. The undercovers working narcotics were assigned to a task force. They also had cases in the pipeline that would have to be put on hold. Taking them away from their other duties also meant they would not be available to assist other agencies in the task force, which often meant acting as essential backup during raids and other operations.

All objections vanished three days later on April 22nd when 23-year-old Courtney Griffin, a prostitute who had been picked up on the stroll downtown, was forced to strip at knifepoint before being raped vaginally and orally. Like the other Canyon Road rapes, she was abused with a dildo and threatened with a knife and a pair of pliers before escaping and running naked to a nearby home for help. In true increaser form the frequency of rapes was rising.

As we worked out the logistics of setting up the surveillance, the Canyon Road rapist struck again. As mentioned before, rapists targeting prostitutes often attack women who are not prostitutes. Approximately 11:00 PM the night of Sunday, April 29th, 2007, 22-year-old Tiffany VanCleeve attended a party at a friend's house near 45th and Saratoga. Around 4:00 the next morning she left the party to walk to her parents' home on William Street. As she walked along the nearly deserted early morning streets she passed by the park-like campus of Omaha Better Together on the southwest corner of 42nd and Bedford Street. A 1990s burgundy-colored van pulled abreast of her as she walked south on 42nd Street. The driver lowered the passenger side window and asked her if she needed a ride. VanCleeve, under the influence of drugs and alcohol after a heavy night of drinking and using heroin, agreed and got into the van.

She didn't recognize the driver and said later that she felt that he was not from the neighborhood. She described him as a short, heavyset white male with close-cropped hair, a partial goatee on the chin only, with "crazy eyes" that were cross-eyed. He said his name was "DJ" and as they pulled away from the curb he asked VanCleeve if she wanted to "smoke some meth." He claimed it was in his house and he wanted to smoke it with her. He was trying to put her at ease by offering drugs to an obvious addict. By enticing her to go to his house for drugs he was using a con approach to disguise his abduction of her so she would not become alarmed as he drove her to the secluded Canyon Road.

Unlike his other victims VanCleeve was not a prostitute he could keep calm as he drove to the site of the rape by claiming he had "a special place in mind" for the sex act. The desire for the money kept most hookers calm and accepting as he drove out of the city. For VanCleeve he resorted to enticing her with drugs. She declined the meth but asked if she could stop at a gas station and get some water. Continuing the con approach out of fear over losing control over his prey if she got out at a gas station, he offered her a drink from a convenience store-type cup with an unknown liquid in it instead. VanCleeve later reported it tasted musty and old, as if it had been sitting in the cup for some time. In her drug-addled state, she drank some of it anyway.

The driver told VanCleeve that he was a suspended driver, had picked up prostitutes twice before and had been in jail. He offered her a cigarette as they proceeded North on 30th Street. As she took it she noticed that he smoked Marlboros. Her senses dulled by alcohol and drugs, VanCleeve didn't realize initially that he was headed in the opposite direction from her home. When she realized it she became concerned and asked where he was headed. He replied that "had to do something real quick" and he would soon be taking her home.

The realization that he was going away from her home raised her awareness of impending danger at least somewhat. Through the alcohol and drug haze she began to study the driver. That was when she saw the large knife with a 6-inch blade and a black handle resting on his lap. VanCleeve later said he became nervous and fidgety as they drove to a remote location on a gravel road she identified as Canyon Road. He then pulled over and put the knife to her throat and ordered her to get out.

VanCleeve described the scene has having a small mound a few feet off the roadway which led to a steep ravine down the other side. He ordered her to undress but got impatient as she stalled and he started to unbutton her top with one hand while holding the knife to her throat with the other. He then pushed her to the ground and she landed on her knees. He continued to hold the knife in his right hand, threatening her as VanCleeve begged him to use a condom. He pulled one out of his pocket and told her to put it on him. She refused so he tried with one hand while still holding the knife but he was unable to put it on. Aggravated, he ripped if off angrily and threw it on the ground. He then vaginally assaulted her from behind as she was on all fours in the dirt before ordering her at knifepoint to orally copulate him. He alternated several times between raping her vaginally from behind and forcing her to orally copulate him.

VanCleeve said that eventually he ejaculated onto her back and her clothing after raping her vaginally. After ejaculating he began to strike VanCleeve with his left hand while holding the knife in his right hand. Fearing that he might start cutting her with the knife, she waited for a chance to escape. He tried to swing his left hand and arm to strike her again but missed as she ducked the blow while still on all fours. The miss caused him to slip and lose his footing. As he stumbled awkwardly down the hill towards the ravine, VanCleeve seized the opportunity and stood up quickly, gathered her clothing, and began to run down the road southbound while screaming for help. The suspect started to chase her but quickly gave up and ran back to his van and drove away in the opposite direction.

VanCleeve ran screaming and clutching her clothes to the closest house. It was again the Matthews' home on Canyon Road. She headed to the front door and began pounding on it while screaming for help. Matthews later told reporters, "We come out looking for her, could not find her, and of course we'd called 911 right away and [deputies] were out here. Well, she happened to go up to our neighbors" (WOWT 2007a).

When she received no immediate response at the Matthews home, and still fearing that her attacker was coming after her, VanCleeve ran to the next house. She ended up at the front door of the James and Jacquelin Dahlin residence also on Canyon Road. There she again frantically pounded on the door while screaming for help. When Jim Dahlin answered, she begged him to help her and to call the police.

Most rapists are opportunists who target victims based on access, vulnerability, and exploitability. Chronic drug or alcohol abuse increases the vulnerability of a potential victim by dulling their senses and clouding their judgment. Although not a prostitute, Tiffany VanCleeve was a chronic alcohol and drug abuser. She had recently moved back to Omaha from Minneapolis to live with her parents. Her mother, Linda Hendrickson, told detectives that VanCleeve lived with them but had not been at the house for three or four weeks. She said it was not unusual for her to disappear for weeks at a time when using drugs. Her stunted sense of danger and lack of awareness of her surroundings, combined with the Canyon Road rapist's predatory instincts to spot a vulnerable woman, converged on April 30th, leading to her assault.

VanCleeve was treated at the ER of Methodist Hospital. Detective Mary Burmeister was notified by patrol deputies and interviewed VanCleeve, who was coming down from the drug high and was very sleepy and groggy. Burmeister later said that VanCleeve fell asleep during the interview and had to be woken up several times to complete it.

The next day Burmeister, assisted by Detective Jen Tinsely, returned VanCleeve to Canyon Road to search for the spot where the rape had occurred. She got out and walked north along the east side of the road and found a place where she said she believed the suspect parked the van. Burmeister and Tinsley found the mound close by. Lying on the ground nearby was a blue condom wrapper torn in half. While searching further they found the discarded condom. The Crime Scene Investigation Division was called, and they photographed and retrieved the items for processing.

After the VanCleeve rape I ordered that a stakeout begin immediately on the Park Avenue stroll, other strolls downtown and on Canyon Road. The operation would begin at 10:00 PM and end at 6:00 AM. Two detectives set up surveillance of the strolls downtown alternating with other locations where hookers were trolling for customers. Two other detectives set up at the southern end of Canyon Road. Nine days later, on Wednesday May 9th, they struck pay dirt. At approximately 2:15 AM Detectives Jay Wineinger and Joe Mainelli of the Narcotics Division were parked on Rainwood Road watching North 31st where it turns into Canyon Road when a dark colored Kia minivan drove by. They noticed that it had Nebraska license plates OYR-239. In the dimly lit area they were unable to see clearly who was inside. When they ran the registration it came back expired to a residence near 50th and Bancroft located on the other side of town.

They began to follow the vehicle as it proceeded northbound on Canyon Road. It turned westbound on Ponca Road before turning southbound on Calhoun Road to 31st Street where it turned northbound on 31st towards Canyon Road again for about four or five blocks. Before reaching Canyon Road it abruptly turned into a residence on the west side of 31st Street, backed out after about 30 seconds, and drove southbound on 31st Street towards Interstate 680. It entered Westbound 680 at 30th street while Mainelli and Wineinger radioed for a marked patrol cruiser to stop the vehicle. The detectives continued to follow the minivan when it exited onto southbound 72nd street until it turned into a gas station at Military Avenue where a patrol vehicle arrived and initiated a traffic stop in the parking lot.

The driver identified himself as Henry Kamphaus. The passenger identified herself as 30-year-old Kaylynn Kirsh. As described by prior victims, Kamphaus had a nickel-sized mole on his right cheek near his ear. He was extremely nervous with sweat forming on his forehead and his hands shaking as he sat in the van. When initially confronted by deputies, Kirsh said they were coming from a friend's house in the 3000 block of Jackson Street. She claimed that she had asked Kamphaus for a ride to her apartment near 108th and Fort Street.

Still denying that she was engaged in prostitution, Kirsh said she didn't know the driver's name. She finally admitted that after she got in the van he offered her $100 for sex. She claimed that he was not specific about what type of sex act he wanted and she asked him to touch her breast to prove he was not a cop. After Kamphaus complied he told Kirsh that his name was DJ and he claimed to be a pharmaceutical rep. She got nervous the farther they drove out of the city and asked Kamphaus where they were going. He replied that he wanted to have sex outdoors and had a specific place in mind. As she began to panic and pester him with questions, Kamphaus became increasingly agitated and said that they would go to his house that he claimed was in the Ponca area. Kirsh said that Kamphaus noticed a vehicle following them and began accusing her of setting him up and working with the police. He then promised to take her to an ATM machine to get money to pay her.

Like all rapists, the AER is good at hiding his predatory side. He exhibits few if any outward signs of his sexual offending. An interview with a former coworker and friend of Kamphaus reveals how effective AERs are at hiding their dark side. D.J. Yechout worked with Kamphaus at a lawn care service in the Ponca Hills area, the same area where four of his victims were raped. It is interesting that Kamphaus used "DJ" as his alias when stalking hookers. According to Yechout, "I always knew Henry as a really nice guy, one of the nicest guys you would ever meet" (WOWT 2007b). Yechout says

Kamphaus hit bottom two years before the rapes began. His mother died and he fell into money troubles.

"I helped this guy out a lot," Yechout said. "I mean the guy owes me a lot of money but he was a friend." They shared an apartment for a year in the same complex where Kamphaus lived with his brother at the time of his arrest. When Kamphaus ran down on his luck, Yechout even invited Kamphaus to move in with his family including three small children. "When I would be working, he would be in the house with my family alone, you know. Who only knows what could happen to them at the time," Yechout said (WOWT 2007b).

Not everyone was as trusting of Kamphaus. Even as Yechout befriended this man down on his luck, others would avoid him. According to Yechout, "People would look at Henry and think he was creepy." Yechout eventually kicked Kamphaus out of his home for messy housekeeping. That was just a few weeks after the first rape. The two haven't spoken since (WOWT 2007b).

Henry Kamphaus hadn't progressed to levels of extreme violence typical of some AERs. Perhaps his sadistic fantasies did not rise to the level of lust murder. Or maybe he lacked the patience, intelligence or criminal sophistication necessary to preplan kidnapping a hooker and holding her hostage to torture and rape her repeatedly before murdering her. He certainly lacked the financial resources to have a secluded place accessible to take his victims for prolonged rape and torture. It is obvious that he had trouble controlling his victims during the rapes, leading most of them to escape his grasp in the middle of the assault. Perhaps his clumsiness, combined with a lack of intelligence and a lack of financial resources, hampered his ability to act on his sadistic urges beyond the crude inept violence displayed.

Sheriff Tim Dunning held a press conference a few days after the arrest. In addition to announcing that a serial rapist had been arrested investigators wanted to find other victims. During the conference Dunning announced, "We know there are other victims but we don't know their identities." The goal was to get anyone with information to come forward. Echoing the pernicious view that prostitutes can't be raped, or that somehow the rape of a prostitute is a less serious offense than other rapes, a reporter asked the sheriff if all of the victims were prostitutes. Dunning's response quickly shut down that line of thinking. Paraphrasing his reply, "We prefer to view them as victims of a violent, serial rapist who is now off the streets." In laying out some of the details of Kamphaus' violence he pointed out, "The suspect threatened mutilation with a pair of pliers and a knife" (WOWT 2007a).

A later search of the van found a vibrating dildo and a pair of pliers in the map pocket of the driver's door.

A horde of reporters descended on Canyon Road after the news conference. Judy and Jim Tyler's home on Canyon Rd is mere yards away from where the rapes occurred. They have lived there for more than 30 years. "We don't like all the stuff that goes on out here. It brings out a bad crowd," Jim Tyler told a reporter (WOWT 2007a).

In tying up loose ends after his arrest, detectives showed Kamphaus pictures of VanCleeve, Green, Riva and Gallup. He identified VanCleeve, Riva and Green as prostitutes he "had been with." In true AER form Kamphaus stated that the point of taking his victims to the remote location was to fulfill his outdoor fantasy and to cause the victims fear so it was easy to dominate them so they would be easy to control. It is important to remember that the hallmark of the Anger Excitation Rapist is sexual sadism involving sexual arousal by causing the extreme pain, suffering or humiliation of others. Claiming that he chose the Canyon Road location to fulfill a fantasy is only partially true, if at all. It is more likely that the dark, isolated and menacing location was chosen to heighten the fear and suffering of his victims to feed his sadistic impulses.

In an obvious attempt to mitigate his crimes Kamphaus denied that he actually intended to harm his victims. Even after using a dildo to torture two victims, and threatening to use a knife and pliers to torture others, Kamphaus steadfastly denied that he would have actually harmed any of them. He did admit that his "role-playing" was so aggressive there would be no way for any of the women to know he would not truly cause them injury. He added that shoving his victims around and forcing them to have sex heightened his sexual pleasure and increased his feelings of power. He claimed that he raped because he was frustrated with women and felt that he couldn't have a normal relationship because he was ugly. Kamphaus also admitted that there were other victims who did not report the rape and that in some cases he paid them afterwards or simply abandoned them in Ponca Hills.

After his arrest in January 2008, Kamphaus was charged with two counts of sexual assault, two counts of false imprisonment, and two counts of terroristic threats. He was sentenced to 6 1/2 to 10 years in prison after pleading no contest to reduced charges of false imprisonment and terroristic threats (Associated Press 2008).

Prosecutors say they made the plea deal after concerns arose about the women's willingness and ability to testify.

Even if they had been able to testify, the fact they were prostitutes meant that their testimony would have been viewed as tainted, especially if Kamphaus' attorney mounted a vigorous criminal defense in a jury trial.

Raymond Hudlemeyer, a family friend of Van Cleeve's, voiced concerns over her welfare after her rape (WOWT 2007a). He said that he had known her since she was a child and said she hadn't been seen by her family since the day after she reported her attack in April. He said, "I would like to know where she's at, at least know she's all right."

Kamphaus was released in June 2012 after serving a little more than 4 ½ years. The fact that he had not been convicted of a sex offense was a huge mistake because serial rapists, especially the most violent and dangerous among them, are widely considered untreatable and will re-offend. Research in 2003 involving incarcerated sex offenders compared to non-sex offenders released from state prisons found that sex offenders were four times more likely to be rearrested for a sex crime within three years following their release (Langan 2003). The numbers aren't any better for supposedly "rehabilitated" rapists. Thirty-nine percent of imprisoned rapists who had undergone sex offender treatment in prison reoffended within two years of release.

Cases like Kamphaus pose many problems to prosecutors. Prostitute witnesses disappear or are unreliable on the stand due to their drug abuse and criminal lifestyle. It is easy for defense attorneys to cast doubt about the veracity of their testimony. And juries often view them as unsympathetic victims. What is certain is that the scandalously minimal prison sentence Kamphaus received, and the fact that he was not convicted of a sex offense, meant that he did not have to register for sex offender monitoring after release. These factors, combined with the high recidivism rate of serial rapists, and the MO-learning that occurs when rapists serve their time and emerge from prison wiser to the mistakes that landed them there in the first place, means that Kamphaus is likely to be an even bigger, more criminally sophisticated and adept threat than he was before.

Chapter Ten
Conclusion

I had the good fortune to work for thirty years in a career that I loved. During that time I was able to put some very deserving predators behind bars with the assistance of a talented group of professionals and a healthy dose of good luck. My passion for investigating sex crimes stemmed from my first encounter with a rape victim. I was a rookie patrol deputy running from call to call on a hot summer night in 1980. Shortly after 2:00 AM I was dispatched to a 24-hour convenience store near 96th and Q Street in Omaha. A bloody and dazed woman had stumbled into the store begging for help. She had been beaten, robbed and raped in the parking lot of a nearby apartment complex. As I pulled up to the scene paramedics were still treating "Mary" in the back of the rescue squad. She was a twenty-something woman who had suffered a broken nose in a vicious beating before and while being raped.

At the hospital Mary told me that she had been bar-hopping with friends. The group ended up at what was then a trendy bar catering to young singles near 108th and Mockingbird Drive. Mary said she "had a little too much to drink" and decided to head for home over the protestations of her friends who wanted to continue partying. It was shortly before bar closing at 1 AM when she walked alone to her car. In the darkened parking lot she didn't see the man hiding on the floor of her backseat. As she was pulling out of the parking lot he grabbed her around the throat from behind and began to choke her. Mary described his fingers around her throat as feeling "like steel." Terrified, and with her wind cut off, she desperately tried to pry his fingers away by clawing at his hands. In the process she deeply scratched her own neck, leaving bleeding lacerations from her fingernails. She was dangerously close to passing out when he finally loosened his grip. He ordered her not to look at him and to shut the car off. When she had done so he ordered her to climb over the console to the passenger side and get on the floor. He then climbed into the driver's seat and started to drive. Whenever Mary looked up her assailant punched her in the face so hard that he broke her nose. He also blackened her right eye, split her lip, and left visible finger-shaped bruises on the front of her throat from the choking.

He drove Mary to a large apartment complex nearby and parked in a dark, secluded area. There he went through her purse, taking her cash before tearing off her clothes and raping her repeatedly during a profanity-laced tirade. After he was done assaulting her he pushed her out of the car and drove off. Her car was found abandoned several days later on the other side of town.

I was angry that a cowardly predator had targeted and terrified an innocent young woman and raped and beat her so viciously. I spent the rest of the shift, and many nights after that, looking for her attacker without success. I checked with detectives working the case and they had no better luck than I did. Research indicates that fewer than one in three reported rapes leads to an arrest (Planty 2013).

Mary's rape inspired me to understand why men rape. It also ignited a passion for investigating sex crimes. Even though I could not arrest Mary's attacker I got a great deal of satisfaction taking predators like him off the street. Not because of the arrest itself, although there was some professional pride in that, but because it meant the rapist could not attack other women. In that regard I worked for the victims.

In spite of my passion investigating rape cases I wasn't able to solve them all. One of the cases that I failed to solve still haunts me. Thirteen-year-old Rebecca Williams disappeared on June 4th, 2003 from the area of her home in the Park Meadows Estates mobile home community at 108th and Ida Street. She was last seen by friends at a park nearby. I was then the lieutenant in charge of detectives looking for Rebecca after her family reported her missing. My detectives searched for her and canvassed the area and surrounding neighborhoods for witnesses who might have seen her or knew anything about what happened to her. They also distributed her picture in and around the mobile home community. It showed a cute young girl with a vivacious smile. She was the embodiment of youthful enthusiasm and potential with big dreams. She had told her mother that she wanted to be a writer or a pediatrician when she grew up.

On June 19th, 2003 three boys picking mulberries in a brushy wooded area adjacent to the mobile home community found Rebecca's badly decomposed body. I supervised the recovery of her remains and forensic processing of the scene. Although in advanced stages of decomposition Rebecca's body showed several apparent wounds indicating that she had been beaten by, or struggled with, her killer. Wounds and ante-mortem injuries decompose faster than uninjured areas of a victim's body (Hanna, 2008:8). Although the exact nature of some of the wounds are confidential hold-back information the advanced decomposition of areas of Rebecca's body relative to the overall state of decomposition are consistent with injuries sustained during a sexual assault. This led me to believe that she was murdered while being raped.

In the days after Rebecca's body was discovered, detectives scoured the area searching for evidence and canvassed the area again for witnesses. They interviewed her family, anyone who knew her and especially her teenage friends. A fourteen-year-old boy soon emerged as a prime suspect. He had expressed a romantic interest in Rebecca and told friends that he was going to meet her the day she disappeared. He lived with his grandmother in a neighborhood near the mobile home community. Detectives met with the grandmother and she agreed to accompany her grandson to be interviewed at the sheriff's office. However, shortly after the interview began, an attorney retained by the grandmother arrived and halted the questioning before a full statement or confession could be elicited.

The boy's attitude and behavior during questioning worried detectives. Even though he was only fourteen years old with no reported criminal history he exhibited a complete lack of nervousness, fear or intimidation in the presence of detectives in the tight confines of the interview room. He appeared to enjoy denying his involvement in Rebecca's disappearance and murder. And his apparent lack of empathy for Rebecca or the suffering of her family led detectives to believe that he might be a sociopath. This suspicion was bolstered by the fact that during the fifteen days Rebecca was missing he showed up in the neighborhood and hung out with mutual friends nearly every day while exhibiting no signs of worry or concern. Unlike Rebecca's other friends he showed no sign of empathy or sorrow over her death.

Lacking eyewitnesses who had seen him with Rebecca on the day of her disappearance and having no physical evidence that linked him to her death meant that we didn't have enough to arrest him. Because the prime suspect was not talking we were desperate to find evidence that tied him to Rebecca's murder. We went so far as to resort to forensic entomology. Forensic entomology focuses on the invasion of the succession of insects that inhabit and feed on decomposed human remains. Different bugs infest decomposing bodies at different times in a predictable order. A common way to estimate how long a victim has been dead is to identify the bugs that are present (Joseph 2011:90). Depending on the region of the country where the body is found, blowflies, flesh flies, and black soldier flies are typical species found on human remains. They home in on moist cavities like the mouth, nose, eyes, and to a lesser extent the anus and genitalia to lay their eggs (Lord 1989:43). The young that hatch out are the maggots which proceed to feed by eating their way through the surrounding soft tissue. It was hoped that DNA could be extracted from the digestive systems of the maggots that had been feeding on the body. The process involved gathering maggots from what was left of the vaginal area and grinding them into a solution and then trying to extract trace DNA from the solution. Unfortunately we couldn't catch a break in the Rebecca Williams case and no useable DNA was recovered.

The case remains open but is now a cold case. Detectives revisited it again in June 2014. They announced a reward for information via the news media (Chapman 2014). They were hoping that the friends and associates of the killer and Rebecca were grown up enough to step forward and give them the tip they needed to solve the case. Lt. Mark Gentile told a reporter, "Back then, there were a lot of teenage children involved in this case. We went down different avenues, different paths, but always [came] back to the same conclusion on who this kid [the prime suspect] was. Now, these kids they're adults, some of them even might have children of their own" (Chapman 2014).

The bane of all sex crimes detectives are the cases that can't be solved, especially those in which a suspect has been identified but evidence sufficient to arrest and prosecute him is out of reach. In Rebecca Williams' case we know who killed her, how he killed her and we have good theories about why he killed her. Her rape-murder haunts me on two levels. As long as the suspect evades arrest Rebecca's family is deprived of the sense of closure that an arrest and trial often provides. Justice for Rebecca demands no less. And it means that her killer is free to commit other crimes. It is my hope that sometime soon the final piece of the puzzle drops into place and the killer can be brought to justice so that Rebecca, forever frozen in time as that bright, smiling thirteen-year-old girl, and her loved ones can rest a little easier knowing that her killer has faced justice.

References

48 Hours, "Todd Kohlhepp Case: Confessions of a Suspected Serial Killer" November 12, 2016, https://www.cbsnews.com/news/todd-kohlhepp-case-48-hours-confessions-of-a-suspected-serial-killer-buried-truth/.

Aamodt, Michael, Serial killer statistics. Serial Killer Information Center, Radford University, 2016, http://maamodt.asp.radford.edu/serial killer information center/projectdescription.htm.

Alper, Mariel, Durose, Matthew R., Markman, Joshua, 2018. Update on Prisoner Recidivism: A 9-Year Follow-up Period (2005-2014). Bureau of Justice Statistics, Special Report, May 2018, NCJ 250975.

Amnesty International, Death Penalty Extra, AMR 51/86/92, Harold Lamont "Wili" Otey, July 8 1992, https://www.amnesty.org/en/documents/amr51/059/1994/en/.

Arias, Jeremy, Sheriff's office charges six with violating terms of sex offender registry 2018, https://www.fredericknewspost.com/news/crime_and_justice/sheriff-s-office-charges-six-with-violating-terms-of-sex/article_dce33734-9570-53d4-8576-386ff84ffcfe.html.

Associated Press, Omaha man accused in rapes sentenced to up to 10 years, Lincoln Journal Star, January 10, 2008, https://journalstar.com/news/state-and-regional/govt-and-politics/omaha-man-accused-in-rapes-sentenced-to-up-to-years/article_6a8b092a-fe72-56aa-b50d-608f0734f667.html.

Aveni, Thomas, "Officer-Involved Shootings: What We Didn't Know Has Hurt Us," The Police Policy Studies Council, http://www.theppsc.org/Staff_Views/Aveni/OIS.pdf.

Babiak, Pinizzoto, et al, Psychopathy: An Important Forensic Concept for the 21st Century, FBI Law Enforcement Bulletin, 81:7, 2012.

Banfield, Edward, The Unheavenly City Revisited: A Revision of The Unheavenly City, Scott Foresman; Glenview, Illinois, 1974.

Baum Bob, Hells Angel On Trial 18 Years After Murders, Spokesman-Review, Spokane, WA, 2012, http://www.spokesman.com/stories/1995/may/14/hells-angel-on-trial-18-years-after-murders/

Bechtel, Laura and Christopher Holstege Criminal Poisoning: Drug-Facilitated Sexual Assault, Emergency Medical Clinics of North America, 2007, 25, 499–525.

Blogger dg1952, John Joubert, Nebraska Boy Snatcher, Blog Post, Sep 27, 2008. https://www.tapatalk.com/groups/watchingrobertpickton88015/john-joubert-nebraska-boy-snatcher-t1815.html.

Bonner, Walter, "Outlaw Chronicles": True Stories with the Hells Angels, 2015, https://www.mensjournal.com/adventure/outlaw-chronicles-true-stories-with-the-hells-angels-20150817/

Brunkow, Angie, Psychiatrist Predicted Man Would Rape Again, Omaha World Herald, at 1A-2A, December 6, 1998.

Brunkow, Angie and Toni Heinzl, Jury Finds Burdette Guilty in Rapes, Omaha World Herald, August 21,1999.

Bunkley, Nick and Joseph Juran, 103, Pioneer in Quality Control, Dies. The New York Times National Edition, Page B7, March 3, 2008.

Burbach, Christopher, 'I won't get back the years of my life that I lost': Judge rules killer must spend at least 22 more years in prison for 1990 murder, Omaha World Herald, Feb 15, 2016, https://www.omaha.com/news/crime/i-won-t-get-back-the-years-of-my-life/article_f0acc812-d1ab-11e5-bb58-b3fb8ef5f4d1.html.

Burdette v. Britten, 8:08CV536 (D. Neb. Jul. 8, 2009).

Carlie, Michael, Into The Abyss: A Personal Journey into the World of Street Gangs, 2002, http://people.missouristate.edu/michaelcarlie/storage/motorcycle_gangs.htm.

Chapman, John, Cash Reward Available For Cold Case Murder, 2014, https://www.wowt.com/home/headlines/Cash-Reward-Available-For-Cold-Case-Murder-263349551.html.

Chiodo, Joe, Mom of Teen Murdered in 1990 Speaks after Killer's Resentencing, 2016, Accessed at URL: www.wowt.com/home/headlines/Killer-faces-resentencing-in-1990-murder-368620461.html

Christensen, Jordan et. al., Gerald Gallego, Serial Killer Research, Radford University, http://maamodt.asp.radford.edu/Psyc%20405/serial%20killers/Gallego,%20Gerald%20-%202005.pdf.

Clendenning, Alan, Trail of Violence Nears its End John Joubert, Scheduled for Execution in Nebraska on Friday, Began His Bloody Attacks in Portland, 1996, https://mylifeofcrime.files.wordpress.com/2007/12/trail-of-violence-nears-its-end-john-joubert-scheduled-for-execution-in-nebraska-on-friday-began-his-bloody-attacks-in-portland.doc.

Date Rape Pamphlet, New York State Police, 2006, https://troopers.ny.gov/Publications/Crime_Prevention/daterape.pdf.

Devin, Jane, Prostitute's Rape Unimportant, 2007, http://janedevin.com.

Dietz, Park, et al., The Sexually Sadistic Criminal and His Offenses. Bulletin of the American Academy of Psychiatry and the Law, 1990, 18(2), 163-178.

Doe, Jane, Who Killed Dallas, Police State Blog post, 2002, https://www.indybay.org/newsitems/2002/10/31/15406201.php.

Douglas, John et. al., Crime Classification Manual: A Standard System for Investigating and Classifying Violent Crime (2nd ed.), San Francisco, Calif.: Jossey-Bass, 2006.

Douglas, John E., et. al., "Crime Classification Manual: A Standard System for Investigating and Classifying Violent Crimes," Jossey-Bass, Hoboken, NJ, 1997.

Drewery, George, Skulls, Wings & Outlaws – Motorcycle Club Insignia & Cultural Identity. Inter-Cultural Studies; A Forum on Social Change & Cultural Diversity, 2003, 3:2.

Ending Exploitation Collaborative, Commercial Sexual Exploitation, http://www.endingexploitation.com/exploitation.html.

Fagan, Kevin, "When Jailbirds Sing," San Francisco Chronicle Staff Writer, December 3, 1995. https://www.sfgate.com/news/article/When-Jailbirds-Sing-It-was-the-pure-savagery-of-3018647.php.

Farley, Melissa and Howard Barkan, Prostitution, violence, and posttraumatic stress disorder. Women Health. 1998; 27(3):37-49.

Farley, Melissa and Emily Buler, Prostitution and Trafficking – Quick Facts, Prostitution Research & Education 2012, http://www.prostitutionresearch.com/Prostitution%20Quick%20Facts%2012-21-12.pdf.

Farley, Melissa, Risks of Prostitution: When the Person Is the Product, Journal of the Association for Consumer Research, Volume 3, Number 1, 2017, https://www.journals.uchicago.edu/doi/abs/10.1086/695670.

FBI, Frequently Asked Questions on CODIS and NDIS, https://www.fbi.gov/services/laboratory/biometric-analysis/codis/codis-and-ndis-fact-sheet.

FBI, National Crime Information Center (NCIC), https://www.fbi.gov/services/cjis/ncic

Forensics Laboratory, Edmond Locard, http://aboutforensics.co.uk/edmond-locard/

Fry, Melissa, Authorities ask for community's help in 1986 unsolved murder, KETV, March 27, 2016. https://www.ketv.com/article/authorities-ask-for-communitys-help-in-1986-unsolved-murder/7209833.

Gardner, David, Rodney Alcala sentenced to death for murders of four women and girl, 12, The Daily Mail, London, 2010,

https://www.dailymail.co.uk/news/article-1262485/Rodney-Alcala-sentenced-death-murders-women-girl-12.html.

Geberth, Vernon, Practical Homicide Investigation Law and Order Magazine, Vol. 46, No. 5, May 1998.

Geberth, Vernon, Sex-Related Homicide and Death Investigation: Practical and Clinical Perspectives, Second Edition, Boca Raton, CRC Press, 2010

Goodman, Walter, Battling Over the Life of a Convicted Killer, NY Times, National Edition, Dec, 1994, 22.

Grace, Erin, She Listened as Baby Sitter was Murdered, Omaha World Herald, February 12, 2016.

Grayson, Betty and Morris Stein, Attracting Assault: Victims' Nonverbal Cues, Journal of Communication, Volume 31, Issue 1, March 1981, Pages 68–75.

Grieg, Charlotte, Evil Serial Killers: In the Minds of Monsters, New York: Barnes & Noble, 2005.

Griffin, Michael and Jim Leusner, Woman Recalls Life as "Property" of Outlaw Enforcer. The Orlando Sentinel, 1995, http://www.orlandosentinel.com/news/os-xpm-1995-12-17-9512160801-story.html.

Griffiths, Mark, Life On A Knife Edge: A Brief Look at Picquerism, Psychology Today Bog, Jan. 1, 2015, https://www.psychologytoday.com/us/blog/in-excess/201501/life-knife-edge.

Groth, A.N., et. al., Rape: Power, Anger, and Sexuality, American Journal of Psychiatry, Vol. 47, Iss. 3., 1977.

Groth, Nicholas, Men Who Rape: The Psychology of the Offender, New York: Plenum Press, 1979.

Guardian, Canada judge resigns over "keep your knees together" comment in rape trial, 2017, https://www.theguardian.com/world/2017/mar/10/canada-judge-resigns-keep-your-knees-together-comment-rape-trial.

Hammel, Paul, Court Rejects Appeal by Man Convicted in 1990 Slaying of West Omaha Baby Sitter, 2018, https://www.omaha.com/news/crime/court-rejects-appeal-by-man-convicted-in-slaying-of-west/article_413ed6aa-f373-59d7-9d05-986dd92e73c6.html.

Hanna, J. and A Moyce, Factors Affecting Human Decomposition, Queens University, Belfast, Ireland, 2008, https://pure.qub.ac.uk/portal/files/4112087/green_grave_report.pdf.

Hazelwood, Roy and Ann Burgess, "Introduction to the Serial Rapist: Research by the FBI," FBI Law Enforcement Bulletin Vol. 56, No. 9, Quantico, VA, 1987.

Hazelwood, Roy and John Douglas, Lust Murderer, FBI Law Enforcement Bulletin, 49:4, 1980, 8-22.

Hazelwood, Roy and Janet Warren, Criminal Behavior of the Serial Rapist, FBI Law Enforcement Bulletin, 59:2, 1990, 11-16.

Heinzl, Toni, August 21. 1982 Burdette Victim Relieved After Verdicts, Omaha World Herald, 1999.

Hunter, Susan and K.C. Reed, K.C., "Taking the side of bought and sold rape," speech at National Coalition against Sexual Assault, Washington, DC, July, 1990.

Hickman, Matthew, Citizen Complaints about Police Use of Force, NCJ 210296, Washington, DC, Bureau of Justice Statistics, 2006.

Hunziker, John, Court-ordered Psychological Examination of David Burdette, Douglas County Hospital, Omaha, NE, November 1982.

Hustmyre, C. and J Dixi "Marked for Mayhem: Street criminals are selective about their victims. Unfortunately, many of us unwittingly give off signals that mark us as easy targets," 2009, https://www.psychologytoday.com/us/articles/200901/marked-mayhem.

Jacksonville Journal Courier, Monday, June 19, 1978, https://newspaperarchive.com/jacksonville-journal-courier-jun-19-1978-p-6/.

Jayne, Brian, The Investigator Anthology: A Compilation of Articles and Essays about The Reid Technique of Interviewing and Interrogation, Chicago, IL: John E. Reid and Associates, 1999.

Jensen, Lorenzo, Wives Of Motorcycle Gang Members On Life As A Biker Bitch, 2015, https://thoughtcatalog.com/lorenzo-jensen-iii/2015/11/10-wives-of-motorcycle-gang-members-on-life-as-a-biker-bitch/.

Joseph, Isaac, The Use of Insects in Forensic Investigations: An Overview on the Scope of Forensic Entomology, Journal of Forensic Dental Science, 3(2), Jul-Dec, 2011, 89–91.

Joubert v. Hopkins, Nos. 94-3687, 94-3849, 1996.

Kaffer, Nancy, 8 years into tests of abandoned rape kits, Worthy works for justice, Detroit Free Press, Dec. 17, 2017, https://www.freep.com/story/opinion/columnists/nancy-kaffer/2017/12/17/rape-kit-detroit/953083001/.

Kansas v. Hendricks, No. 95-1649, June 23, 1997.

Kelly, Michael, Joan McManus, Mrs. Nebraska of 1961 and mom of 10, had a life marked by tragedy, Omaha World Herald, Sept. 20, 2017, https://www.omaha.com/columnists/kelly/kelly-joan-mcmanus-mrs-nebraska-of-and-mom-of-had/article_8146badb-2764-53e0-ad8e-13eb4d3d4bf7.html.

Kemling, Mark, and David M. Kanive, Nebraska Penal and Correctional Complex Intake Classification Study, Lincoln, NE, January 1983.

Kentsmith, David K, Court-ordered Psychological Examination of David Burdette, Douglas County District Court, Omaha, NE, 1982

Keppel, Robert, The Riverman: Ted Bundy and I Hunt for the Green River Killer. New York: Pocket Books, (Paperback ed), 2005.

Kiehl and Hoffman, The Criminal Psychopath: History, Neuroscience, Treatment, and Economics, Jurimetrics, 51: 357, 2011.

King, M. L. Jr. "I Have a Dream," Address Delivered at the March on Washington for Jobs and Freedom, 1963,

https://kinginstitute.stanford.edu/king-papers/documents/i-have-dream-address-delivered-march-washington-jobs-and-freedom.

Kirchner, Paul, "Jim Cirillo's Tales Of The Stakeout Squad," Boulder, Colorado, Paladin Press, 2008.

Kocsis, Richard, ed, Criminal Profiling: International Theory, Research, and Practice, Humana Press, Totowa, NJ, 2006.

Kristof, Nicholas, The Pimps' Slaves, New York Times, Op-ed, March 16, 2008, WK-12.

Langan, P. et. al., Recidivism of Sex Offenders Released From Prison in 1994. Washington, DC: U.S. Department of Justice, Office of Justice Programs, Bureau of Justice Statistics, 2003.

Lapan, Tovin, Pimp Subculture Filled with Money, Manipulation, Violence. Las Vegas Sun, March 11, 2013. https://lasvegassun.com/news/2013/mar/11/sex-sells/.

Lavigne, Yves, 1989. Hells Angels: Three Can Keep a Secret if Two Are Dead, Lyle Stuart, New York, NY, 1989, 114.

Lee, Jooyoung and Sasha Reid. Serial Killers and Their Prey, Contexts, Vol. 17, Iss. 2, 2018, 46-51.

Linn, Katie, Pimp Controlled Trafficking & The Grooming Process, Exploit No More, 2016, https://www.exploitnomore.org/blog/pimp-controlled-trafficking-the-grooming-process.

Lord, Wayne, and William Rodriguez, Forensic Entomology: The Use of Insects in the Investigation of Homicide and Untimely Death, The Prosecutor, Winter, 1989. https://www.ncjrs.gov/pdffiles1/Photocopy/116278NCJRS.pdf.

292

Maas, Kimberley, Making Sense Of Motorcycle Brotherhood: Women, Branding, and Construction Of Self. Minnesota State University – Mankato, All Theses, Dissertations, and Other Capstone Projects, Paper 2013, 238.

Megan's Story http://www.meganslaw.com/megans-story.html.

Mullen, Kris, McManus Family Hopes Finality Brings Solace, Omaha World Herald, September 2, 1994, News, 8,

https://www.laguardia.edu/lesson/files/Otey/Lexis%20Nexis%20 OTEY/otey%2010.pdf.

Murderpedia, Harold Lamont Otey http://murderpedia.org/ male.O/o1/otey-harold-lamont.htm.

Mullen, Kris, McManus Family Hopes Finality Brings Solace, Omaha World Herald, September 2, 1994, News, 8,

https://www.laguardia.edu/lesson/files/Otey/Lexis%20Nexis%20 OTEY/otey%2010.pdf.

Nesbitt v. Hopkins, No.95-2061, 1996.

Nesbitt v. Frakes, S-16-931, 2018.

New York State Police, Date Rape Pamphlet, 2016. https://troopers. ny.gov/Publications/Crime_Prevention/daterape.pdf.

Newton, Josh, Woman caught shooting up, sex offender taken to jail, February 20, 2014, https://www.tahlequahdailypress. com/news/local_news/woman-caught-shooting-up-sex-offender-taken-to-jail/article_1e552436-623a-594f-bd92-d4727c65c9c6.html.

Olson, D. Clinical Forensic Psychology, BJ559, FBI National Academy, Quantico, VA, 1998.

Olson, Dean, Ethics, Douglas County Sheriff Training Bulletin 97-016.34, 1997, 2.

Olson, Dean, Crime Scene Protocol, Douglas County Sheriff Training Bulletin 99-01.50, 1999, 1.

Olson, Dean, Deadly Force Action/Reaction Gap, Douglas County Sheriff Training Bulletin 96-03.08, 1996, 4.

PCAR, The Intersection between Prostitution and Sexual Violence, Pennsylvania Coalition Against Rape, 2013. https://www.pcar. org/sites/default/files/pages-pdf/the_intersection_between_ prostitution_and_sexual_violence.pdf.

People v. Diaz, First Appellate District of California, No. A107118, 2007, https://www.fearnotlaw.com/wsnkb/articles/p-vdiaz-10555.html.

Peralta, Eyder, In Minnesota, Jacob Wetterling's Killer is Sentenced to 20 Years, 2016, https://www.npr.org/sections/thetwo-way/2016/11/21/502900632/jacob-wetterlings-killer-is-sentenced-to-20-years-in-minnesota.

Petherick, W A., et al., Forensic Criminology. London: Elsevier Academic Press, 2010.

Pettit, Mark, A Need to Kill: The True-Crime Account of John Joubert, Nebraska's Most Notorious Serial Child Killer, Create Space Online Publishing, 2013.

Pinnizotto, Anthony, Class notes: Organized/Disorganized Offenders, Clinical Forensic Psychology, CJ 559, FBI National Academy, 193rd Session, 1998.

Pinnizotto, Anthony, Lecture notes, Forensic Psychology, CJ559, FBI National Academy, 193rd Session, Quantico, VA., 1998.

Planty, Michael and Lynn Langton, Female Victims of Sexual Violence, Washington, DC: Bureau of Justice Statistics, 2013.

Powers, William, "Enforcement Odyssey, Massachusetts State Police. A new Commemorative History of One of the Nation's Premiere State Law Enforcement Agencies," Paducah, Kentucky: Turner Publishing, 1998.

Quay, H. C. (1965). Psychopathic personality as pathological stimulation-seeking. The American Journal of Psychiatry, 122(2), 180-183.

Ramsland, K. and P. McGrain, Inside the Minds of Sexual Predators, Santa Barbara CA: Greenwood, 2009.

Ramsland, Katherine, Erotica for Serial Killers, Blog post: April 10, 2017. https://www.psychologytoday.com/us/blog/shadow-boxing/201704/erotica-serial-killers.

Ressler, Robert and Tom Shachtman, Whoever Fights Monsters: My Twenty Years Hunting Serial Killers for the FBI, New York: St. Martin's Press, 1992, 93-112.

Rooney, Paula, Microsoft's CEO: 80–20 Rule Applies To Bugs, Not Just Features, CRN Magazine, 2002, https://www.crn.com/

news/security/18821726/microsofts-ceo-80-20-rule-applies-to-bugs-not-just-features.htm.

Russo, Francine, 2017. Sexual Assault May Trigger Involuntary Paralysis, Scientific American, https://www.scientificamerican.com/article/sexual-assault-may-trigger-involuntary-paralysis/

Samenow, Stanton, Sex Crimes Are Not About Sex, Psychology Today Blog Post, Inside the Criminal Mind, 2011,

https://www.psychologytoday.com/us/blog/inside-the-criminal-mind/201106/sex-crimes-are-not-about-sex.

Shamus, Kristen, What happened to Detroit's untested rape kits? Detroit Free Press, April 1, 2017, https://www.freep.com/story/news/local/michigan/detroit/2017/04/01/untested-detroit-rape-kits/99845762/.

State v. Burdette, A-99-1210, Ne Sup. Ct. 1999.

State v. David E. Burdette, No. S-99-1210, 1999.

State v. Garza, 492 N.W.2d 32 (Neb. 1992)

State v. Joubert, 399 N.W.2d 237 (1986), 224 Neb. 411.

State v. Joubert, 603 A.2d 861 (Me. 1992).

State v. Nesbitt, 226 Neb. 32•409 N.W.2d 314 (1987).

State v. Nesbitt, S-09-000350, 2009.

State v. Otey, 464 N.W.2d 352 236 Neb. 915 (Neb. 1991)

State v. Robertson, 394 N.W.2d 635 223 Neb. 825 (1986).

State v. Steven Garza, 459 N.W.2d 739, 236 Neb. 202 (1990).

State of Nebraska v. Garza, 492 N.W.2d 32, , 264 Neb. 612, 241 Neb. 934 (1992).

State of Nebraska v. Nesbitt, 650 N.W.2d 766, 264 Neb. 612 (2002).

Stewart, Potter, "The Road to Mapp v. Ohio and beyond: The Origins, Development and Future of the Exclusionary Rule in Search-and-Seizure Cases," Columbia Law Review, 1983: Vol. 83, No. 6,1365–1404.

Thorsen, Leah, Inmate Who Sought Liver Transplant Dies, Lincoln Journal Star, Jan 20, 2005. https://journalstar.com/news/local/inmate-who-sought-liver-transplant-dies/article_68bc8b12-9fc6-b1fa-56373366280e.html.

United Nations Development Program, 1992 Human Development Report, New York: Oxford University Press.

UPI, Child killer executed in Nebraska, July 17, 1996, https://www.upi.com/Archives/1996/07/17/Child-killer-executed-in-Nebraska/9576837576000/.

UPI Archive, Rapist of "Most eligible" Women Sentenced, December 2, 1982, https://www.upi.com/Archives/1982/12/02/Rapist-of-Most-eligible-women-sentenced/3971407653200/.

U.S. v. Nesbitt, 852 F.2d 1502 (7th Cir. 1988).

Valdemar, Richard, Protecting Gang Witnesses. Police Magazine Blog post: Gangs, 2009. https://www.policemag.com/373270/protecting-gang-witnesses.

State of Nebraska v. Nesbitt, 650 N.W.2d 766, 264 Neb. 612 (2002).

Waltz, Emily, How Genealogy Websites Make it Easier to Catch Killers, 2018, https://spectrum.ieee.org/the-human-os/biomedical/ethics/criminals-getting-easier-to-find-thanks-to-genealogy-websites.

Weide, Sean, Twenty Years Ago: Another Tragic Disappearance, Blog, April 06, 2006. http://nebraskamedianotes.blogspot.com/2006/04/twenty-years-ago-another-tragic.html

Welborn, Larry, "O.C. death row: 11 murders, maybe more," The Orange County Register, 2011. https://www.ocregister.com/2011/02/25/oc-death-row-11-murders-maybe-more/

Williams, John, "Outlaw Motorcycle Gangs," Los Angeles, CA, Los Angeles County Sheriff's Department, 2010.

Wolbert Burgess, Ann and Linda Lytle Holmstrom, Rape Trauma Syndrome, 131 Am J Psych 981, 1974.

Wolfe, Rojek. et al, "Characteristics of Officer-Involved Vehicle Collisions," Policing; 38(3): 460, 2015.

WOWT, Assault Suspect Arrested, 2007a, https://www.wowt.com/home/headlines/7417986.html.

WOWT, Alleged Rapist Charged, 2007b https://www.wowt.com/home/headlines/7466002.html.

SEP 0 3 2019

9 781947 521124